GREAT DESSERTS

From the Editors of
Food & Wine Magazine

Edited and Written by
Mardee Haidin Regan

Photography by
Irvin Blitz

Art Direction by
Leslie Smolan

Stewart Tabori & Chang,
New York

GREAT DESSERTS

Food & Wine Great Desserts

Publisher: Claire Gruppo
Editorial Director: Susan Crandell
Writer/Editor: Mardee Haidin Regan
Photographer: Irvin Blitz
Art Director: Leslie Smolan
Designer: Allison Cary Muench
Managing Editor: Victoria Walsh
Photo Stylist: Francesca Bacon
Food Stylist: Alice Cronk
Food Stylist Assistant: Leslie Baxter
Photography Assistants:
    Tarryn Ackor, Laurie Vogt

The text of this book was set in
Bembo and Gill Sans by Typogram,
New York, N.Y. The four color
separations were done by International
Color, Rochester, N.Y. The book
was printed and bound in
Milan, Italy by Amilcare Pizzi S.p.a.

Published in 1989 by
Stewart, Tabori & Chang, Inc.
740 Broadway
New York, New York 10003

Distributed by Workman Publishing
708 Broadway
New York, New York 10003

Pommes Grand'mère de Hilo from
New Menus from Simca's Cuisine,
copyright © 1978, 1979 by Simone
Beck and Michael James. Reprinted
by permission of Harcourt Brace
Jovanovich, Inc.

Library of Congress
Cataloging-in-Publication Data
Food & Wine Great Desserts.
Originally published: New York:
American Express Pub. Corp., c1987.
Includes index.
1. Desserts. I. Regan, Mardee Haidin.
II. Title: Food and wine great desserts.
TX773.F65 1989 641.8′6 88-24883
ISBN 1-55670-064-4

Contents

About This Book

■ What's for dessert? It's one of the most frequently asked questions in America. And it can be among the most frustrating, if you're the one who has to come up with the

perfect answer every time. More often than not, you choose a particular dessert not because it's a pie, but because it complements other courses you're serving, and it fits both the spirit of the occasion and the amount of time you have to spend making it. Because these are the things you consider in making your choice, they're the criteria we've applied in setting up this cookbook. Instead of arranging our recipes under category heads like pies, cakes, cookies and such, we've grouped them into chapters that can really help you decide which dessert to make.

When you're searching for a truly special, really elegant dessert, you don't want to wade through pages and pages of blueberry muffins and peanut butter cookies just to find a few possibilities. In this book, you won't have to. If it's a spectacular looking dessert you seek, just page to our chapter titled *Works of Art* (and you'll be delighted to know that some of these dazzlers are actually quite easy to make).

If it's a special event you're creating, check our chapter on *Celebrations*, a compendium of desserts that exude a spirit of revelry. But if it's rainy and cold outside and you feel glum, our *Old Favorites* chapter can provide a recipe to lift your spirits.

Our *Lightweights* chapter spotlights desserts that are light in texture (to follow a hearty meal), low in calories (for those dieting days) or light in spirit (just for fun). There are easy-to-make desserts in *Simple Pleasures* (yet some of them look downright complicated when you're through). The great dessert teams that make up our *Perfect Partners* reveal inventive new pairings of ingredients and flavors that are surprisingly tasty in combination.

Chapter 7 is called *Savories*, so named because here we concentrate on great salads and cheese – wonderfully palate-pleasing ways to end a meal. Whoever said every conclusion has to be a sweet one? We close with *Liquid Assets*, a word or two about beverages – dessert wines, liqueurs, *eaux-de-vie*, brandies, ports – that are most appropriate for fine dining and entertaining.

Because you sometimes do make choices by category ("I know I want to serve pie tonight, but which kind shall I make?"), we've also included a comprehensive index to all of our recipes. Just page to the back for listings of every pie (or cake, or cookie or even flavor of ice cream) that appears in the book.

All of these recipes have been tested in the kitchen at *Food & Wine* magazine. Many of them have been contributed by noted cookbook authors and food authorities from all over the world. They represent the excellence of the individual authors as well as the high editorial and culinary standards of *Food & Wine* magazine. We chose these recipes – more than 200 of them – from over 700 possibilities, to bring you great desserts – exciting conclusions for virtually every meal.

Mardee Haidin Regan

Celebrations

Celebrations

If the whole idea of a celebration is purposeful revelry, then let the fun begin with a good idea. Celebrating the traditional holidays of the year – anniversaries,

birthdays, Christmas, Thanksgiving – is terrific of course, but creating a special occasion has distinct merits of its own. All it takes is a moment of inspiration followed by a burst of cleverness, and perhaps a tiny jolt of humor. No matter what the occasion, it will benefit from an extra flash of spirit.

The inventiveness – and the fun – comes in figuring out the best way, say, to fete a lawyer friend who's just made partner (see our suggestion on page 18), or what to bring for a celebratory first meal in a friend's finally finished, newly renovated home (we recommend a flambéed dessert to ignite the occasion). These are just a few examples of the kinds of special celebrations the desserts in this chapter bring to mind. Surely, you'll think of other fitting occasions for our celebratory desserts as well.

Indeed, food often can be the "hook" on which a party is hung. When you think about what events are coming up, consider what foods are in season. Will the celebration be inside or outside, small or large? Look at a calendar – is it National Apple Week? If so, perhaps apple blossoms can be used for table decoration, or the foods can be chosen along an apple theme.

Will a friend who's mad for chocolate be visiting soon? There's no nicer way to welcome him or her than by highlighting a favorite food; have a go at Narsai's Original Chocolate Decadence, Peter Sussman's Chocolate-Chocolate-Chocolate-Chip Fudge Cake or even White Chocolate Mousse.

For a friend who's running in a marathon, plan a regain-your-strength victory reception to congratulate the runner for finishing (if not winning) the race. Serve up lots of quick energy treats to help combat exhaustion, and set up several do-it-yourself Ice Cream Fritter stations on the lawn or patio and let all the celebrants batter and fry the flavor of their choice.

Good homemade ice cream is reason enough to celebrate, as the 11 very special flavors in this chapter illustrate. With the profusion of easy-to-use ice cream makers available these days – from fancy electric machines by Gaggia and Simac to nifty little inexpensive ones you pre-chill in the freezer, like the Donvier – serving up eight or nine different flavors of homemade ice cream has become no problem at all. Chop up some special but vital ingredients for mash-ins and mix-ins. We suggest M & Ms, peanut butter cups, chocolate chips, nuts, mini chocolate truffles and toffee bars. And don't forget the toppings – bananas, sliced fresh straw-berries, nuts, whipped cream and loads of sauces. Our favorite sauce recipes (Bittersweet Double Chocolate, Butterscotch, Hot Fudge, Caramel) begin on page 174.

More formal celebrations can be shaped around the deli-cacy of certain foods. Certainly, anybody who shares fond memo-ries with you – the members of your book club, French course or college class – would enjoy madeleines on an afternoon filled with fond recollections. Indeed, the idea behind Proust's favorite shell-shaped cookies is "remembrance of things past."

For intimate, two-person-only trysts, seek out sweets with sensual flavors and textures, such as our *crème brûlée*. No doubt you'll want to have the right romantic accompaniment, which may mean a bottle of pink Champagne or antique crystal brandy snifters holding a very special Cognac – maybe Paradis (it's said to take a definite part in creating just that). ■

Hazelnut Succès

You could hardly find a more aptly named dessert than Hazelnut Succès to fete a newly graduated M.B.A. or a budding entrepreneur. Invite a group for drinks and coffee, bring out this star-studded cake, and join your friends in wishing the honoree all the best. This extremely elegant dessert can be made in stages. Once assembled, it keeps well in the refrigerator for up to 24 hours before serving.

1 cup plus 2 tablespoons (5 ounces) lightly toasted and skinned hazelnuts
1 cup confectioners' sugar
6 egg whites, at room temperature
Pinch of cream of tartar
1 cup granulated sugar
Hazelnut Praline Buttercream, at room temperature (recipe follows)
⅔ cup Hazelnut Praline (recipe follows)
12 hazelnuts in their skins, for garnish

1 Preheat the oven to 250°. Line 2 large baking sheets with parchment paper and trace a 10-inch circle onto each piece of parchment.

2 Finely grate the toasted hazelnuts (a rotary nut grater works best) into a bowl. Sift in ¾ cup of the confectioners' sugar and toss to mix thoroughly.

3 In a large bowl, beat the egg whites and cream of tartar on low speed until foamy, about 2 minutes. Increase the speed to high and beat until the whites nearly double in volume and stiff peaks form. Gradually beat in the granulated sugar, 1 tablespoon at a time. Beat until the whites are dense and glossy and form stiff peaks.

4 With a large rubber spatula, lightly fold in the nut mixture until no white streaks remain.

5 Use a tiny amount of the nut meringue to anchor the corners of the parchment to the baking sheet. Spoon half of the meringue onto one of the circles and, with a thin metal spatula, spread into an even layer to fill the circle. Form a second circle with the remaining meringue on the other baking sheet.

6 Bake the nut meringues in the upper and lower thirds of the oven, switching positions once, until lightly browned and crisp throughout when tapped, 1 to 1½ hours. The amount of time it takes to dry out will depend on the humidity of the day. Let cool to room temperature. (The recipe can be prepared to this point up to 2 days ahead.) Wrap the meringue layers, with the parchment still attached to the bottom (for stability), in a large sheet of foil to seal.

To assemble the dessert:

7 Peel off the parchment paper from the meringue layers. Set one layer on a flat surface and spread evenly with 2 cups of the Hazelnut

Recipe continues on the next page

Hazelnut Succès Continued

Praline Buttercream. Place the second layer, flat-side up, on top of the buttercream and press gently. With a metal spatula, spread the remaining buttercream evenly on the top and sides of the cake.

8 To decorate, press the Hazelnut Praline around the sides of the cake and sift the remaining ¼ cup confectioners' sugar evenly over the top or use stencils to create a design. Garnish with the whole hazelnuts. Refrigerate uncovered for at least 1 hour, or up to 24 hours to firm up. Serve chilled.

Serves 12 to 16
Recipe by Diana Sturgis

3 Gradually beat the boiling syrup into the eggs in a thin steady stream. Beat until the mixture cools to room temperature, 6 to 8 minutes.

4 Gradually beat in the butter, 4 tablespoons at a time, and continue to beat until the buttercream is fluffy.

5 Fold in the Hazelnut Praline. Use at once or cover and refrigerate overnight. Remove from the refrigerator at least 1 hour before using, to return to room temperature.

Makes about 3⅔ cups
Recipe by Diana Sturgis

Hazelnut Praline Buttercream

¾ cup granulated sugar
5 egg yolks
1 whole egg

¾ pound unsalted butter, softened and lightly beaten
1⅔ cups Hazelnut Praline (recipe follows)

1 In a small heavy saucepan, combine the sugar with ½ cup of water. Bring to a boil over moderately high heat, stirring to dissolve the sugar. Boil without stirring until the syrup reaches the soft-ball stage, 244° on a candy thermometer, about 6 minutes.

2 Meanwhile, in a bowl, beat the egg yolks and whole egg on high speed until pale, fluffy and quadrupled in volume, about 5 minutes.

Hazelnut Praline

1 cup plus 2 tablespoons (5 ounces) lightly toasted and skinned hazelnuts

1¼ cups granulated sugar

1 Lightly oil a baking sheet and place the nuts in a single layer in the middle of the tray.

2 In a heavy medium saucepan, combine the sugar with ½ cup of water. Bring to a boil over moderately high heat, stirring to dissolve the sugar. Boil without stirring until the sugar turns golden, about 10 minutes.

3 Drizzle the boiling caramel over the nuts and set aside until hard and cool, about 20 minutes.

4 Break the nuts and caramel into chunks by hitting the bottom of the tray. Grind to a powder in a food processor, about 20 seconds. Use at once or store in an airtight container for up to 3 weeks.

Makes about 2⅓ cups
Recipe by Diana Sturgis

Narsai's Original Chocolate Decadence

Sometimes all that's lacking is an excuse for a party – a reason to make a special effort. If Valentine's Day is just too far away, aim for Ground Hog's Day – almost two weeks earlier. Whatever the occasion, for the tried and true chocolate devotee, this recipe is a party in itself.

1 pound high-quality bittersweet or semisweet chocolate
¼ pound plus 2 tablespoons unsalted butter
4 whole eggs
1 tablespoon sugar
1 tablespoon all-purpose flour

1 cup heavy cream, whipped
Shaved bittersweet chocolate
1 package (10 to 12 ounces) frozen raspberries, thawed

1 Flour and butter an 8-inch round cake pan. Cut a round of waxed paper to fit the bottom, butter it and place in the pan. Preheat the oven to 425°.

2 In a small saucepan over very low heat or in a microwave oven, melt the chocolate with the butter. Set aside. In the top of a double boiler over very hot water, whisk the eggs with the sugar. Beat over hot water until the sugar dissolves and the mixture is just luke-warm. Remove the top of the double boiler from the heat and beat the eggs until they quadruple in volume and become quite thick.

3 Fold the flour into the eggs. Stir one-fourth of the egg mixture into the chocolate. Then, fold the chocolate back into the rest of the egg mixture. Pour the batter into the prepared cake pan. Bake for 15 minutes; the cake will still be liquid in the center. Cover and freeze the cake in the pan overnight.

4 To unmold the cake, carefully dip the bottom of the pan in hot water and invert onto a cake plate. Remove the pan and gently peel off the waxed paper. Decorate the cake with the whipped cream and shaved chocolate. Refrigerate until serving.

5 Puree the raspberries and their juice in a blender or food processor. Pass the puree through a fine sieve and serve a tablespoon of the sauce with each portion.

Serves 12
Recipe by Narsai David

American Chocolate Cake with Fudge Frosting

Here is a tall, tender-crumbed cake with a mild chocolate flavor and a thick coating of dark fudge frosting – just the right refreshment for a gallery opening.

2¾ cups plus 2 tablespoons cake flour
2 cups sugar
1¾ cups solid vegetable shortening
½ cup unsweetened Dutch-process cocoa
4 tablespoons plus 2 teaspoons powdered milk
2½ teaspoons baking powder
1 teaspoon baking soda
1½ teaspoons vanilla extract
1 teaspoon salt
6 egg whites, at room temperature
Fudge Frosting (recipe follows)

1 Preheat the oven to 350°. Lightly grease and flour three 8-inch cake pans.

2 In a large mixer bowl, combine the flour, sugar, vegetable shortening, cocoa, powdered milk, baking powder, baking soda, vanilla, salt and 1 cup of water. Beat, beginning on low speed and gradually increasing to high, until smooth and light, about 4 minutes.

3 Add the egg whites and ½ cup of water. Beat until very smooth and light in texture, about 4 minutes. Divide the batter among the pans; smooth the tops evenly.

4 Bake in the center of the oven for 25 to 30 minutes, until the cakes are puffed and a tester inserted in the center comes out clean. Let the cakes cool in the pans for 10 minutes. Invert to unmold onto a wire rack; let cool completely, about 3 hours. (The cake layers may be baked a day ahead. Store at room temperature in plastic wrap.)

5 To assemble the cake, generously cover the top of one layer with some of the frosting. Place another layer on top and slather on another layer of frosting. Set the third layer in place and frost the top and sides with the remaining frosting. To give the frosting a shiny glaze, dip the knife in warm water and lightly swirl in a decorative pattern. Store under a domed cake cover until ready to serve.

Serves 12
Recipe from Bun's Restaurant
Delaware, Ohio

Le Cirque's Crème Brûlée

Fudge Frosting

**8 ounces unsweetened chocolate,
coarsely chopped**
¼ cup solid vegetable shortening
8 cups confectioners' sugar

½ teaspoon salt
1¼ cups milk
1 teaspoon vanilla extract

1 In the top of a double boiler, combine the chocolate and the shortening. Warm over low heat, stirring, until smooth. Immediately remove from the heat.

2 In a large bowl, combine the confectioners' sugar, salt, 1 cup of the milk and the vanilla. Stir until smooth.

3 Scrape the melted chocolate into the sugar mixture and beat with a spoon until well blended. Let the frosting stand for 1 minute; it will thicken considerably. Beat in the remaining ¼ cup milk until smooth. Cover with plastic wrap and hold at room temperature until ready to use.

Makes about 5 cups
Recipe from Bun's Restaurant
Delaware, Ohio

To cheer a major career celebration – like a friend's being made partner – serve what you might choose if you went out to one of New York's finest restaurants, Le Cirque.

4 cups heavy cream
1 vanilla bean
Pinch of salt
8 egg yolks

**¾ cup plus 2 tablespoons
granulated sugar**
8 tablespoons light brown sugar

1 Preheat the oven to 300°. In a heavy medium saucepan, combine the cream, vanilla bean and salt. Warm over moderate heat until the surface begins to shimmer, about 5 minutes.

2 In a large bowl, stir the egg yolks and sugar with a wooden spoon until blended. Pour in the hot cream and stir gently to avoid forming air bubbles until the sugar dissolves. Strain the custard into a large measuring cup or pitcher and skim off any surface bubbles. (Rinse the vanilla bean and reserve for another use.)

3 Place eight ¾-cup ramekins in a roasting pan. Pour the custard into the ramekins, filling them to the rim. Place the roasting pan in the oven and pour in enough warm water to reach halfway up the sides of the ramekins. Cover loosely with foil and bake for 1 hour and 15 minutes, or until the custard is firm around the edges. (It may still be wobbly at the center; it will firm up as it chills.)

4 Remove the ramekins from the water bath and let cool. Cover and refrigerate until cold, at least 3 hours. (The custards can be prepared to this point up to 2 days ahead. If small pools of liquid develop on the surface, blot with a paper towel before proceeding.)

5 Preheat the broiler. Set the ramekins on a baking sheet. Sieve 1 tablespoon of brown sugar over the top of each custard in a thin layer. Using a metal spatula or a sharp knife, spread the sugar evenly. Broil the custards as close to the heat as possible until the sugar is caramelized, 30 seconds to 2 minutes; watch carefully. Let cool and serve immediately or refrigerate for up to 4 hours.

Serves 8
Recipe from Le Cirque, New York City

Blueberry-Nectarine Skillet Pizza

Why not invite friends over for an array of New Wave pizzas and surprise them with this – a fruit pizza for dessert. In fact, make several – using this recipe and changing the fruit combinations, using, say, clementine and pineapple or kiwi and strawberry.

6 tablespoons unsalted butter	1 tablespoon vegetable oil
1 envelope (¼ ounce) active dry yeast	2 large nectarines, peeled and thinly sliced
3 to 4 tablespoons sugar	½ cup blueberries
1½ cups lukewarm water (105° to 110°)	Unsweetened whipped cream, sour cream or crème fraîche (optional)
4½ cups all-purpose flour	
½ teaspoon salt	

1 In a small saucepan, melt 4 tablespoons of the butter. Let cool to room temperature.

2 In a small bowl, blend the yeast and 1 tablespoon of the sugar with ½ cup of the warm water. Let stand for 5 minutes, until it begins to bubble. Stir in the cooled melted butter and the remaining 1 cup water.

3 Place 4 cups of the flour in a food processor and add the salt. Turn the machine on and add the yeast mixture through the feed tube. When the dough forms a ball, remove and knead for 5 minutes, working in the remaining ½ cup flour.

4 Lightly oil a large bowl. Form the dough into a ball and place it in the bowl, turning it once to coat it all over with oil. Cover with plastic wrap and let rise in a warm, draft-free place until doubled in bulk, about 1 hour. (If you're making the dough the night before, cover it with plastic wrap and refrigerate overnight.) Unless you are making two tarts (see Note), divide the dough in half and freeze half for future pizza (thaw the dough in the refrigerator before using).

5 Preheat the oven to 450°. Coat a 12-inch cast-iron skillet or griddle with the oil and place it in the oven to heat.

6 Form the dough into an even ball, flatten and then roll into a round 13 to 14 inches in diameter. Sprinkle with 1 tablespoon of the sugar.

7 Remove the hot pan from the oven; pour out any excess oil. (Leave the oven on.) Transfer the round of dough to the hot pan, arranging the dough so that there is a small, even rim extending up the sides of the pan.

8 Arrange the nectarine slices in concentric circles starting at the outside. Fill the center with a single layer of blueberries. Sprinkle with 1 to 2 tablespoons of sugar, depending on the sweetness of the fruit. Dot with the remaining 2 tablespoons butter.

9 Return the pan to the bottom shelf of the oven and reduce the temperature to 400°. Bake for 15 to 20 minutes, until the crust is very pale brown.

10 Remove the pizza from the oven and preheat the broiler. Place the pizza 3 or 4 inches from the heat for about 5 minutes, until the edges of the nectarines are browned.

11 To serve, cut into slices and serve as is or with unsweetened whipped cream, sour cream or crème fraîche.

Note:

This recipe makes enough dough for two fruit pizzas. If you want to make both, double the quantities of fruit and sugar for the topping. If you want to make only one, halve the dough in Step 4 and freeze one half for another time.

Serves 6
Recipe by Anne Disrude

White Chocolate Mousse

For the social break between rubbers of bridge, bring out a bevy of wine glasses gently mounded with this white chocolate mousse. Add a cup of tea or coffee and perhaps a cookie or two for an easy and appealing made-ahead round of refreshments.

1 pound white chocolate, coarsely chopped
2 tablespoons unsalted butter, at room temperature
6 egg yolks
¼ cup plus 2 tablespoons sugar
⅔ cup heavy cream

1 In a double boiler or microwave oven, melt the chocolate with the butter until smooth. Set aside to cool to room temperature.
2 In a double boiler or large bowl over simmering water, beat together the egg yolks and the sugar with an electric hand mixer until thickened, about 4 minutes. Remove from the heat and continue to beat until cooled and very thick and pale, about 5 minutes.
3 Beat the cream until stiff. Add the egg yolk mixture to the chocolate and stir until blended. Fold in the whipped cream until lightened and smooth. Spoon the mousse into stemmed glasses and chill until firm before serving.

Serves 6
Recipe by Diana Sturgis

The Ice Cream Party

Though an ice-cream party might once have been expressly for children, this one includes some definitively "adult" flavors, such as Armagnac and double espresso. Just about any occasion is reason enough to celebrate – the first day of summer, the last day of summer, Father's Day or Valentine's Eve. Choose flavors that suit your taste and ones that work well in combination – fresh lemon and blackberry, say, or cinnamon and hazelnut – and then churn out a flurry of batches all at once or prepare slowly, making, say, a batch a day for a week.

Hazelnut Ice Cream

The color of this ice cream is a pretty, pale tan, and the texture is either nubbly or silken depending on whether you leave the ground hazelnuts in or strain them out of the mixture before freezing. If you are serving the ice cream on its own, leave the nutty bits in. If you are serving it alongside hazelnut cookies or hazelnut cake (a wonderful combination), strain the nuts out for a contrast of texture.

¾ cup (3 ounces) hazelnuts
2 cups half-and-half
½ cup sugar

1 teaspoon Frangelico (hazelnut liqueur)
About ¼ teaspoon fresh lemon juice

1 Preheat the oven to 350°. Spread the hazelnuts on a jelly roll pan and toast in the middle of the oven until the nuts are pale brown beneath the skin, about 12 minutes; shake the pan midway through baking to ensure even browning. Place the hot nuts in a dry kitchen towel and rub briskly to remove as much of the brown skin as possible. (Don't worry about getting off every bit. Those bits lend a good color and flavor in the end.)

2 In a food processor, grind the nuts to a smooth, oily paste, about 60 seconds, scraping down the bowl midway.

3 Add the half-and-half and the sugar; process for 30 seconds to blend the mixture and dissolve the sugar. If you want a smooth-textured ice cream, strain through a fine sieve to remove the nuts.

4 Add the liqueur and stir to blend; then add the lemon juice, several drops at a time, stirring and tasting frequently until the flavor peaks on your tongue. Freeze in an ice cream maker according to the manufacturer's instructions.

Makes about 2½ cups
Recipe by Barbara Tropp

Cinnamon Ice Cream

One of the beauties of this dessert is the flavor and fragrance of freshly ground cinnamon, which you can obtain by grinding thin-barked, crumbly whole cinnamon sticks in a coffee or spice grinder. For a lovely contrast, serve this aromatic beige ice cream with thin chocolate cookie wafers or alongside a small wedge of plain chocolate cake.

1 tablespoon plus 2½ teaspoons freshly ground cinnamon

2 cups half-and-half
6 tablespoons sugar

1. In a small heavy saucepan, combine the cinnamon, half-and-half and sugar. Bring to a foaming near-boil over moderately low heat, stirring to dissolve the sugar. Remove the pan from the heat, cover tightly and allow the mixture to steep for at least 30 minutes or until cool.
2. Pass the mixture through a sieve lined with several layers of dampened cheesecloth, pressing on the cinnamon grounds and scraping the bottom of the strainer to garner every drop. Freeze in an ice cream maker according to the manufacturer's instructions.

Makes about 2½ cups
Recipe by Barbara Tropp

Blackberry Ice Cream

Barbara Tropp on this recipe: "To make this gorgeous deep blue-purple ice cream, I use a giant blackberry imported from New Zealand called 'berryfruit.' Any plump and sweet blueberry, blackberry or ollalieberry will work as well. When berries are in season, I freeze them on a baking sheet, bag them in plastic and store them in the freezer for those berry-less months when the blue ice cream urge hits."

¾ pound (about 2½ cups) plump and sweet berryfruit, blueberries or blackberries
¾ cup plus 2 tablespoons sugar

2 cups half-and-half
1 tablespoon crème de cassis
About 1 teaspoon fresh lemon juice

1. Pick over the berries to remove any that are bruised or moldy. Rinse briefly with cool water, then shake gently in a colander to drain.
2. In a food processor, process ¾ cup of the sugar until very fine. Add the berries and blend for 45 seconds to puree the berries and dissolve the sugar, stopping once to scrape down the bowl.
3. Add the half-and-half and crème de cassis and process for 10 seconds to blend.
4. Taste, then add the remaining 2 tablespoons sugar and/or the lemon juice, ¼ teaspoon at a time, if required to bring out the taste of the berries.
5. Pass the mixture through a fine-mesh strainer to remove the seeds, pressing down and scraping the bottom of the strainer to garner every drop. Freeze in an ice cream maker according to the manufacturer's instructions.

Makes about 5 cups
Recipe by Barbara Tropp

Pomegranate Ice Cream

Fresh Lemon Ice Cream

Here is an unusual ice cream, with a delicious tang of sourness underscoring the sweetness. The color is soft pink, and the texture is exceedingly smooth. Serve it on a ring of thin blood orange slices garnished with fresh pomegranate seeds. Unsweetened pomegranate juice can be found in health food stores. It has a rather odd smell, which – happily – disappears in the freezing process.

1 cup unsweetened bottled pomegranate juice
2 cups half-and-half
½ cup plus 1 tablespoon sugar

1 tablespoon grenadine or crème de cassis
3 to 4 teaspoons fresh lemon juice

1 Blend the pomegranate juice and half-and-half in a food processor. Add the sugar and grenadine and mix for 15 seconds to dissolve the sugar.

2 Stir in 3 teaspoons of the lemon juice, taste, then add additional lemon juice ¼ teaspoon at a time, stirring and tasting, until the flavor peaks on your tongue. Freeze in an ice cream maker according to the manufacturer's instructions.

Makes about 5 cups
Recipe by Barbara Tropp

This is a superbly refreshing ice cream, alive with the tang of fresh lemon. Look for plump, juicy lemons with a smooth and pretty peel. The bits of zest left in the ice cream give it color, texture and character.

2 or 3 large, or 3 or 4 smaller, lemons with unblemished skin
1 cup sugar

2 cups half-and-half
Pinch of salt

1 Wash and dry the lemons. Using a swivel-bladed vegetable peeler, remove the zest from the lemons, taking care not to remove any of the white pith.

2 Combine the zest and sugar in a food processor and grind for about 4 minutes, scraping down the bowl once or twice, until the zest is finely minced and the sugar melts slightly.

3 Squeeze and strain enough lemon juice to yield ½ cup plus 1 tablespoon. Add the strained juice to the processor and mix briefly just to combine. Scrape the mixture into a medium bowl, add the half-and-half and salt and stir well. Let sit for 15 to 30 minutes, stirring occasionally, to allow the mixture to thicken slightly and the sugar to dissolve.

4 Taste and adjust, if necessary, with a bit more lemon juice or sugar. Freeze in an ice cream maker according to the manufacturer's instructions.

Makes about 3½ cups
Recipe by Barbara Tropp

Armagnac Ice Cream

A scrumptiously subtle variation on vanilla, laced with this distinctive French brandy, that's almost too good to share.

2 cups heavy cream	**3 egg yolks**
1 cup milk	**1 teaspoon vanilla extract**
½ cup sugar	**3 tablespoons Armagnac**
Pinch of salt	

1 In a heavy medium saucepan, combine the cream, milk, sugar and salt. Cook over moderate heat, stirring frequently with a wooden spoon, until the sugar dissolves and the mixture is hot, 6 to 8 minutes.

2 In a large bowl, beat the egg yolks lightly. Gradually whisk in the hot cream in a thin stream. Return the mixture to the saucepan and cook over moderately low heat, stirring constantly, until the custard thickens enough to lightly coat the back of a metal spoon, 5 to 7 minutes. (Do not let the temperature exceed 180°.)

3 Strain the custard into a metal bowl. Set the bowl in a basin of ice and water and let stand, stirring occasionally, until cooled to room temperature. Stir in the vanilla and Armagnac. Cover and refrigerate for at least 4 hours, or until very cold.

4 Pour the custard into an ice cream maker and freeze according to the manufacturer's instructions.

Makes about 1 quart
Recipe by Leslie Newman

Double Espresso Ice Cream

This is an easy no-cook ice cream with real flavor and texture appeal. Chocolate-covered espresso beans are available at candy and specialty shops. If you can't find them, your ice cream will still be wonderful without them. Do not substitute coffee bean-shaped candies, coffee-flavored chocolates or chocolate chips, though; they are much too sweet for a real espresso ice cream.

1 can (14 ounces) sweetened condensed milk	**1 teaspoon vanilla extract**
2 cups heavy cream	**½ cup (about 3 ounces) chocolate-covered espresso beans, coarsely crushed**
½ cup brewed very strong espresso, cooled	

1 In a medium bowl, combine the condensed milk, cream, espresso and vanilla. Stir well, cover and refrigerate for 4 hours, or until very cold.

2 In an electric mixer on medium speed, beat the chilled espresso cream until it is thick and custardlike, 6 to 8 minutes.

3 Pour the mixture into an ice cream maker and freeze according to the manufacturer's instructions until partially frozen. Stop the machine and quickly stir in the crushed chocolate-covered espresso beans. Continue churning until the ice cream is frozen.

Makes about 1 quart
Recipe by Leslie Newman

Cardamom Ice Cream

Although the flavor sounds exotic, this cardamom-scented ice cream will appeal to less adventurous palates as well.

3 cups milk	**6 egg yolks**
1 cup heavy cream	**1 cup sugar**
16 cardamom pods	**¾ teaspoon vanilla extract**

1 In a large heavy saucepan, combine the milk, cream and cardamom pods. Bring to a boil over high heat. Remove from the heat, cover and let steep for 10 minutes.

2 Meanwhile, in a medium bowl, combine the egg yolks and sugar. Beat together until the mixture is pale and falls in thick ribbons when the beater is lifted.

3 Gradually beat the hot milk (with the cardamom) into the egg-sugar mixture. Return the custard to the saucepan and cook over moderate heat, stirring constantly, until thick enough to coat the back of a spoon; do not let boil. Remove from the heat. Stir in the vanilla extract.

4 Strain the custard into a bowl; discard the cardamom pods. Place over a larger bowl of ice and water and stir until cool. (The mixture can be made ahead to this point. Cover and refrigerate for up to 3 days.) Freeze in an ice cream maker according to the manufacturer's instructions.

Makes 1 quart
Recipe by Dorie Greenspan

Spiced Pumpkin Ice Cream

Whether with a wedge of pie or in place of it, this ice cream is a crowd pleaser. Don't be shy about using canned pumpkin – its flavor frequently is better than fresh.

2 egg yolks	**1½ teaspoons ground cinnamon**
¾ cup sugar	**1½ teaspoons freshly grated**
1½ cups milk	**nutmeg**
1 cup solid-pack pumpkin puree,	**1 cup heavy cream**
pressed through a fine sieve	

1 In a medium bowl, whisk the egg yolks with ½ cup of the sugar until well blended, about 1 minute.

2 In a small heavy saucepan, stir together 1 cup of the milk with the remaining ¼ cup sugar over moderate heat until the liquid boils and the sugar dissolves. Slowly whisk the hot milk into the egg-sugar mixture.

3 Transfer to a medium saucepan. Cook, stirring, over moderately low heat until the custard thickens slightly, about 5 minutes; do not allow to boil. Immediately pour into a large bowl set over ice.

4 Stir in the pumpkin puree, cinnamon, nutmeg, cream and the remaining ½ cup milk until blended. Continue to stir over ice until cool.

5 Freeze in an ice cream maker according to the manufacturer's directions.

Makes about 1½ pints
Recipe by Diana Sturgis

Apricot Brandy Ice Cream

No need to buy apricot brandy for this ice cream – all you need is fresh apricots and a good brandy to fine-tune your own combination.

1½ pounds fresh apricots	8 egg yolks
3 tablespoons fresh lemon juice	2 cups heavy cream
½ cup brandy	1 cup milk
1¼ cups sugar	⅛ teaspoon salt
½ teaspoon ground allspice	

1 In a large saucepan of boiling water, blanch the apricots, 3 or 4 at a time, for about 1½ minutes to loosen the skins. Transfer with a slotted spoon to a bowl of ice water. Add the lemon juice to another bowl of cold water. One by one, peel the apricots and place in the acidulated water to prevent browning. When all are peeled, pit the apricots and cut into ⅜-inch dice; there will be about 2 cups.

2 In a medium nonreactive saucepan, combine the apricots and brandy. Bring to a boil over moderate heat and simmer for 1 minute. Drain the apricots through a sieve set over a bowl and return the brandy to the saucepan. Transfer the apricots to a bowl.

3 Add ½ cup of the sugar and the allspice to the brandy in the saucepan. Bring to a boil over high heat, reduce the heat to moderate and boil, stirring frequently, until reduced to ⅓ cup, about 5 minutes. Remove the syrup from the heat and pour over the apricots, stirring well to coat. Cover and refrigerate until cooled.

4 In a double boiler, over gently simmering water, combine the egg yolks and the remaining ¾ cup sugar. Blend in 1 cup of the cream, the milk and the salt. Cook, stirring constantly, until the custard coats a spoon and is the consistency of heavy cream, 5 to 7 minutes. Remove from the heat and set the top of the double boiler into a bowl of ice to prevent further cooking. Cover and refrigerate until cooled.

5 Combine the cold apricot mixture, custard and the remaining 1 cup cream. Freeze in an ice cream maker according to the manufacturer's instructions.

Makes about 1 quart
Recipe by Jim Fobel

Chocolate Ice Cream Deluxe

The extreme richness of this delectable homemade ice cream is offset by the fact that it is served in very small portions, usually in demitasse cups.

8 ounces high-quality semisweet chocolate, coarsely chopped	Mix-ins, such as semisweet chocolate chips, crushed
2 cups heavy cream	toffee bars, crushed
1 cup milk	cookies, chopped nuts,
2 eggs	orange zest,
¼ cup dark rum	etc. (optional)
1 teaspoon vanilla extract	

1 In the top of a double boiler over barely simmering water, melt the chocolate with 1 cup of the cream over moderate heat, stirring occasionally, until completely smooth.

2 Slowly add the remaining 1 cup cream and the milk and stir until smooth. Remove from the heat and refrigerate until almost cold, about 2 hours.

3 Meanwhile, in a mixing bowl, beat the eggs until slightly foamy, about 1 minute. Add the rum and vanilla and chill until cold.

4 Stir together the chocolate and egg mixtures and add any of the optional mix-ins, if using.

5 Pour the mixture into an ice cream maker and freeze according to the manufacturer's instructions.

Makes about 1 quart
Recipe by Henry Koehler

Three-Layer Celebration Cake with Apricot Glaze

Whether it's for a bridal shower or small wedding party itself, this cake will make the attendees glad they came. Its three layers are not difficult to construct and the tasteful decoration relies on fresh flowers nested upon easy-to-manage loops of buttercream. Serve it with huge quantities of apricot nectar mixed with sparkling wine and watch the celebration shine.

Cake:
¾ pound unsalted butter, at room
    temperature
3¾ cups granulated sugar
6 eggs
4½ teaspoons vanilla extract
6¾ cups sifted cake flour
7½ teaspoons baking powder
3 teaspoons salt
3 cups milk
6 tablespoons orange liqueur

Glaze:
2 jars (12 ounces each)
    apricot preserves
½ cup orange liqueur

Frosting:
Vanilla Buttercream
    (recipe follows)

Prepare the cake layers:

1 Preheat the oven to 375°. Butter a heavy-duty 18-x-13-inch jelly-roll pan and line the bottom with parchment or waxed paper. Butter the paper and dust with flour.

2 In a large bowl, beat ¼ pound of the butter and 1¼ cups of the sugar with an electric mixer on medium speed until light and fluffy. One at a time, add 2 of the eggs, beating well after each addition. Beat in 1½ teaspoons of the vanilla.

3 In a large bowl, combine 2¼ cups of the sifted flour with 2½ teaspoons of the baking powder and 1 teaspoon of the salt. In a small bowl, combine 1 cup of the milk and 2 tablespoons of the orange liqueur. Beat about ½ cup of the flour mixture into the butter mixture until thoroughly incorporated. Beat in about ¼ cup of the liquids. Continue alternating additions of the flour and milk mixtures, beating well after each addition, until you have used all the ingredients.

4 Pour the batter into the sheet pan and tap the pan to level the mixture. Bake for 20 to 25 minutes, until the top springs back when touched and a toothpick inserted in the center comes out clean. Cool in the pan for 10 minutes; then invert on a rack and remove the parchment. Let cool completely.

Recipe continues on the next page

Three-Layer Celebration Cake with Apricot Glaze Continued

5 Repeat two more times with the remaining cake ingredients to make 3 layers.

Make the glaze:

6 Strain the preserves into a small saucepan. Add ¼ cup of the liqueur. Cook, stirring, over low heat until smooth and warm.

Assemble and frost the cake:

7 Make the frosting. Arrange one cake layer on a large serving platter. Brush the top with half of the warm apricot glaze. Place a second layer on top and brush it with the remaining glaze. Place the third layer on the cake and brush the top with the remaining ¼ cup orange liqueur.

8 Trim the brown edges off the sides of the cake with a long sharp knife. Frost the top and sides with half of the frosting. Use the remainder to decorate the cake.

Serves 32
Recipe by W. Peter Prestcott

Vanilla Buttercream

2 egg yolks
⅓ cup potato starch*
2 cups cold milk
5 cups sifted confectioners' sugar
1¼ pounds unsalted butter,
    at room temperature

2 teaspoons vanilla extract
*Available in the kosher
    food section of
    supermarkets and delis

1 In a medium bowl, whisk the egg yolks, potato starch and 1 cup of the cold milk until smooth. In a heavy saucepan, stir the remaining 1 cup milk into 2 cups of the confectioners' sugar until blended. Heat to boiling; remove from the heat.

2 Gradually whisk the hot milk mixture into the egg-yolk mixture in a thin, steady stream. Strain through a fine sieve into a clean heavy saucepan. Bring to a boil, stirring constantly, over moderately low heat. Reduce the heat to low and simmer, stirring, until the mixture becomes very thick, 5 to 7 minutes. Remove from the heat and scrape into a small bowl. Cover the surface with waxed paper; let cool to room temperature.

3 Beat the butter and the remaining 3 cups sugar with an electric mixer until light and fluffy, 8 to 10 minutes. Add the cooled milk mixture, ¼ cup at a time, beating until blended after each addition.

Makes about 5½ cups
Recipe by W. Peter Prestcott

Pomander Cake

Inspired by those pretty, clove-spiked oranges that are made to hang in closets, this cocoa party cake is a variation on the classic gènoise. Serve it to announce the beginning of the holiday season.

½ cup plus 2 tablespoons all-purpose flour	4 tablespoons unsalted butter, melted and cooled to room temperature
½ cup unsweetened Dutch-process cocoa powder	8 whole cloves
¼ cup cornstarch	2 thin-skinned, seedless oranges, thinly sliced
1 teaspoon baking powder	
1½ teaspoons ground cloves	1½ tablespoons orange liqueur, such as Grand Marnier
6 whole eggs	
1 egg yolk	1½ cups heavy cream
3 cups granulated sugar	⅓ cup confectioners' sugar

1 Preheat the oven to 350°. Lightly butter two 8-inch round cake pans, 2 inches deep. Line the bottoms of each with parchment or waxed paper and butter the paper. Dust the pans with flour; tap out any excess.

2 Sift together the flour, cocoa, cornstarch, baking powder and ground cloves.

3 In a large metal bowl, combine the whole eggs, egg yolk and 1 cup of the granulated sugar. Whisk together until light in color. Place over a saucepan of simmering water and whisk until the sugar is dissolved and the mixture is slightly warm to the touch.

4 Remove the bowl from the heat and beat until tripled in volume and thick enough to form a ribbon that holds for 10 seconds when the beater is lifted, about 5 minutes.

5 Sift one-third of the dry ingredients over the eggs and fold in until just blended. Fold in half the melted butter. Repeat with half the remaining dry ingredients and the remaining butter. Fold in the last of the dry ingredients.

6 Divide the batter between the 2 prepared pans. Bake in the center of the oven for 25 to 30 minutes, until the tops are springy and a cake tester inserted in the center comes out clean. Remove from the oven and let cool on a rack for 10 minutes. Unmold the cake and remove the parchment. Turn and cool right-side up. (The cakes can be made ahead to this point. Cool completely, wrap in plastic and store at room temperature or in the refrigerator for up to 3 days or freeze for one month.)

7 In a medium saucepan, combine the remaining 2 cups granulated sugar and the whole cloves with 2½ cups of cold water. Bring to a boil over high heat and cook until the sugar dissolves and the liquid is clear. Add the orange slices. Return to the boil, reduce the heat to moderately low and simmer until the orange rinds are softened, about 20 minutes. Remove from the heat and let the oranges cool in the syrup for 10 minutes.

8 Remove the oranges and finely chop. Measure out 1 cup of the syrup and stir in the orange liqueur; discard any remaining syrup.

9 Cut each cake layer in half horizontally. Break one of the top layers into pieces, place in a food processor and grind to fine crumbs. Reserve for garnish.

10 Beat the cream until it stands in stiff peaks. Sift the confectioners' sugar over the whipped cream and fold in. Fold the chopped orange into half the whipped cream. Set the remaining whipped cream aside.

11 To assemble, place a bottom layer of the cake, cut-side up, on a platter or cake stand. Brush one-third of the reserved poaching syrup over the layer. Cover evenly with half the whipped cream-chopped orange mixture. Place the other bottom layer, cut-side up, over the filling. Brush with ⅓ cup of the syrup and spread with the remaining orange-cream mixture. Brush the cut side of the top layer with the remaining syrup and place on top, cut-side down.

12 Cover the entire cake with the reserved whipped cream. Press the cake crumbs into the sides of the cake. Refrigerate for 2 to 6 hours before serving. (This cake is best eaten the day it is assembled.)

Serves 8 to 10
Recipe by Dorie Greenspan

Chocolate-Chocolate-Chocolate-Chip Fudge Cake

This grown up rendition of a chocolate birthday cake is just the thing for a friend who's still a kid at heart. Forego the dozens of candles and serve some spirited liqueurs instead. The cake, with fudge filling, chocolate cream, a layer of chocolate chips and a final drizzle of syrup, is worth its weight in chocolate.

Cake Layers:
¼ pound plus 2⅔ tablespoons unsalted butter, at room temperature
2 cups granulated sugar
3 eggs
2 cups sifted all-purpose flour
¾ cup unsweetened cocoa powder, preferably Dutch process
1¼ teaspoons baking soda
¼ teaspoon baking powder
½ teaspoon salt
1½ cups milk
1 teaspoon vanilla extract
¼ cup chocolate-mint flavored liqueur, such as Vandermint

Chocolate Fudge Filling:
⅔ cup granulated sugar
½ cup heavy cream
2½ ounces unsweetened chocolate
1 tablespoon light corn syrup
2 tablespoons unsalted butter

Chocolate Cream:
2½ cups heavy cream
3½ tablespoons unsweetened cocoa powder, preferably Dutch process
7 tablespoons confectioners' sugar

Assembly and Chocolate Syrup:
3 tablespoons chocolate chips
2 tablespoons unsweetened cocoa powder, preferably Dutch process
2 tablespoons light corn syrup
1 tablespoon granulated sugar

Prepare the cake layers:

1 Preheat the oven to 350°. Line two 9-inch round cake pans with waxed paper; butter and flour the pans; tap out any excess flour.

2 In a mixer bowl, beat the butter until light and fluffy. Gradually add the sugar and continue beating until smooth. One at a time, beat in the eggs until well blended.

3 Sift together the flour, cocoa, baking soda, baking powder and salt. Add to the egg mixture in thirds, alternating with the milk, mixing only until blended. Blend in the vanilla and liqueur.

4 Divide the batter between the two prepared pans. Bake until the tops of the cakes are springy to the touch, 40 to 45 minutes. Remove from the oven and set on racks to cool for 30 minutes. Loosen the edges with a knife and unmold. Peel off the waxed paper. Set the cakes on a rack and let cool completely.

Recipe continues on page 34

Chocolate-Chocolate-Chocolate-Chip Fudge Cake Continued

Prepare the filling:

5 Combine the sugar, cream, chocolate and corn syrup in a small heavy saucepan. Bring to a simmer over moderate heat, stirring frequently. Reduce the heat to low and cook for 10 minutes, or until the mixture thickens. Remove from the heat, dot the top with the butter and let cool to room temperature, about 15 minutes. When cool, stir in the butter until the fudge filling is smooth and creamy.

Prepare the chocolate cream:

6 Beat the cream and cocoa until soft peaks form. Gradually add the confectioners' sugar and continue beating until stiff.

Assemble the cake:

7 Cover one cake layer with all of the fudge filling. Sprinkle evenly with the chocolate chips. Spread ½ cup of the chocolate cream on top of the chips. Top with the second cake layer and cover the top and sides of the cake with half of the remaining chocolate cream. Use the remainder in a pastry bag to decorate the cake as desired. Refrigerate for up to 3 hours before serving time.

Prepare the syrup:

8 Combine the cocoa, corn syrup, sugar and 2 tablespoons of water in a small heavy saucepan. Bring to a simmer over low heat and cook, stirring constantly, for 2 minutes. Transfer the syrup to a small bowl and let cool to room temperature, stirring once or twice, to prevent a skin from forming.

9 Just before serving, drizzle the syrup over the top of the cake in a lacy design.

Serves 10 to 12
Recipe by Peter Sussman
The Phoenix
Warren, Vermont

Christmas Pudding

You don't have to be British to follow the charming holiday custom of a steamed Christmas Pudding. Make it with friends up to a year ahead – age improves its flavor – and don't forget, for tradition's sake, to stir the batter *clockwise only,* with a wooden spoon. If you like, wrap a dime in foil and stir it into the pudding. It isn't a sixpence but finding it offers a dickens of a good time.

2 cups dark raisins
2 cups golden raisins
2 cups currants
½ cup finely chopped blanched almonds (about 2 ounces)
1½ cups grated suet, loosely packed (about 4 ounces)
2 cups fresh bread crumbs
2 teaspoons grated orange zest
1 teaspoon grated lemon zest
½ cup (packed) brown sugar
½ cup grated carrot
1 cup all-purpose flour
1 teaspoon ground cinnamon
1 teaspoon freshly grated nutmeg
½ teaspoon ground ginger
¼ teaspoon ground cloves
4 eggs, lightly beaten
½ cup dark ale or milk
⅓ cup brandy
Hard Sauce (recipe follows), Brandy Sauce (recipe follows) or whipped cream

1 In a large bowl, mix the dark and golden raisins, currants, almonds, suet, bread crumbs, orange and lemon zests, brown sugar and carrot. Sift in the flour, cinnamon, nutmeg, ginger and cloves; mix well. Stir in the eggs and ale until well blended.

2 Butter a 6- to 8-cup pudding basin. Line the bottom with a small circle of buttered waxed paper. Spoon the pudding mixture into the basin. Place a 14- x 12-inch sheet of foil on a flat surface. Cover with a sheet of waxed paper the same size and butter the waxed paper. Treating the foil and waxed paper as a single thickness, make a 1-inch pleat in the center to form a 12-inch square which will allow space for expansion. Place the cover, buttered side down, on top of the pudding basin and twist and crimp the foil tightly around the rim or tie securely with string to seal. Tie the basin in a cotton or linen kitchen towel "sling" by knotting

opposite corners together and lower it onto a rack or folded towel in a steamer or large, deep pot filled with enough boiling water to reach halfway up the sides of the basin.

3 Cover and steam over moderate heat for 7 hours, replenishing the boiling water as needed, about every 30 minutes. This pudding will get darker the longer it steams.

4 Store the pudding in its basin, covered, until ready to use. Before serving, steam for up to 2 hours to reheat. Just before serving, unmold the pudding onto a platter. Heat the brandy, light it with a match and pour it over the top of the pudding. When the flames subside, cut the pudding into wedges and serve with Brandy Sauce, Hard Sauce or whipped cream.

Serves 16
Recipe by Diana Sturgis

Brandy Sauce

1 tablespoon cornstarch	1 tablespoon unsalted
1¼ cups milk	butter
2 tablespoons granulated sugar	3 tablespoons brandy

1 Place the cornstarch in a small, heavy saucepan. Blend in ¼ cup of the milk with a wooden spoon until smooth. Stir in the remaining milk; add the sugar and butter.

2 Bring the mixture to a boil over moderate heat, stirring constantly. Reduce the heat to low and simmer, stirring, for 4 minutes. Remove from the heat and stir in the brandy.

3 Pour into a bowl or pitcher and serve at once; or pour into a small bowl, cover with waxed paper and hold in a saucepan of hot water for up to 1 hour.

Makes about 1⅓ cups
Recipe by Diana Sturgis

Hard Sauce for Christmas Pudding

¼ pound unsalted butter, at room temperature	½ cup (packed) brown sugar
	3 tablespoons brandy

Beat the butter with the sugar until they are soft and well combined. Gradually beat in the brandy. Place the sauce in a small crock or bowl, cover and refrigerate for at least 1 hour or for several days.

Note:

To prepare well in advance, chill the sauce until almost firm, form into a log 1 inch in diameter, wrap tightly and freeze.

Makes about 1 cup
Recipe by Diana Sturgis

Basic Madeleines

Whether it has been 10 years or 50, seeing old friends is truly a pleasure. When remembering the past is appropriate, serve up pots of hot tea and platefuls of Proust's well-remembered madeleines. Whether you choose basic, tea-scented, spice or cocoa, these soft cookies set the stage for comfortable wanderings into the past.

3 eggs, at room temperature
¾ cup sugar
1 teaspoon vanilla extract
2 teaspoons grated lemon zest
¼ teaspoon fresh lemon juice
1⅓ cups sifted all-purpose flour
¾ cup clarified unsalted butter

1 In a large bowl, whisk the eggs with the sugar until light colored and thick enough to fall in ribbons. Beat in the vanilla, lemon zest and lemon juice.

2 Using a rubber spatula, fold the flour into the eggs. Fold in ½ cup of the butter until just incorporated; do not overfold. Tightly cover the bowl with plastic wrap and refrigerate for at least 1 hour or until chilled through. (The recipe can be prepared to this point up to 24 hours ahead.)

3 Preheat the oven to 425°. Using a small pastry brush, coat the indentations of two 12-inch madeleine molds with 2 tablespoons of the butter. Place the mold upside-down over a baking sheet to catch drips so that the butter will evenly coat the molds and won't pool in the bottom; refrigerate until the butter is set, about 10 minutes. Brush again with the remaining 2 tablespoons butter and let chill until set.

4 Spoon rounded tablespoons of the batter into the mold; do not smooth the batter. Bake in the center of the oven for 5 minutes; then reduce the heat to 375° and bake for 7 to 10 minutes, until the madeleines are golden in the center and browned around the edges.

5 Remove from the oven. Sharply rap the mold against a flat surface to loosen the madeleines. Turn out and let cool slightly on a wire rack. Serve warm. (The madeleines can be loosely wrapped in waxed paper and stored in a loosely covered container for up to 24 hours.)

Makes 2 dozen
Recipe by John Robert Massie

Tea-Scented Madeleines

Perfect, no doubt, if Earl Grey tea is being served.

¾ cup clarified unsalted butter	1 teaspoon finely grated
2 tablespoons Earl Grey tea leaves	lemon zest
3 eggs, at room temperature	¼ teaspoon fresh lemon juice
¾ cup sugar	Pinch of salt
	1⅓ cups sifted all-purpose flour

1 In a small saucepan, combine ½ cup of the butter with the tea. Gently steep over low heat for 10 minutes to release the aromatic oils; do not boil. Remove from the heat and set aside, uncovered, to infuse for 30 minutes. Strain the butter and discard the tea leaves.

2 Continue from Step 1 of the Basic Madeleines, substituting the tea-flavored butter for the plain clarified butter in Step 2.

Makes 2 dozen
Recipe by John Robert Massie

Spice Madeleines

An interesting switch – you don't normally expect a madeleine to be spicy, but you'll love the difference it makes.

¾ cup clarified unsalted butter	3 eggs, at room temperature
3-inch cinnamon stick, broken	¾ cup sugar
into pieces	Pinch of salt
1 tablespoon whole cloves	1⅓ cups sifted all-purpose flour

1 In a small saucepan, combine ½ cup of the butter with the cinnamon and cloves. Gently warm over low heat for 10 minutes to release the aromatic oils; do not boil. Remove from the heat and set aside, uncovered, to infuse for 30 minutes. Strain the butter and discard the spices.

2 Continue from Step 1 of the Basic Madeleines, substituting the spice-flavored butter for the plain clarified butter in Step 2.

Makes 2 dozen
Recipe by John Robert Massie

Cocoa Madeleines

Extra-homey looking, cocoa madeleines will please those who like every dessert to include chocolate.

3 eggs, at room temperature	**½ cup unsweetened cocoa powder,**
¾ cup sugar	**preferably Dutch process**
1 teaspoon rum extract	**¾ cup clarified unsalted**
1 cup sifted all-purpose flour	**butter**

1 In a large bowl, beat or whisk the eggs with the sugar until light colored and thick enough to fall in ribbons. Beat in the rum flavoring.
2 Sift together the flour and the cocoa. Gently fold into the eggs.
3 Fold ½ cup of the butter into the batter until just incorporated; do not overfold. Tightly cover with plastic wrap and refrigerate for at least 1 hour until chilled through.
4 Continue from Step 3 of the Basic Madeleines recipe.

Makes 2 dozen
Recipe by John Robert Massie

Belle Epoque Cherries Jubilee

For the friends who just put the final finishing touches on their Victorian house, offer a fittingly Victorian dessert in celebration. This one couldn't be simpler, and it shines with all the fireworks of a much more elaborate effort.

1 can (1 pound) pitted Bing	**1 pint vanilla ice cream,**
cherries	**frozen hard**
½ cup sugar	**Chocolate curls, for garnish**
2 tablespoons grated orange zest	**Strips of orange zest,**
1 tablespoon arrowroot	**for garnish**
⅓ cup kirsch	

1 Drain the cherries, reserving the juice. Measure the juice and add enough water to equal 1½ cups; pour into a small saucepan. Add the sugar and orange zest and simmer uncovered over low heat for 10 minutes.
2 Add 2 tablespoons of water to the arrowroot, stirring to dissolve. Gradually stir the arrowroot mixture into the cherry liquid in the pan. Simmer, stirring frequently, until thick, about 10 minutes. Add the cherries.
3 In a small saucepan, warm the kirsch over moderate heat, about 1 minute. Meanwhile, scoop the ice cream into a serving bowl or individual dessert dishes. At table, pour the warm kirsch into the cherry sauce and ignite. Carefully pour the flaming sauce over the ice cream and garnish with the chocolate curls and strips of orange zest if desired.

Serves 4
Recipe by W. Peter Prestcott

Ice Cream Fritters with Raspberry Sauce

When quick energy is in order, no dessert suits as well as ice cream. Welcome runners home from a race with a backyard full of friends and some ice cream fritters. Each fritter has a hot, crispy nut coating encasing a frozen ice-cream center. And don't be hesitant about frying ice cream. If you follow our procedure, the results will be exciting. The ice cream balls can be prepared ahead of time and frozen, but the fritters must be served immediately after frying.

Ice Cream Fritters:
1 pint high-quality vanilla
   ice cream
1 egg white, lightly beaten
1 cup chopped toasted almonds

Raspberry Sauce:
½ cup seedless raspberry jam
2 tablespoons framboise or
   raspberry liqueur

Prepare the ice cream balls:

1 Using an ice cream scoop, shape the ice cream into ten 1½-inch balls and freeze them for at least 1 hour.

2 Quickly roll the ice-cream balls in the beaten egg white, the almonds, again in the egg white, and again in the almonds; replace the balls in the freezer until ready to deep-fry. They will keep for as long as a week stored in airtight containers.

Prepare the raspberry sauce:

3 In a small saucepan, heat the jam over moderate heat, stirring constantly until it has melted. Stir in the framboise.

4 In a deep-fryer with a deep-frying basket inserted, heat about 3 inches of oil to 375°. Using a slotted spoon, lower up to four fritters into the basket in the oil; fry for 15 seconds. Remove with the basket and drain briefly. Immediately place two fritters each in small, stemmed serving dishes. Repeat with the remaining ice-cream balls. Spoon raspberry sauce over the fritters and serve immediately.

Serves 5
Recipe by Jim Fobel

L'Ile Flottante Pralinée

What could be more appropriate to the occasion than serving Floating Island at a Bon Voyage Party? You might not be able to carry it down to the pier but for at-home farewells, it couldn't be more fitting.

Crème Anglaise:
6 egg yolks
⅓ cup granulated sugar
2 cups milk, scalded and cooled
   slightly
2 tablespoons vanilla extract
½ cup heavy cream, very lightly
   whipped

Hazelnut Praline:
½ cup hazelnuts
½ cup granulated sugar
Pinch of cream of tartar

Caramel Syrup:
½ cup granulated sugar
Pinch of cream of tartar

Meringue:
10 egg whites (about 1¼ cups),
   at room temperature
⅛ teaspoon salt
⅛ teaspoon cream of tartar
¾ cup superfine sugar
1½ teaspoons vanilla extract

Prepare the crème anglaise:

1 Using an electric mixer, beat the egg yolks lightly and add the sugar, beating until the mixture forms a ribbon when the beaters are lifted. Slowly stir in the scalded milk as you continue to beat. Transfer the mixture to a heavy pan and cook over moderately low heat, stirring constantly, until thickened to the consistency of heavy cream. Remove from the heat and stir in the vanilla. Transfer to a bowl, cover with a round of waxed paper placed directly on the surface, and let cool to room temperature for 1 hour or as long as overnight.

Prepare the hazelnut praline:

2 Preheat the oven to 350°. Spread the hazelnuts over a shallow baking pan and roast, stirring once or twice, for about 25 minutes, or until the nuts are golden. Place the nuts in a towel and rub briskly to remove the skins.

3 In a skillet, combine the sugar with ¼ cup water and the cream of tartar; bring the mixture to a boil, washing down any sugar that clings to the pan with a wet pastry brush. Cook the syrup only until it is a golden-colored caramel.

4 Add the hazelnuts to the syrup and tilt the skillet to coat the nuts. Pour the mixture onto an oiled marble surface or oiled baking pan and let it cool until brittle. Break up the praline into chunks and pulverize in a food processor or blender; set aside.

Prepare the caramel syrup:

5 In a small saucepan, combine the sugar with ¼ cup water and the cream of tartar and bring the mixture to a boil over low heat, washing down any sugar that clings to the pan with a wet pastry brush. Increase the heat and cook the syrup only until it is a golden-colored caramel; remove the pan from the heat. Standing back from the pan, quickly pour ¼ cup hot water into the caramel and stir to make a thick syrup. Then quickly divide the syrup among eight 1-cup molds or custard cups, tilting the molds to coat the bottoms evenly with the caramel. There will be about 2 tablespoons of syrup for each mold.

Prepare the meringue:

6 Preheat the oven to 325°. In a large bowl, beat the egg whites with the salt and cream of tartar until soft peaks form. Gradually add the superfine sugar and the vanilla and beat until stiff but not dry. Fold in ¾ cup of the hazelnut praline (reserve the remainder for another use). Divide the meringue mixture among the caramelized molds, mounding it slightly.

7 Arrange the molds in a roasting pan and add enough hot water to reach two-thirds of the way up the sides of the molds. Bake for 30 minutes, or until the meringues are puffed and golden.

8 Remove the molds from the baking pan, cool to room temperature, and cover with rounds of waxed paper. Refrigerate until well chilled, at least 1 hour or as long as overnight.

9 To serve, loosen the edges of the molds with the point of a knife and turn the "islands" out of the molds onto chilled dishes. Gently fold the lightly whipped cream into the crème Anglaise, and spoon it around the islands.

Serves 8
Recipe by Sally Darr

Old
Favorites

Old Favorites

If this chapter were a song, it might be Stephen Collins Foster's "My Old Kentucky Home" or some equally sweet and memorable melody that has a timeless grace. Our old favorites are timeless too, with an enduring appeal that ensures they will be eagerly prepared by generation after generation of cooks. This collection of recipes is where we share our favorite versions of those familiar desserts that are beloved by all, hoping that you will find the renditions we've chosen as delicious as we do.

Not content to offer up just any Banana Cream Pie, we highly recommend that you give Jim Fobel's a try. It's superlative – sweet and creamy, topped with a cloud of lightly sweetened fresh whipped cream. It makes a perfect ending to a wintertime beef stew dinner or a plateful of barbecued ribs.

Some homespun dishes smell as good while they're cooking as they'll taste later on, and the temptation to sneak a spoonful is almost irresistible. Consider our Old-Fashioned Bread Pudding, all puffed and golden as it comes out of the oven, or a fresh-baked Spiced Pumpkin Pie – how many pie-tops have been marred by a telltale fingerprint? Or maybe it's the fragrance of cookies baking that recalls the past for you. If so, we suggest you try the Buttery Tea Balls, Petite Macaroons or Dark Fudge Cookies.

These soothing recipes might not be sophisticated, but they're seldom short on style. You need only one bite of the fudgy Pepper Mill Squares to know that something spicy and sweet and quite special is happening here. We dare you to come away from a wedge of Elizabeth Schneider's rendition of a classic French country sugar pie – La Galette Pérougienne – without feeling you're actually sitting in Pérouges, a tiny and ancient walled town on the road from Lyon to Geneva.

There's a voluptuousness about homespun desserts that comes straight from the heart – the little extra effort of a Grandmother who glazed the piecrust so it would shine, or who cut out your initials in pastry to mark a tart as yours alone. It's the generosity of spirit that shines through all three layers of Aunt Charlotte's Milk Chocolate Cake, thickly slathered with frosting.

Our Super Double-Cream Cheesecake is as smooth and creamy as the puddings and purees mothers love to serve their kids. In addition to texture, a food's very flavor can say homespun too. Perhaps it's fresh and lemony, like Ruth Spear's sprightly Lemon Curd Tart, or the shock of the goodness of sweet purple grapes in Wild Wind Farm's simple Concord Grape Tart, or the mingling of spicy, sweet and fruit flavors to be found in a crockery bowl heaped with a serving of Dorie Greenspan's Gingered Brown Betty, with a soothing scoop of Vanilla Custard Ice Cream alongside.

Perhaps the very best qualities of old favorite desserts are embodied in the tin of Sweetheart Cookies you carried off to college – a touch of home to help you brave your new world. ■

Aunt Charlotte's Milk-Chocolate Cake

School can be many years behind you, but this tall chocolate cake will take you back. It makes a major treat after a hard day in the classroom or office.

Cake:
¼ **pound unsalted butter, at room temperature**
¼ **cup white vegetable shortening**
2 cups granulated sugar
3 ounces semisweet chocolate, melted and cooled
1½ **teaspoons vanilla extract**
4 whole eggs
1 egg yolk
3 cups all-purpose flour
¾ **teaspoon baking powder**
¾ **teaspoon salt**
1½ **teaspoons baking soda**
1½ **tablespoons distilled white vinegar**
1½ **cups buttermilk**

Frosting:
¾ **pound unsalted butter, at room temperature**
2 eggs
1 tablespoon vanilla extract
2 pounds (2 boxes) confectioners' sugar, sifted
6 ounces unsweetened chocolate, melted and cooled

Prepare the cake:

1 Preheat the oven to 350°. Lightly grease three 9-inch round cake pans. Line the bottom of each pan with a circle of parchment or waxed paper. Grease the pans again, applying a generous layer to the sides and the paper. Flour the pans and tap out any excess.

2 In a medium bowl, beat together the butter, shortening and granulated sugar until very light and creamy, about 5 minutes.

3 Beat in the melted chocolate and the vanilla. One at a time, add the eggs, beating well after each addition. Beat in the egg yolk.

4 Sift together the flour, baking powder and salt.

5 Place the baking soda and vinegar in a small bowl and stir while it foams; add the buttermilk.

6 Working quickly and lightly, fold about ½ cup of the dry ingredients into the chocolate mixture. As soon as it is incorporated, fold in about ¼ cup of the buttermilk mixture. Repeat until all of the flour and buttermilk have been added.

7 Divide the batter among the three cake pans and spread it evenly. Place in the oven immediately and bake for about 30 to 35 minutes, until the center of each cake springs back when lightly touched. Shift pan positions halfway through to allow for even baking.

Recipe continues on the next page

Aunt Charlotte's Milk-Chocolate Cake Continued

Allow the layers to cool in the pans for 20 minutes. Unmold and cool on a wire rack; peel off the waxed paper.

Meanwhile, make the frosting:

8   Beat together the butter, eggs and vanilla until fluffy. Gradually beat in the sugar and chocolate and mix until well blended.

9   Brush any loose crumbs from the cakes. Place one cake layer, flat-side up, on a cake plate. Spread with a thick layer of the frosting. Set another layer on top and spread with more frosting. Place the remaining cake layer flat-side down, over the frosting. Frost the top and sides of the cake. Chill to set the frosting.

Serves 14
Recipe by Jim Fobel

Carrot Pecan Coffee Cake with Praline Streusel

This type of dessert has several advantages – it's portable, it's tasty and it's excellent for breakfast the next morning.

Praline Streusel:
½ cup all-purpose flour
¼ cup (packed) dark brown sugar
4 tablespoons unsalted butter, chilled
⅓ cup chopped pecans

Coffee Cake:
1 cup all-purpose flour
1 cup whole wheat flour
1 tablespoon baking powder

1½ teaspoons baking soda
1 teaspoon salt
½ teaspoon ground cinnamon
½ teaspoon freshly grated nutmeg
½ teaspoon ground mace
½ pound unsalted butter, softened
1¼ cups (packed) dark brown sugar
4 eggs
2 cups shredded carrots
1 cup chopped pecans

1   Preheat the oven to 350°. Generously oil a 9-inch springform pan.

Make the streusel:

2   In a large bowl, combine the flour and sugar. Cut in the butter until it is the size of small peas. Add the pecans and toss with a fork to mix.

Make the cake:

3   In a large bowl, sift together the flours, baking powder, baking soda, salt, cinnamon, nutmeg and mace.

4   In another large bowl, cream the butter and sugar until fluffy. One at a time, beat in the eggs and stir in the carrots. Add the dry ingredients and stir until well blended. Fold in the pecans. Turn the batter into the prepared pan and spread it evenly. Sprinkle the streusel evenly over the top of the batter.

5   Bake the cake in the center of the oven for 1 hour, or until a tooth-pick inserted in the center comes out clean. Cool in the pan on a rack for 1 hour. Carefully remove the sides of the springform and allow the cake to cool for at least 30 minutes. Serve warm or at room temperature.

Serves 12 to 14
Recipe by Maria Piccolo Stern

Super Double-Cream Cheesecake

The epitome of cheesecakes – you won't find a creamier, tastier or better one anywhere. Don't open the oven door during baking if you want to keep the top from cracking. Make this cake at least a day before you want to serve it to allow the flavors to develop.

Crust:
1 box (8½ ounces) chocolate
   wafer cookies
¼ cup sugar
1 teaspoon ground cinnamon
Pinch of salt
6 tablespoons unsalted butter,
   melted

Filling:
3 large packages (8 ounces each)
   cream cheese, softened

⅔ cup sugar
½ teaspoon salt
3 eggs
3 cups sour cream
1 tablespoon fresh lemon juice
1½ tablespoons bourbon or
   dark rum
1 teaspoon vanilla extract
2 tablespoons unsalted butter,
   melted

Make the crust:

1 In a food processor or blender, grind the cookies into moderately fine-textured crumbs. Add the sugar, cinnamon and salt and process briefly to blend. Transfer to a bowl, pour the butter over the crumbs and toss with a fork to moisten evenly. Gently press the crumbs evenly over the bottom and sides of a 9-inch springform pan.

Prepare the cheesecake filling:

2 Preheat the oven to 350°. In a food processor, combine the cream cheese, sugar, salt and eggs; blend until smooth, scraping down the sides of the container as necessary. Add the sour cream (see Note), lemon juice, bourbon, vanilla and butter and blend.

3 Pour the filling into the cookie-crumb shell and bake in the middle of the oven for 45 minutes. Turn off the oven, prop the oven door open slightly and allow the cake to rest in the oven for 1 hour. Cool on a rack and refrigerate for at least 8 hours.

Note:

If the container of the food processor is not large enough, add only 1 cup of sour cream in Step 2. Pour about half the mixture into a mixing bowl; add the remaining 2 cups of sour cream to the processor and blend. Combine both batches in the mixing bowl and stir to blend.

Serves 10 to 12
Recipe by Kate Slate

Dark Fudge Cookies

Godiva Chocolates developed this recipe – the Lady would have been proud.

6 ounces dark sweetened chocolate, preferably bittersweet	2 eggs
	1½ cups all-purpose flour
	½ teaspoon salt
1 cup sugar	1½ cups coarsely chopped
¼ pound unsalted butter, softened	pecans or walnuts

1 In a double boiler or microwave oven, melt the chocolate over low heat; remove from the heat and let cool for 10 minutes.

2 Meanwhile, in a large bowl, cream the sugar, butter and eggs until smooth. Beat in the cooled chocolate until well blended.

3 Gradually add the flour and salt, mixing until smooth. Stir in the nuts. Cover and chill until firm, about 1 hour.

4 Preheat the oven to 375°. Lightly grease 2 baking sheets. Drop the cookie dough by rounded teaspoons 2 inches apart onto the prepared sheets.

5 Bake for 10 to 12 minutes, until the cookies are slightly firm when touched. Let cool for 5 minutes before removing to a cooling rack.

Makes about 3 dozen
Recipe from Godiva Chocolates

Pecan Icebox Cookies

Since this dough can hold for a week, it's a good one to keep in the fridge ready to slice and bake at a moment's notice.

¼ pound unsalted butter, softened	2½ cups all-purpose flour
1 cup (packed) dark brown sugar	½ teaspoon baking soda
1 egg	½ teaspoon salt
1 teaspoon vanilla extract	½ cup chopped pecans

1 In a medium bowl, cream the butter and sugar together until light and fluffy. Beat in the egg and vanilla.

2 Combine the flour, baking soda and salt and sift into the butter mixture. Blend thoroughly. Stir in the pecans.

3 Shape the dough into a roll 2 inches in diameter. Wrap tightly in plastic wrap and refrigerate overnight or for up to 1 week.

4 Preheat the oven to 350°. Using a sharp thin knife, cut the dough into ¼-inch slices and place on ungreased cookie sheets. Bake in the center of the oven for about 15 minutes, or until lightly browned and set. Transfer to wire racks to cool.

Makes about 4 dozen
Recipe by Joanna Pruess

Cottage Butter Cut-Out Cookies

Here's a basic butter cookie that makes a perfect jumping-off point for your most artistic decorating ideas. Think of them as a blank canvas and get ready to paint.

½ pound unsalted butter, softened	2½ cups all-purpose flour
⅔ cup sugar	1 teaspoon baking powder
1 teaspoon vanilla extract	Colored crystal sugar or Sugar
½ teaspoon lemon extract	Glaze (recipe follows),
1 egg	for decoration

1 In a large bowl, beat the butter and sugar until smooth and fluffy, 3 to 4 minutes. Add the vanilla and lemon extracts and the egg; beat until smooth and light, 2 to 3 minutes.

2 Add 1¼ cups of the flour and ½ teaspoon of the baking powder. Beat until just smooth; add the remaining 1¼ cups flour and ½ teaspoon baking powder and mix to combine. Cover the dough with plastic wrap and refrigerate until firm, at least 1 hour.

3 Preheat the oven to 325°. On a lightly floured surface, roll out the dough, one-quarter at a time, about ⅛ inch thick. Cut out the dough with decorative cookie cutters and place 1 inch apart on ungreased cookie sheets.

4 Bake the cookies for 20 minutes, or until lightly golden around the edges. To decorate: sprinkle the cookies with crystal sugar while still warm and then transfer to a rack to cool. Or, let the cookies cool and then decorate with Sugar Glaze. Store in layers, separated by sheets of waxed paper, in an airtight tin.

Makes about 4 dozen
Recipe by Quinith Janssen

Sugar Glaze

3 tablespoons milk	3½ cups (1-pound box)
½ teaspoon vanilla extract	confectioners' sugar
	Food coloring (optional)

1 In a medium bowl, combine the milk and vanilla. Slowly stir in the sugar, beating constantly until the frosting becomes thick and creamy. The more this frosting is beaten, the shinier it becomes.

2 Divide the frosting among several small bowls. Stir a few drops of the desired food coloring into each bowl. If the frosting becomes too thin, stir in a few teaspoons of confectioners' sugar. Spread on cooled cookies with a broad flat knife. Let the glaze harden completely before storing the cookies.

Note:

To prevent the frosting from forming a crust while decorating, keep covered with a dampened cloth.

Enough for 4 to 5 dozen
Recipe by Quinith Janssen

Strawberry Peach Pie

Say goodbye to summer in the most graceful way we know, by taking advantage of the season's last strawberries and peaches. Combine the two in this luscious lattice-topped pie and toast the vigor of the upcoming autumn and winter months.

Pastry:
3 cups all-purpose flour
½ teaspoon salt
¼ pound cold unsalted butter, cut into bits
½ cup vegetable shortening, cut into bits
1 egg
¼ cup ice water

Filling:
2 pints strawberries, left whole if small, halved if large
1 pound ripe fresh peaches, peeled, stoned and cut into crescent-shaped slices
¾ to 1 cup sugar (depending on the sweetness of the fruit)
¼ cup all-purpose flour
2 teaspoons grated lemon zest
1 tablespoon milk mixed with 1 teaspoon sugar, for glaze (optional)
Finely chopped toasted pecans, for decoration

Make the pastry:

1 Combine the flour and salt in a large mixing bowl. Scatter the butter and shortening on top and cut in until the mixture resembles coarse meal with several pea-size bits of fat remaining.

2 Lightly beat the egg with the ice water and pour it over the flour mixture. Stir with a fork just until the mixture forms a mass. Place the dough on a lightly floured surface, divide in half (making one half slightly larger than the other) and flatten into 6-inch disks. Wrap separately in plastic and chill for 1 hour.

3 Preheat the oven to 400°. On a lightly floured surface, roll out the larger portion of dough into a 12-inch round. Transfer to a 10-inch pie plate and fit the dough into the pan without stretching. Refrigerate.

Make the filling:

4 In a large bowl, combine the strawberries and peach slices. Sprinkle the sugar, flour and zest over the top and toss gently, just to mix. Take care that you don't break up the fruit. Turn the filling into the chilled pie shell.

5 On a slightly floured surface, roll out the remaining portion of dough. Using a fluted pastry wheel, cut long strips for a lattice top. Create a twisted lattice top by arranging twisted strips of pastry at 1¼-inch intervals, crossing the pie on its two diagonals. Weave the strips in and out as with any lattice top. Fold the overhanging dough over the ends of the strips and crimp decoratively. If desired, sprinkle with the toasted pecans.

6 Place the pie on a baking sheet and brush lightly with the glaze, if desired. Place on the center rack of the oven and reduce the heat to 350°. Bake for 35 to 45 minutes, or until the crust is golden and the juices are bubbling.

Serves 6-8
Recipe by Mardee Haidin Regan

Sweetheart Cookies

Joanna Pruess's great grandmother handed down the recipe and technique for making these buttery cookies filled with a spot of raspberry jam.

¼ pound plus 4 tablespoons unsalted butter, softened	1½ cups all-purpose flour
½ cup sugar	¼ teaspoon salt
1 egg yolk	About 2 tablespoons raspberry jam
½ teaspoon grated lemon zest	

1 In a medium bowl, cream the butter and sugar until fluffy and light. Beat in the egg yolk and lemon zest.

2 Combine the flour and salt and sift into the butter mixture. Stir until well blended. Cover and refrigerate the dough until firm, 2 to 3 hours.

3 Preheat the oven to 350°. Shape the dough into balls 1¼ inches in diameter and place them on ungreased cookie sheets. With your fingertip or the end of a wooden spoon, make a small depression in the center of each cookie. Fill each hollow with ⅛ to ¼ teaspoon raspberry jam.

4 Bake in the middle of the oven for 15 minutes, or until the cookies are lightly browned around the edges. Transfer to wire racks and let cool.

Makes about 2 dozen
Recipe by Joanna Pruess

Cream Wafers

Everyone loves sandwich cookies and since you're in charge here, you might want to double the filling recipe so that you can use twice as much between the cookies.

Wafers:	¼ pound unsalted butter, at room temperature
2 cups all-purpose flour	
½ pound unsalted butter, softened	1 egg yolk
⅓ cup heavy cream	1 teaspoon vanilla extract
Granulated sugar	Food coloring (optional)
	Confectioners' sugar or colored crystal sugar, for decoration
Filling:	
¾ cup confectioners' sugar	

Make the wafers:

1 In a large bowl, combine the flour, butter and cream. Beat until smooth, 3 to 4 minutes. Divide the dough into quarters and flatten each into a disk. Wrap the disks individually in waxed paper and refrigerate for several hours or overnight.

2 Preheat the oven to 375°. On a lightly floured surface, working with one disk at a time, roll the dough out ⅛ inch thick. Cut into 1½- inch rounds. Place 1 inch apart on ungreased cookie sheets. Prick the top of each cookie 4 times with a fork. Sprinkle lightly with sugar.

3 Bake the cookies for 15 to 17 minutes, until light golden and puffed. Transfer to a rack to cool.

Meanwhile, make the filling:

4 Beat the confectioners' sugar, butter, egg yolk and vanilla in a medium bowl until light and fluffy. Color, if desired, with food coloring.

5 To assemble, mound about 1 rounded teaspoon of the filling onto a wafer. Gently press a second wafer on top of the filling. Repeat with all the cookies and filling. Before serving, dust with sifted confectioners' sugar or colored crystal sugar.

Makes about 20
Recipe by Quinith Janssen

Orange Cut-Out Cookies

Make these cookies suit the occasion by cutting out specially chosen shapes or piping colorful icing on top.

¾ cup confectioners' sugar
¼ pound plus 3 tablespoons unsalted butter, softened
2 tablespoons grated orange zest
¼ cup fresh orange juice

1¾ cups all-purpose flour
Pinch of salt
Piping Icing (recipe follows), for decorations

1   In a large mixer bowl, cream together the sugar and butter until smooth and fluffy, 3 to 4 minutes. Add the orange zest and juice and beat until smooth.

2   Gradually add the flour and salt, beating until just smooth. Gather the dough into a ball, cover with plastic wrap and refrigerate until the dough is firm, at least 1 hour.

3   Preheat the oven to 325°. On a lightly floured surface, roll out one-quarter of the dough ⅛ inch thick. Cut out cookies with decorative cookie cutters and place 1 inch apart on ungreased cookie sheets.

4   Bake the cookies for 25 minutes, or until lightly golden around the edges. Continue rolling out and cutting cookies until all of the dough is used. Let the cookies cool on a rack before decorating with Piping Icing. Store in layers, separated by sheets of waxed paper, in an airtight tin.

Makes about 3 dozen
Recipe by Quinith Janssen

Piping Icing

1 egg white, lightly beaten
2 to 3 cups confectioners' sugar, sifted

Several drops of fresh lemon juice
Food coloring (optional)

1   Place the egg white in a medium bowl. Gradually stir in the sugar and lemon juice until the mixture is stiff.

2   Divide the sugar mixture among several small bowls. Stir a few drops of the desired food coloring into each bowl. If the frosting becomes too thin, stir in a few teaspoons of sifted confectioners' sugar. Fit a pastry bag with a small (#0 or #1) plain tip and pipe decorations onto cooled cookies. Let the icing harden completely before storing.

Note:

To prevent the frosting from forming a crust while decorating, keep covered with a dampened cloth.

Makes about 2 cups
Recipe by Quinith Janssen

La Galette Pérougienne

In the tiny town of Pérouges, France, this age-old sugar pie is made and sold, still warm, in big wedges. Here, you might want to serve it with crème fraîche or whipped cream and fresh or "put-up" fruit.

Dough:
1 package active dry yeast
⅓ cup lukewarm water (105°
    to 115°)
2¼ cups all-purpose flour
2 tablespoons sugar
Grated zest of 1 lemon (or ½
    orange – which is not authentic,
    but delicious)
¾ teaspoon salt
6 tablespoons unsalted butter,
    chilled
1 whole egg
1 egg yolk

Topping:
5 tablespoons unsalted butter,
    frozen
¼ cup sugar

Make the pastry:

1 Combine the yeast and a pinch of sugar with the lukewarm water and stir until the yeast dissolves. Let stand for about 5 minutes, or until foamy. If the yeast does not foam, begin again with fresh ingredients.

2 Place the flour, sugar, zest and salt in a food processor. Process, turning the motor on and off several times, to mix well. Remove the processor top and slice the butter, by ½ tablespoonfuls, into the container. Turn the machine on and off several times, until the bits of butter are no longer discernible.

3 Lightly beat together the egg and egg yolk. With the motor running, add the yeast mixture to the processor and immediately add the egg. Process for 45 seconds to knead the dough.

4 Form the dough into a ball and set it in a lightly floured bowl. Sprinkle the top of the ball lightly with flour. Cover the bowl with plastic wrap and let stand at room temperature for about 1½ hours, or until doubled in bulk.

5 Preheat the oven to 425°. Adjust the oven racks to both the lowest and highest positions in the oven. Place the dough on a lightly floured surface and flatten evenly with your hand. With a rolling pin, gradually press out the dough into a 19-inch circle. Fold the dough in quarters, center the point in a 17-inch pizza pan, and unfold the dough to cover the pan. Fold a ½-inch rim of dough inward to make a neat border, and make a decorative edge.

Make the topping:

6 With a swivel-bladed peeler or sharp knife, shave the frozen butter evenly over the dough, right out to, but not on, the border. Sprinkle on the sugar.

Recipe continues on the next page

La Galette Pérougienne Continued

7 Set the galette on the lower oven rack and bake for about 6 minutes, or until the border is lightly browned and the surface bubbles. Increase the heat to 475° and move the pan to the higher oven rack. Bake for about 4 minutes, or until the top surface is browned in parts.

8 Slice into wedges and serve; the galette should be eaten while hot and soft.

Note:

To make two smaller galettes, follow the recipe through Step 4. Then halve the dough. Roll out one half to form a circle 12 to 13 inches in diameter; repeat with the second half. Place one of the circles on an ungreased baking sheet and proceed as for the large galette, but using only half the topping. Place the second circle on a large, foil-covered plate or tray, form the border and then place it in the freezer for about an hour, or until frozen solid. Wrap the foil tightly around the dough, remove it from the tray and replace it in the freezer, where it will keep for several weeks. To bake the frozen galette: Open the foil wrapper and let the dough come to room temperature – 1 to 1½ hours. Set it on a lightly floured baking sheet and continue with recipe Steps 6 and 7, adding 2 minutes to the initial baking time at 425°.

Makes one 16-inch galette or
two 10-inch galettes
Recipe by Elizabeth Schneider

Petite Macaroons

Macaroons make the perfect surprise treat that can be pulled out of a tin to accompany a cup of tea or to quell a midnight craving.

1 cup whole unblanched almonds (about 5 ounces)	2 tablespoons plus 4 teaspoons sugar
¾ cup confectioners' sugar	½ teaspoon almond extract
2 egg whites	¼ teaspoon vanilla extract
Pinch of salt	

1 Combine the almonds and confectioners' sugar in a food processor and whirl to an extremely fine texture. Scrape the nut-sugar powder into a medium bowl.

2 Preheat the oven to 325°. Cover a large baking sheet with parchment paper or use a nonstick baking sheet. In the small bowl of an electric mixer beat the egg whites with the salt until soft peaks form. Add the 2 tablespoons sugar, 1 tablespoon at a time, beating for 1 minute on high speed after each addition. Beat in the almond and vanilla extracts.

3 Fold in the almond powder with a rubber spatula.

4 Fit a pastry bag with ½-inch plain tube and fill it with the almond mixture. Press out 40 to 50 rounds, each about 1¼ inches in diameter, onto the baking sheet. With a wet spoon or fingertip, smooth the top of each round. Sprinkle the cookies with the remaining 4 teaspoons sugar to give them shiny, crackled tops.

5 Bake the cookies in the center of the oven for about 15 minutes, or until firm and colored a very pale beige, but not browned. Remove from the oven and let stand 10 to 15 minutes.

6 Transfer the macaroons to a wire rack and let cool completely. Packed in an airtight tin, they'll keep for weeks.

Makes about 4 dozen
Recipe by Elizabeth Schneider

Sally's Sesame Crisps

These crisp wafers have the old-fashioned look of a benne wafer, but the sesame seeds are lightly toasted and dark rum perks up the flavor.

1 cup sesame seeds
¼ pound plus 4 tablespoons unsalted butter, melted and cooled to room temperature
¾ cup (packed) light brown sugar
1 egg
2 tablespoons dark rum

1¼ cups sifted all-purpose flour
¼ teaspoon baking powder
½ teaspoon freshly grated nutmeg
¼ teaspoon salt
⅛ teaspoon white pepper

1 Place the sesame seeds in a large skillet and cook over moderate heat, tossing frequently until light brown and toasted, about 5 minutes. Spread out on a plate and let cool.

2 Preheat the oven to 375°. Butter 2 baking sheets. In a medium bowl, combine the butter, sugar, egg, rum and sesame seeds.

3 Combine the flour, baking powder, nutmeg, salt and white pepper and sift over the butter mixture. Blend well.

4 Drop by rounded ½ teaspoon measures about 2 inches apart onto the prepared baking sheets. Bake in the center of the oven for about 10 minutes, or until the cookies are golden brown with darker edges. Transfer to wire racks and let cool.

Makes about 5 dozen
Recipe by Joanna Pruess

Buttery Tea Balls

They're tiny, they're buttery, they're delicious — and they couldn't be simpler to make.

½ pound unsalted butter, at room temperature
4 cups confectioners' sugar
1 teaspoon vanilla extract

2¼ cups all-purpose flour
¼ teaspoon salt
¾ cup finely chopped walnuts

1 Preheat the oven to 375°. In a large bowl, mix the butter, ½ cup of the sugar, the vanilla, flour, salt and walnuts until they form a dough.

2 Roll the dough into 1-inch balls in the palm of your hand. Place on ungreased baking sheets and bake for 10 to 12 minutes, or until the bottoms are slightly brown.

To coat:

3 Place the remaining 3½ cups sugar in a shallow dish. Using a spatula, remove the balls from the baking sheet and, while still hot, roll them around in the sugar. Let cool and roll again, until thoroughly coated.

Makes about 4 dozen
Recipe by Anna Mae Hubert

Aunt Myra's Butterscotch Pie

Made with patience and a little flair, this pie can be unspeakably beautiful. Try to contour the meringue into big floppy petals that will turn shades of brown and tan at the edges.

Pastry:
1½ cups all-purpose flour
¼ teaspoon salt
½ cup white vegetable shortening
About 3 tablespoons ice water

Butterscotch Filling:
1 cup (packed) light brown sugar
½ cup all-purpose flour
¼ teaspoon salt
1 can (13 ounces) evaporated milk

4 egg yolks
4 tablespoons unsalted butter
1 teaspoon vanilla extract

Meringue:
4 egg whites, at room
   temperature
¼ teaspoon salt
¼ teaspoon cream of tartar
½ cup superfine sugar

Prepare the pastry:

1 Combine the flour and salt in a mixing bowl. Cut in the shortening until the mixture resembles coarse meal. Sprinkle on the ice water and stir rapidly with a fork until the pastry can be gathered into a ball. Shape the pastry into a 6-inch disk, wrap tightly in plastic and chill for 1 hour.

2 Preheat the oven to 425°. On a lightly floured surface, roll out the pastry ⅛ inch thick. Loosely fit the pastry into a 9-inch pie pan and trim the edge, leaving a 1-inch border. Fold the pastry in to make a raised edge and flute or decoratively crimp the edge. Prick the pastry all over with the tines of a fork and bake in the center of the oven, pricking several times if the bottom bubbles, for about 12 minutes, or until crisp and golden brown; cool on a wire rack.

Prepare the filling:

3 Combine the brown sugar, flour and salt in a medium bowl. Add enough water to the evaporated milk to make 2 cups. In a small bowl, lightly beat the egg yolks together and then whisk in ½ cup of the diluted evaporated milk. Whisk the egg-milk mixture into the dry ingredients until thoroughly blended and then whisk in the remaining diluted milk. Transfer to a double boiler and cook, whisking constantly, over simmering water, until very thick, 10 to 15 minutes. Remove from the heat and stir in the butter and vanilla. Cover with a round of waxed paper placed directly on the surface and let cool for 15 minutes. Pour the filling into the baked pie shell and cover with a round of waxed paper. Let cool to room temperature and then refrigerate until well chilled, about 3 hours.

Prepare the meringue:

4 Preheat the oven to 350°. Beat the egg whites with the salt and cream of tartar until soft peaks form. Gradually add the sugar and continue beating until the whites are stiff and glossy; do not over-beat or the meringue will be dry.

Assemble and bake the pie:

5 Remove the waxed paper from the pie filling and pile the meringue on top, mounding it in the center and spreading it out to overlap the crust slightly all around.

6 Bake the pie in the center of the oven for 12 to 15 minutes, or until the meringue turns slightly golden. Chill for 3 hours before serving. When slicing, dip a sharp knife into very hot water before making each cut.

Serves 6-8
Recipe by Jim Fobel

Southern-Style Pecan Pie

The liquor one chooses for pecan pie might have something to do with geography or then again it might not. If you prefer bourbon in your pecan pie, by all means substitute it for the rum – and add a touch to some lightly whipped cream while you're at it.

Pastry:
1½ cups all-purpose flour
2 tablespoons sugar
¼ teaspoon salt
6 tablespoons unsalted butter, chilled and cut into bits
2 tablespoons vegetable shortening, chilled
2 to 3 tablespoons ice water

Filling:
3 eggs
1 cup dark corn syrup
1 cup sugar
1 teaspoon vanilla extract
4 tablespoons unsalted butter, melted and slightly cooled
1 tablespoon dark rum
6 ounces (about 1½ cups) pecan halves

Prepare the pastry:

1 In a food processor, process the flour, sugar, salt, butter and shortening, pulsing on and off until the mixture resembles coarse meal. With the motor running, gradually add the ice water until the dough gathers into a soft ball. Shape the dough into a ball and flatten into a 6-inch round. Wrap in waxed paper and chill for at least 1 hour.

2 Place a baking sheet in the center of the oven and preheat the oven to 350°. Lightly butter a 9-inch pie plate. On a lightly floured surface, roll out the pastry into a 12-inch round. Without stretching, carefully fit the pastry into the pie plate. Trim, leaving a ½-inch border all around. Fold under and crimp decoratively; set aside.

Prepare the filling:

3 In a large bowl, lightly beat the eggs. Stir in the corn syrup, sugar, vanilla, melted butter and rum. Evenly arrange the pecans, flat sides down, over the bottom of the pie shell and pour the filling over them. Place the pie on the preheated baking sheet and bake for 1 hour, or until the filling is set and the center puffed. Cool to room temperature and serve.

Serves 8
Recipe by Ruth Spear

Gingered Brown Betty

Since you have to chill this Brown Betty overnight before baking, you should have plenty of time to mix up a batch of Pat Buckley's homemade vanilla ice cream to serve with it (page 72).

5 cups coarsely cubed brioche or challah, crusts removed (made from a 1-pound loaf of egg bread)
¼ pound plus 2 tablespoons unsalted butter, melted
⅓ cup sugar

2 teaspoons ground ginger
1½ pounds baking apples, such as Cortland – peeled, cored and thinly sliced
Crème fraîche, whipped cream or vanilla ice cream, as accompaniment

1 Generously butter a 6-cup charlotte mold or soufflé dish. Line the bottom of the mold with a circle of waxed paper. Butter well.

2 Place the bread cubes in a large bowl and drizzle with the melted butter while tossing with a fork to moisten.

3 In another large bowl, combine the sugar and ginger. Add the apple slices and toss to coat evenly.

4 Place one-fourth of the bread cubes in the bottom of the mold so that they cover the base in an even layer. Distribute one-third of the apple slices over the bread. Repeat twice more, ending with a layer of bread. Cover with aluminum foil, fit a plate or piece of cardboard cut to size inside the mold and weigh down with a 2-pound can. Refrigerate, weighted, overnight.

5 Preheat the oven to 375°. Remove the weights and the plate or cardboard from the dessert and bake, still wrapped in foil, for 25 minutes. Remove the foil and bake until the top is nicely browned, about 30 minutes.

6 Let stand at room temperature for 5 minutes, then loosen the sides with a knife and invert onto a large plate. Peel off the waxed paper and serve warm with cream or ice cream.

Serves 6
Recipe by Dorie Greenspan

Rhubarb and Strawberry Pie

Pack a perfect picnic pie to please your friends. The pastry recipe makes enough for two pies; so, you can freeze half for later use or make two pies while rhubarb is still in season.

Pastry:
3 cups all-purpose flour
½ teaspoon salt
¼ pound cold unsalted butter, cut into small pieces
½ cup vegetable shortening, cut into small bits
1 egg
¼ cup ice water

Filling:
2 pints strawberries, cut into large chunks
1 pound rhubarb, cut into 1-inch pieces (about 4 cups)
⅔ cup sugar
1 teaspoon finely grated lemon zest (optional)
¼ cup instant tapioca

Crumb Topping:
1 cup all-purpose flour
4 tablespoons unsalted butter, chilled and cut into bits
¼ cup sugar

Make the pastry:

1 Place the flour and salt in a large mixing bowl. Scatter the butter and shortening on top and cut in until the mixture resembles coarse meal with several pea-size bits of fat remaining visible.

2 Lightly beat the egg with the ice water and pour it over the flour mixture. Stir just until the mixture forms a mass. Place the dough on a lightly floured surface, divide in half and shape the halves into two 6-inch disks. Wrap separately in plastic and chill for at least 30 minutes or overnight. (If you are making only one pie, freeze one disk for later use.)

3 Preheat the oven to 400°. On a lightly floured surface, roll out one of the pastry disks into a 13-inch circle. Transfer to a 10-inch pie plate and fit the pastry into the dish without stretching; refrigerate.

Make the filling:

4 In a large bowl, place the strawberries, rhubarb, the ⅔ cup sugar, lemon zest and tapioca; toss to combine. Place the fruit filling in the chilled pie shell.

Make the crumb topping:

5 In a bowl, combine the flour, butter and sugar. Rub together to make a crumbly topping. Sprinkle the crumb topping over the filling to cover completely.

6 Place the pie in the middle of the oven. Reduce the temperature to 350° and bake for 1 hour, or until golden. Remove to a rack and let cool to room temperature.

Serves 8
Recipe by Diana Sturgis

Best Apple Pie

Whether you have it with a wedge of cheddar, a scoop of vanilla or nothing at all, this apple pie is equal to Mom's best efforts.

1 recipe Flaky Pie Pastry (recipe follows), made with vegetable shortening
2½ pounds (5 to 7) tart cooking apples, such as Granny Smith or Greening
1 cup plus 2 tablespoons sugar
¼ cup all-purpose flour
1½ teaspoons ground cinnamon
½ teaspoon freshly grated nutmeg
1 tablespoon unsalted butter
1 egg white, lightly beaten, for egg wash

1 Prepare and roll out the pastry as directed in the recipe. Refrigerate the bottom crust and the unrolled top crust while you prepare the apples.

2 Peel, core and quarter the apples lengthwise. Cut the quarters lengthwise into ½-inch-thick wedges (you will have about 7 cups).

3 In a medium bowl, mix together 1 cup of the sugar, the flour, cinnamon and nutmeg. Add the apples and toss to coat well. Turn the apples into the pie shell, mounding them in the center. Dot with the butter.

4 Preheat the oven to 425°. On a lightly floured surface, roll out the remaining pastry into a 12-inch circle. Moisten the edge of the bottom crust lightly with cold water and place the top crust over the apples. Trim both crusts evenly to ½ inch. Turn the excess pastry under the rim and crimp decoratively. Cut three steam vents in the top crust with the tip of a small knife. Decorate with cutouts made from scraps of dough, if desired.

5 Lightly brush the pastry with the egg wash and sprinkle the remaining 2 tablespoons sugar evenly over the top. Bake the pie for 40 minutes, or until the top is golden brown and the apples are tender when pierced with a knife through a vent. Transfer the pie to a rack and cool before serving.

Serves 6 to 8
Recipe by Jim Fobel

Flaky Pie Pastry

For the flakiest results, use lard. Shortening or butter makes for richer, but still flaky, pastry.

2 cups all-purpose flour
¼ teaspoon salt
⅔ cup vegetable shortening, butter or lard, chilled
3 to 4 tablespoons ice water

1 In a large bowl, combine the flour and salt. Cut in the shortening, lard or butter until the mixture resembles coarse meal. Sprinkle the ice water over the mixture 1 tablespoon at a time, tossing with a fork, until the pastry can be gathered into a ball. (Use additional drops of water if necessary.)

2 Divide the ball of dough in half; flatten each half into a 6-inch disk, wrap individually in waxed paper and chill for at least 45 minutes. (Tightly wrapped in plastic wrap, this pastry will keep for up to 3 days in the refrigerator and for up to 3 months in the freezer.)

To roll out the pastry:

3 On a lightly floured surface, roll out one of the pastry rounds into an 11- to 12-inch circle. Fold the circle into quarters or roll loosely over a lightly floured rolling pin and transfer to a 9-inch pie pan. Unfold and ease the pastry into the pan without stretching it. If you are making a double-crust pie, keep the remaining, unrolled portion chilled until needed.

Makes two single 9-inch shells
or one double-crust pie
Recipe by Jim Fobel

Spiced Pumpkin Pie

Ginger, allspice, cinnamon and a good jolt of molasses add the spice and spark that make this pie special. Chill before serving if you'd like a stronger, more intense flavor.

Pie Crust:
1 cup plus 2 tablespoons
   all-purpose flour
¼ teaspoon baking powder
¼ teaspoon salt
6 tablespoons unsalted butter,
   chilled and cut into pieces
1 tablespoon sugar
1 egg yolk
1 tablespoon ice water

Filling:
1⅓ cups canned solid-pack
   pumpkin

3 whole eggs
1 cup sour cream
½ cup heavy cream
½ cup light unsulphured molasses,
   such as Mott's or Grandma's
1 teaspoon ground ginger
1 teaspoon ground cinnamon
1 teaspoon ground allspice

Accompaniment:
½ cup heavy cream, chilled
2 teaspoons sugar
1 egg white
Ground cinnamon

Make the crust:

1 In a large bowl, mix together the flour, baking powder and salt. Cut in the butter until the mixture resembles coarse meal. Mix in the sugar. Add the egg yolk and ice water and stir to form a dough. Pat the dough into a 6-inch disk; wrap and refrigerate until chilled, about 20 minutes.

2 Butter a 9-inch metal pie plate. On a lightly floured sheet of waxed paper, roll out the dough into an 11-inch circle. Invert the pastry into the prepared pie plate and peel off the paper. Fit the pastry evenly in the dish, trim away any excess and decoratively crimp the edge. Refrigerate the pie shell while you make the filling. (The crust can be made a day ahead.)

Make the filling:

3 Preheat the oven to 400°. In a large bowl, lightly beat the pumpkin, eggs, sour cream, heavy cream, molasses, ginger, cinnamon and allspice until well blended.

4 Place the pie plate on a baking sheet and pour the filling into the prepared pie shell. Bake in the center of the oven for 20 minutes. Reduce the oven temperature to 325° and continue to bake for 25 to 30 minutes, until the pie is set but slightly wobbly in the center. Let cool on a rack. Serve at room temperature or chilled.

As accompaniment:

5 In a large bowl, beat the heavy cream with 1 teaspoon of the sugar until stiff. In another bowl, beat the egg white until soft peaks form. Whisk in the remaining 1 teaspoon sugar and beat until stiff peaks form. Fold the beaten egg white into the whipped cream. (The cream can be prepared and refrigerated 2 hours before serving.) Lightly dust the cream with cinnamon and serve on the side.

Serves 8 to 10
Recipe by Diana Sturgis

Orange Meringue Pie

Though lemon meringue pie may be the norm, try this orange version right away. It has the tartness of lemon with the added flavor of orange juice and zest.

Pie Pastry:
2 cups all-purpose flour
½ teaspoon salt
⅔ cup vegetable shortening
2 to 3 tablespoons ice water

Filling:
6 tablespoons cornstarch
3 tablespoons all-purpose flour
1 cup sugar
¼ teaspoon salt
1 cup boiling water
5 egg yolks, lightly beaten

2 cups fresh orange juice
12 tablespoons unsalted butter
  (1½ sticks), sliced
1½ tablespoons grated orange zest
½ cup fresh lemon juice
2 teaspoons grenadine syrup

Meringue:
5 egg whites, at room
  temperature
¼ teaspoon salt
½ teaspoon cream of tartar
½ cup plus 2 tablespoons sugar

Prepare the pastry:

1 Combine the flour, salt and shortening in a large mixing bowl, and cut in the shortening until the mixture resembles coarse meal. With a fork, stir in only enough ice water to enable the dough to be gathered into a ball. Flatten the ball into a disk, wrap in waxed paper and refrigerate for at least 1 hour.

2 On a lightly floured surface, roll out the pastry into an 11-inch round. Without stretching, fit the pastry into a 9-inch pan. Trim, leaving a ½-inch overhang all around; discard the pastry scraps or reserve for another purpose. Tuck under the excess pastry and crimp to make a decorative edge. Refrigerate for 30 minutes before baking.

3 Preheat the oven to 425°. Line the pastry with aluminum foil and weigh down with aluminum pie weights or dried beans to prevent the pastry from bubbling. Bake for 15 to 20 minutes, or until crisp and golden. Cool on a rack.

Prepare the filling:

4 In a large mixing bowl, combine the cornstarch, flour, sugar and salt. Stirring constantly, pour in the boiling water and blend until smooth. Add the egg yolks and orange juice and beat until smooth. Transfer the filling to the top of a double boiler over, but not touching, boiling water and cook, stirring frequently, for 15 to 20 minutes. When the mixture is very thick, remove it from the heat. Add the butter, orange zest, lemon juice and grenadine; stir until the butter melts. Cover with a round of waxed paper placed directly on the surface and let the filling cool to room temperature. Pour into the pre-baked pie shell, cover with waxed paper and chill for at least 5 hours or overnight.

Prepare the meringue:

5 Preheat the oven to 350°. Place the egg whites in a bowl, add the salt and beat until the whites are foamy. Add the cream of tartar and beat until soft peaks form. Gradually add the sugar and continue beating until the whites are stiff and very glossy. Do not overbeat or the meringue will be dry. Pile the meringue on the filling, mounding it in the center and spreading it out to the edge of the crust to seal well.

6 Bake in the center of the oven for 15 minutes, or until the meringue is golden. Let cool and chill for 3 hours before serving. To slice neatly, use a knife dipped into boiling water before making each cut.

Serves 8
Recipe by Jim Fobel

Best Banana Cream Pie

Next time your best pal needs a bit of cheering up, this pie should do the trick. The texture is just about as smooth and creamy and sweet as any you'll find.

1 Cookie Crumb Crust (recipe
   follows), made with vanilla
   wafers
6 tablespoons all-purpose flour
1 cup granulated sugar
¼ teaspoon salt
2 cups milk, scalded
3 egg yolks, well beaten and at
   room temperature

4 tablespoons unsalted butter, cut
   into ¼-inch slices and at room
   temperature
1 teaspoon vanilla extract
4 small bananas
2 cups heavy cream
¾ cup confectioners' sugar

1 Prepare and bake the pie crust as directed in the recipe that follows.

2 In a heavy saucepan, combine the flour, granulated sugar and salt. Gradually stir in the scalded milk until the mixture is smooth. Bring to a boil over moderate heat, stirring constantly. Boil, stirring, for 1 minute and remove from the heat.

3 Gradually stir about ¼ cup of the hot milk mixture into the egg yolks to warm them, and then stir the yolk mixture back into the pan. Cook, stirring constantly, over moderate heat for about 3 minutes, or until the custard is very thick. Remove the pan from the heat and stir in the butter and vanilla until smooth. Place a sheet of plastic wrap directly on the surface of the custard to prevent a skin from forming, and allow the custard to cool at room temperature for 15 minutes.

4 Cut the bananas into ¼-inch slices and arrange half of them, overlapping slightly, over the bottom of the pie shell. Cover evenly with half the custard. Arrange the remaining bananas over the custard layer and cover evenly with the remaining custard. Cover the custard with a round of waxed paper and refrigerate for at least 2 hours.

5 Using a chilled bowl and beaters, beat the heavy cream until soft peaks form. Gradually add the confectioners' sugar ¼ cup at a time, beating on low speed after each addition until thoroughly incorporated. Beat on high speed until the cream is stiff.

6 Spoon all of the whipped cream over the pie, or spread two-thirds of it over the surface, place the remainder in a pastry bag fitted with a decorative tip and pipe decorations over the top of the pie.

Serves 6 to 8
Recipe by Jim Fobel

Cookie Crumb Crust

Use whatever type of plain, dry cookie you choose – vanilla wafers, "Famous" wafers or gingersnaps.

1⅓ cups crushed cookie crumbs,
   or 1 cup cookie crumbs plus
   ⅓ cup finely chopped nuts

2 tablespoons sugar
5 tablespoons unsalted
   butter, melted

1 Preheat the oven to 350°. In a medium bowl, combine the cookie crumbs, or crumbs and chopped nuts, with the sugar. Pour the butter over and blend with a fork until the crumbs are moistened.

2 Butter the bottom of a 9-inch pie plate (but not the sides or the shell may fall during baking) and gently press the crumbs evenly over the bottom and then up the sides of the pan. Bake in the center of the oven for 8 minutes. Let the pie crust cool to room temperature before filling.

Makes one 9-inch shell
Recipe by Diana Sturgis

Pear Brandy Tart

The serene beauty of this tart makes it an artful ending to a late
night supper. Take advantage of red-skinned pears when they're
available to add a touch of color to your tart.

Tart Shell:
1 cup all-purpose flour
1½ tablespoons sugar
¼ teaspoon salt
5 tablespoons plus 1 teaspoon cold
   unsalted butter
1 egg yolk, lightly beaten with 2
   teaspoons brandy

Filling:
¾ cup sugar
1¼ pounds Anjou pears (about 4
   medium) – peeled, cored and
   cut into ½-inch slices
3 whole eggs
1 cup heavy cream
1 teaspoon grated lemon zest
2 tablespoons fresh lemon juice
3 tablespoons melted
   unsalted butter, cooled to
   room temperature
¼ cup brandy

Garnish:
2 tablespoons unsalted butter
1 medium or 2 small red, green or
   yellow pears – peeled, cored and
   cut into ½-inch slices
1 teaspoon sugar
2 tablespoons brandy
Lemon zest, cut into fine julienne
   (optional)
Ground cinnamon (optional)

Prepare the tart shell:

1 In a medium bowl, combine the flour, sugar and salt. Cut in the
cold butter until the mixture resembles coarse meal. Gradually add
the egg yolk mixture to the flour mixture, stirring with a fork, until
the dough begins to mass together. If necessary, add a few drops
of cold water. Flatten the dough into a 6-inch disk, wrap in waxed
paper and chill for at least 1 hour.

Make the filling:

2 In a medium skillet, dissolve the sugar in ¼ cup of water over low
heat. Add the pear slices and bring to a boil. Reduce the heat, cover
and simmer the pears for about 35 minutes, or until soft; drain.
Transfer the pears to a medium bowl, and mash into a puree with a
wooden spoon.

3 Preheat the oven to 400°. Oil or butter a 9½-inch tart pan with a
removable bottom. Roll out the pastry between two sheets of generously floured waxed paper to an 11-inch round, about ⅛ inch
thick. Carefully peel off the top sheet of waxed paper. Invert the
pastry into the tart pan and without stretching, gently ease the
pastry into the pan, fitting it against the sides. Peel off the waxed
paper and remove the excess pastry by pressing the rolling pin over
the rim of the pan. With a fork, lightly prick the dough all over.
Refrigerate for 15 minutes.

Recipe continues on page 70

Pear Brandy Tart Continued

4 Line the pastry shell with aluminum foil and fill with pie weights or dried beans. Bake for 12 minutes; remove the foil and weights. Reduce the oven temperature to 350° and bake the shell for another 2 minutes, or until the bottom of the pastry is dry. Let the shell cool in its pan on a rack while you finish the filling.

5 In a large bowl, beat the eggs until frothy. Stir in the cream, lemon zest, lemon juice, melted butter, brandy and pear puree. Set the tart pan on a baking sheet; pour the pear custard into the tart pan and bake until the custard is set, about 30 minutes. Let cool for 2 hours at room temperature.

Prepare the garnish:

6 Melt the butter in a small skillet. Add the pear slices, sprinkle with the sugar and sauté until lightly browned and tender. Pour in the brandy and ignite, shaking the pan until the flames subside. With a slotted spoon transfer the pears to a shallow dish and let cool to room temperature.

7 Before serving, remove the sides of the tart pan. Arrange a spiraled circle or ring of pear slices on top of the tart, about 2 inches in from the edge. Sprinkle the pears with the lemon zest, if desired, and dust the pie with ground cinnamon. Serve at room temperature, or chilled, with Pat Buckley's Vanilla Custard Ice Cream if desired (recipe on page 72).

Serves 8
Recipe by W. Peter Prestcott

Moravian Sugar Bread

This kind of recipe is fun and it serves a crowd of people. You get to pat the dough into a big baking pan with your fingers, and then it's baked with butter, brown sugar and cinnamon on top. It'll make your house smell wonderful.

1 cup lukewarm water (105° to 115°)	2 eggs, lightly beaten
1 envelope (¼ ounce) active dry yeast	½ pound unsalted butter, at room temperature
⅓ cup plus 1 teaspoon granulated sugar	¾ teaspoon salt
1 cup mashed potatoes (about 2 medium all-purpose potatoes)	1 tablespoon milk
3½ cups all-purpose flour	1 cup (packed) light brown sugar
	1 teaspoon ground cinnamon

1 Place the water in a mixer bowl. Add the yeast and 1 teaspoon granulated sugar; stir until the yeast dissolves. Stir in the mashed potatoes, 2 cups of the flour, the remaining ⅓ cup granulated sugar, the eggs, ¼ pound of the butter and the salt. Beat on medium speed for 5 minutes. Using a dough hook, gradually add the remaining flour and continue beating for another 5 minutes; alternatively, if you do not have a dough hook, stir in the flour, turn out onto a floured surface and knead until the dough is soft and very elastic, 10 to 15 minutes. Cover and let rise in a warm place until doubled in bulk, about 2 hours.

2 Butter a 15- x 10-inch jelly roll pan. With lightly oiled hands, spread the dough evenly into the prepared pan. Cover and let rise for 1 hour, or until the dough appears light and bubbly.

3 Preheat the oven to 350°. Brush the dough with the milk. Combine the brown sugar and cinnamon and sprinkle over the top. With two floured fingers together, make 30 evenly spaced indentations in the dough. Melt the remaining ¼ pound butter and spoon over the surface of the dough and into each indentation. Bake for 35 minutes, or until golden brown and firm to the touch. Serve warm.

Serves 24
Recipe by Judith Olney

Lemon Curd Tart

A big lemon curd tart – there's hardly a friendlier looking dessert. If you'd rather, why not make individual tartlets – there's enough pastry for more than a dozen.

Lemon Curd:
3 whole eggs, at room
   temperature
2 egg yolks, at room temperature
1 cup sugar
¼ pound unsalted butter, at room
   temperature
Finely grated zest and juice of 2
   large lemons

Pâte Brisée Tart Shell:
1½ cups all-purpose flour
2 tablespoons sugar
¼ teaspoon salt
¼ pound unsalted butter,
   chilled and cut into small
   pieces
1 egg yolk
2 to 3 tablespoons ice water

Make the lemon curd:

1 Whisk together the eggs and egg yolks in the top of a double boiler set over, but not touching, boiling water. Add the sugar and continue whisking over moderate heat until the curd is thick and lemon-colored, 10 to 12 minutes.

2 Cut the butter into 8 slices and add it, a piece at a time, stirring until each piece melts before adding the rest. Add the zest and lemon juice and cook the mixture, stirring constantly, over simmering water until thick and creamy, about 4 minutes. Let cool. Place a sheet of plastic wrap directly on the surface of the curd and chill for several hours. (The lemon curd can be made several days ahead and stored airtight in the refrigerator.)

Make the pâte brisée:

3 In a food processor, combine the flour, sugar, salt, butter and egg yolk, and process briefly, pulsing on and off, until the mixture resembles coarse meal. With the motor running, add 2 tablespoons of the ice water and process a few seconds more, or until the dough begins to pull away from the sides. Add just enough of the remaining ice water to make a cohesive mass.

4 Gather the dough into a ball and pat into a 6-inch disk. Wrap in waxed paper and refrigerate for at least 1 hour.

5 Preheat the oven to 350°. Place the dough between two sheets of waxed paper and quickly roll out into a 13-inch round. Without stretching, fit the dough into an 10½- or 11-inch tart pan with a removable bottom; trim away the excess dough. Place the tart pan on a baking sheet and refrigerate for 15 minutes.

6 Pierce the pastry all over with a fork and line the shell with a sheet of aluminum foil. Weigh down with aluminum pie weights or dried beans. Bake in the center of the oven for 9 minutes. Remove the foil and pie weights, prick again and bake for another 10 minutes, or until light golden brown. Let cool on a rack.

7 When the shell is completely cooled, fill with the chilled lemon curd, slice and serve.

Serves 6 to 8
Recipe by Ruth Spear

Pat Buckley's Vanilla Custard Ice Cream

Flavored with vanilla bean, this ice cream presents authentic, old-fashioned goodness – made from a rich egg custard base.

1 cup sugar	**½ teaspoon salt**
1 vanilla bean, coarsely chopped	**3 cups milk, scalded**
6 egg yolks	**2 cups heavy cream**

1 Combine ¼ cup of the sugar and the vanilla bean in a blender. Process until the vanilla is finely ground.
2 In a large bowl, beat the egg yolks and salt. Stirring constantly, add the hot milk in a thin stream.
3 Pour the custard into a heavy nonreactive saucepan. Add the vanilla sugar and the remaining ¾ cup sugar and cook over moderate heat, stirring constantly, until the custard thickens enough to thickly coat the back of the spoon, 5 to 7 minutes. (Do not boil, or the eggs will curdle.)
4 Remove from the heat. Place over a bowl of ice and stir until cool, about 5 minutes. Blend in the cream. Pour into an ice cream maker and freeze according to the manufacturer's instructions.

Makes about 2 quarts
Recipe by Pat Buckley

Lemon Butter Mousse

Butter is the secret – and unexpected – ingredient in this mousse, making it unusually creamy, smooth and satisfying.

⅓ cup plus 3 tablespoons fresh lemon juice	**6 eggs, separated and at room temperature**
1 teaspoon finely grated lemon zest	**¼ teaspoon salt**
1 envelope (¼ ounce) unflavored gelatin	**3 cups sifted confectioners' sugar**
1 cup heavy cream	**¼ pound unsalted butter, at room temperature**

1 In a small heatproof bowl, stir together the ⅓ cup lemon juice and the lemon zest. Sprinkle on the gelatin and set aside to soften for 10 minutes. Set the bowl in a saucepan of hot water over low heat and stir to dissolve the gelatin. Remove from the heat and let cool to room temperature.
2 In a large bowl, whip the cream until just stiff. Cover and refrigerate until needed.
3 In a deep bowl, combine the egg whites with the salt. Beat until soft peaks form. Gradually add 1 cup of the confectioners' sugar and beat until stiff peaks form.
4 In another large bowl, beat the butter until soft and fluffy. Add 1 cup of confectioners' sugar and beat until smooth. One at a time, add the egg yolks, alternating with the dissolved gelatin and the remaining 1 cup confectioners' sugar. Continue to beat until smooth. Fold in one-third of the egg whites. Quickly but gently fold in the remaining egg whites.
5 Beat the remaining 3 tablespoons lemon juice into the whipped cream and fold into the mousse. Turn into a serving dish or stemmed wine glasses, cover and refrigerate until chilled and set, about 3 hours.

Serves 10 to 12
Recipe by Jim Fobel

Wild Wind Farm's Concord Grape Tart

Because you shape this tart using your fingertips and without a baking pan, it takes on a handmade look that's really appealing after a late dinner with friends.

Crust:
1 cup all-purpose flour
2 tablespoons sugar
¼ cup very finely chopped walnuts
4 tablespoons unsalted butter
3 tablespoons vegetable
   shortening
1 whole egg, beaten
1 egg yolk, beaten

Filling:
½ cup red currant jelly
1 tablespoon fresh lemon juice
3 cups Concord grapes (see Note),
   halved and seeded

Make the crust:

1 In a large bowl, combine the flour, 1 tablespoon of the sugar and the walnuts. Cut in the butter and shortening until the mixture resembles coarse meal. Mix in the beaten whole egg and gather the dough into a ball. (If the dough does not mass together easily, sprinkle with up to 1 tablespoon of ice water.) Flatten into a 6-inch disk and wrap in waxed paper; refrigerate for at least 2 hours or overnight.

2 Use your fingers to pat or roll out the dough between two lightly floured sheets of waxed paper into a 10-inch circle. Peel off the top layer of waxed paper and invert the pastry onto a baking sheet; peel off the second sheet of paper. Fold in about ½ inch of the dough all around the edges; turn up and pinch to form a ½-inch-high side around the crust. Brush the inside of the crust with the egg yolk and sprinkle with the remaining 1 tablespoon sugar. Prick the dough in several places with a fork. Refrigerate until thoroughly chilled, about 30 minutes. Preheat the oven to 375°.

3 Bake the crust in the lower part of the oven for 20 to 30 minutes, or until lightly browned. Set aside to cool.

Make the filling:

4 In a nonreactive medium saucepan, such as stainless steel, melt the jelly with the lemon juice over moderately low heat; remove from the heat. Add the grapes and toss gently to coat. Pour into the prepared crust. Turn the top grapes skin-side up. Let the tart cool. Serve at room temperature.

Note:

If Concord grapes are unavailable, use whole Ribier seedless black grapes.

Serves 6
Recipe from Wild Wind Farm
Naples, New York

Ginger-Molasses Skillet Cake

Use your most cherished, well-seasoned cast-iron skillet for this easy-to-make cake. Top it with mock crème fraîche, made from heavy cream mixed with sour cream.

1⅓ cups all-purpose flour
1 teaspoon baking powder
¼ teaspoon baking soda
2 teaspoons ground ginger
½ teaspoon salt
½ teaspoon coarsely
　ground pepper
¼ teaspoon ground cinnamon
¼ teaspoon ground allspice
¼ teaspoon ground cloves
1 cup (packed) dark brown sugar
8 tablespoons unsalted butter
⅔ cup plus 2 tablespoons
　unsulphured molasses
⅔ cup milk
½ teaspoon vanilla extract
¼ cup pine nuts
1 cup heavy cream, chilled
½ cup sour cream

1　Preheat the oven to 350°. In a large bowl, blend together the flour, baking powder, baking soda, ginger, salt, pepper, cinnamon, allspice and cloves.

2　In a small saucepan, combine ¾ cup of the brown sugar, 6 tablespoons of the butter and ⅔ cup of the molasses. Stir over moderate heat until melted and well combined. Stir in the milk and vanilla and set aside.

3　Place the remaining ¼ cup brown sugar, 2 tablespoons butter and 2 tablespoons molasses in a 12-inch cast-iron skillet. Place the skillet in the oven to melt the butter and sugar and heat the skillet. Stir to combine.

4　Stir the brown sugar and milk mixture into the dry ingredients. Beat with a spoon just until smooth. Pour the batter into the skillet. Sprinkle the pine nuts on top and bake for 25 to 30 minutes, until a tester inserted in the center of the cake comes out clean.

5　Beat the heavy cream until soft peaks form. Add the sour cream and continue beating until stiff. Serve the cake warm from the skillet. Pass the whipped cream separately.

Serves 8
Recipe by Anne Disrude

Old-Fashioned Bread Pudding

The minute the weather turns the slightest bit chilly, thoughts turn to soothing desserts that warm the heart. Bread pudding is one of those – a shoo-in for homey-dessert-of-the-month.

⅓ cup raisins	2 egg yolks
12 slices of stale French, Italian or other firm-textured white bread, cut ½-inch thick (about 6 ounces)	½ cup sugar
	½ teaspoon freshly grated nutmeg
	1 cup heavy cream
	1¼ cups milk
2 to 3 tablespoons unsalted butter, softened	Apricot Sauce (recipe follows) or maple syrup
3 whole eggs	

1   Lightly butter a 6- to 8-cup baking dish. Sprinkle half of the raisins over the bottom. Spread the bread with the butter and arrange the slices in the dish, overlapping as necessary. Scatter the remaining raisins on top.

2   In a large bowl, whisk together the whole eggs, egg yolks, sugar and nutmeg until well blended.

3   In a medium saucepan, combine the cream and milk and bring to a simmer. Gradually whisk the hot liquid into the beaten eggs in a thin stream. Pour the custard over the bread and set aside until the bread is saturated, about 15 minutes. (The recipe can be prepared to this point up to 4 hours ahead.)

4   Meanwhile, preheat the oven to 350°. Place the baking dish in a roasting pan and add enough water to reach halfway up the side of the dish. Bake in the center of the oven for 30 to 35 minutes, or until the custard is set. Serve warm or at room temperature with apricot sauce or maple syrup.

Serves 4
Recipe by Diana Sturgis

Apricot Sauce

2 ounces dried apricots (about ⅓ cup)	1 tablespoon dark rum

1   Combine the apricots and 1 cup water in a small saucepan and bring to a boil over low heat. Cover and let soak for about 30 minutes.

2   Return to a boil, reduce the heat and simmer, covered, until soft, about 20 minutes.

3   Pour the apricots and the liquid into a blender or food processor and puree until smooth. Stir in the rum. Serve the pudding warm or at room temperature.

Makes about 1 cup
Recipe by Diana Sturgis

Peaches-and-Cream Rice Pudding

Here's a dish that will take you to a tree-shaded street in Savannah. In a contest for "Most Soothing Food" this pudding would be a serious contender. Make it in late summer when peaches are at their very best.

Rice:
2 cups milk
²/₃ cup white rice, preferably short-grain
½ teaspoon salt

Custard:
1 cup milk
1 cup heavy cream
3 whole eggs
2 egg yolks
⅓ cup sugar
½ teaspoon vanilla extract

⅛ teaspoon each of freshly grated nutmeg, ground cloves, cinnamon and ginger
1 medium peach (about 6 ounces)

Peach Puree:
3 medium peaches (about 1 pound)
1½ teaspoons fresh lemon juice
1½ teaspoons raspberry or distilled white vinegar
2 to 3 teaspoons kirsch
1 to 2 tablespoons sugar

Prepare the rice:

1 Bring the milk to a simmer in a medium saucepan over moderate heat. Stir in the rice and salt, reduce the heat to low and cook, covered, for 20 minutes; set aside.

Prepare the custard:

2 Preheat the oven to 325°. Butter eight 1-cup custard cups or small ramekins. In a heavy saucepan over low heat, scald the milk and heavy cream. Remove from the heat and set aside.

3 In a large bowl, whisk together the whole eggs, egg yolks and sugar until thick and fluffy, 3 to 5 minutes.

4 Whisking constantly, add the warm milk and cream mixture in a slow, steady stream. Add the vanilla and spices and mix for 1 minute; fold in the rice. Peel and pit the peach. Cut the fruit into fine dice; fold into the custard.

5 Divide the custard among the eight cups, filling each to within ½ inch of the top. Set the cups in a baking pan and add hot water to reach 1 inch up the sides of the cups. Bake in the center of the oven for about 1 hour, or until a knife inserted in the center comes out clean. Remove the cups from the water and set aside to cool. To unmold, run a knife tip around the inside of each cup, invert over a dessert plate and shake sharply.

Make the puree:

6 Peel the peaches, cut the fruit from the pits and coarsely chop. In a blender or food processor, puree the peaches with the lemon juice, vinegar, kirsch and sugar, adding more kirsch and sugar if desired. Spoon some of the puree around each custard and serve.

Serves 8
Recipe by Maria Piccolo Stern

Apple Pandowdy

Though this all-American dessert may look a bit dowdy, its flavor and plain old appeal are universal. Make it in the fall when you can try some of the "new" apple varieties, such as Newtown Pippin, that farmers are beginning to cultivate.

3 pounds tart cooking apples, such as Granny Smith or Stayman – peeled, cored and sliced into ½-inch wedges
1 tablespoon fresh lemon juice
1 teaspoon finely grated lemon zest
½ cup (packed) light brown sugar
2 teaspoons ground cinnamon

⅛ teaspoon ground mace
6½ tablespoons unsalted butter, chilled
2 cups all-purpose flour
3 tablespoons granulated sugar
1 tablespoon baking powder
¾ cup plus 1 tablespoon heavy cream

1 In a large bowl, toss together the apples, lemon juice, lemon zest, brown sugar, cinnamon and mace.

2 Lightly butter a 7- to 8-cup deep dish pie pan. Spoon the apples into the dish and dot with 1½ tablespoons of the butter.

3 Sift together the flour, granulated sugar and baking powder. Cut the remaining 5 tablespoons butter into small bits and cut into the flour until the mixture resembles coarse meal.

4 Add ¾ cup of the cream and quickly stir it into the butter-flour mixture. Knead the dough lightly until smooth, about 45 seconds.

5 Preheat the oven to 425°. On a lightly floured surface, roll out the dough ¼ inch thick. Trim to a circle about ½ inch larger than the diameter of the pie pan and cut a small steam vent in the center. Carefully place the crust over the apples in the pie dish. (Do not press the dough into the edges of the pan.) Collect the scraps of dough, roll them out ⅛-inch thick and cut out decorations. Brush these lightly with water and attach them to the crust. Brush the top of the pandowdy with the remaining 1 tablespoon cream.

6 Bake the pandowdy for 10 minutes. Reduce the oven temperature to 350° and continue baking for 35 to 45 minutes, until the crust is golden brown and the filling bubbly. To serve, cut a piece of the crust, place it upside down in a bowl and top with apples and juice.

Serves 8
Recipe by Dorie Greenspan

Pepper Mill Squares

These squares have it all—lots of chocolate, butter, raisins and a smear of cream cheese frosting on top.

½ cup plus 2 tablespoons all-purpose flour
1 teaspoon Pepper Mix (recipe follows)
Pinch of salt
¼ pound plus 2 tablespoons unsalted butter, at room temperature
½ cup granulated sugar
⅓ cup (packed) light brown sugar

4 ounces semisweet chocolate, coarsely chopped
2 ounces unsweetened chocolate, coarsely chopped
1½ teaspoons vanilla extract
2 eggs
⅓ cup golden raisins
4 ounces cream cheese, at room temperature
1 cup confectioners' sugar

1 Preheat the oven to 350°. Lightly butter an 8-inch square baking pan. In a small bowl, sift together the flour, pepper mix and salt.
2 In a large heavy saucepan, melt ¼ pound of the butter over moderately high heat. Add the granulated and brown sugars and, stirring constantly, bring just to a boil. Stir in the semisweet and unsweetened chocolates and remove from the heat. Continue stirring until the chocolate melts. Let cool for 5 minutes, until tepid.
3 Stir in 1 teaspoon of the vanilla. One at a time, mix in the eggs until blended. Gradually stir in the flour mixture. Add the raisins. Pour the batter into the prepared pan.
4 Bake in the center of the oven for 30 minutes, or until the cake begins to pull away from the sides of the pan.

5 Meanwhile, prepare the frosting. In a medium bowl, beat together the cream cheese and the remaining 2 tablespoons butter. Beat in the confectioners' sugar and the remaining ½ teaspoon vanilla.
6 Remove the cake from the oven and let cool in the pan on a rack for 10 minutes. Loosen the edges with a blunt knife. Unmold and turn right-side up; let cool completely on the rack. Spread the frosting over the top. Trim the edges and cut into 2-inch squares.

Makes 16 squares
Recipe by Dorie Greenspan

Pepper Mix

1 tablespoon black peppercorns
1 tablespoon white peppercorns
1½ teaspoons whole allspice berries

Mix the black and white peppercorns and the allspice berries together. Grind to a powder in a pepper or spice mill.

Makes about 2½ tablespoons
Recipe by Dorie Greenspan

Lightweights

Lightweights

This group of desserts approaches the concept of lightness in three different ways: Some recipes are low in calories, others are light in texture, and still others are light in spirit. The dessert that suits your taste at any given time will depend on how and when you plan to serve it.

A lightweight concoction can become an impromptu success. More than one host or hostess can remember an occasion when, by the time it came round to dessert, the planned Baked Alaska or Crème Caramel seemed too, too heavy. The cook who was quick-witted churned out a pint or two of Pink Grapefruit Ice from fruit that had been earmarked for the next day's breakfast.

Aside from offering such last-minute inspiration, our lightweight desserts can help you plan menus that have the proper "rhythm." They allow you to follow a heavy main course, whether it's a saddle of venison, a big bowl of cassoulet or even an old-fashioned chicken pot pie, with a light conclusion – say, Orange-Apricot Chiffon. You needn't be following a diet to opt for a low-calorie choice, such as Granita di Limone or Oranges in Rosemary Syrup, after such weighty precedings.

If you're looking for light texture but have a calories-be-damned attitude because it's your birthday or a going-away party for your best friend, you'll want to try Lydie Marshall's Summer Fruits with Sweet Cheese. The mascarpone and cream cheese are whipped together with sugar and heavy cream to make an incredibly luscious mixture that's long on flavor and style. The new-age equivalent of a creamy cheesecake, it's divine served with a mélange of summer or winter fruits. And our Crystallized Lemon Tart makes an appropriate and beautiful ending to a moderately heavy meal. It's rich and tart, yet somehow light.

Many of the recipes in this chapter have the intensity we associate with diet-crushing desserts but just "happen" to be low in calories. Jean Anderson is a genius at creating such deceptively lightweight recipes. The Frozen Berry Yogurt with Cardinal Sauce is hers, as is the Celestial Lemon Roll and rich Chocolate Silk. You'll never know that hundreds of calories are missing.

Without a doubt, these lightweights are the recipes for people who claim they don't like dessert. Typically, such sugar-shunning folks do like fruit, so we offer several interesting and flavorful treatments that make serving fruit a bit more festive. Ambrosia Mariposa is a fancy name for a fresh fruit salad topped with fresh coconut; Paula Wolfert's Peaches Poached in Raspberries and Red Wine will make the end of your summer a bit less sad; and Chuck Williams's Baked Apples with Raspberry Vinegar offer a surprisingly big payoff in flavor with almost no investment in effort.

Sometimes light means little. Take, for example, Christopher Idone's Miniature Berry and Cherry Tartlets. Tiny two-inch molds make magnificent pop-them-in-your-mouth, one- or two-bite treats – the best. And don't forget that some cookies were never meant for the cookie jar. The ones we offer here – Tuiles, Tulip Cups and Chocolate Lace Almond Cookies, among them – are elegant light bites that offer the perfect finish to the most formal of dinners. ■

Berry Custard Tart

Whether you make a round, square or rectangular tart, the fresh berries, sweet custard and rich pastry combine to create a colorful and flavorful, summery dessert.

Rich Tart Shell:
1 cup all-purpose flour
1½ tablespoons sugar
Pinch of salt
¼ pound chilled unsalted butter,
    cut into ½-inch cubes
½ teaspoon grated lemon zest

Filling:
3 ounces cream cheese, preferably
    fresh (with no vegetable gum
    added),* at room temperature
½ cup crème fraîche
2 egg yolks, at room temperature
3 cups ollalieberries, raspberries,
    blueberries or huckleberries,
    or a mixture
3 tablespoons cassis, raspberry
    syrup or kirsch
1 tablespoon sugar
½ teaspoon fresh lemon juice
*Available at cheese and health-
    food stores

Make the tart shell:

1 In a mixer fitted with a dough paddle or in a food processor fitted with the steel blade, combine the flour, sugar and salt. Scatter the butter and lemon zest on top, and then blend until the dough masses around the blade; it will be crumbly. Press into a compact ball. (The dough can be prepared ahead. Wrap tightly and freeze or refrigerate. Let return to room temperature before proceeding.)

2 Press the dough into a 9-inch round, square or rectangular tart pan with a removable bottom to form a ⅛-inch-thick bottom crust and a slightly thicker wall around the sides. Scrape any excess dough cleanly from the rim. Cover and refrigerate the tart shell until cold and firm, 30 to 60 minutes. (The shell can be refrigerated overnight or frozen.)

3 Preheat the oven to 375°. Place the chilled tart shell on a baking sheet. Line the dough with a sheet of foil and fill to the rim with aluminum pie weights or dried beans. Bake the shell in the center of the oven for 20 to 25 minutes, or until the rim of the shell is dry and the sides shrink away slightly from the pan. Remove the foil and weights. Return the shell to the oven and bake until the crust is golden, 12 to 15 minutes. Let cool before filling.

Recipe continues on the next page

Berry Custard Tart Continued

Make the filling:

4 Preheat the oven to 375°. In a medium bowl, beat the cream cheese until smooth and light. Add the crème fraîche and egg yolks and beat until smooth. Slide the cooled tart shell onto a baking sheet and scrape the custard into the shell. Bake in the center of the oven for about 8 minutes, until barely set. The custard will be quivery, not firm. Gently slip the tart from the baking sheet onto a rack. Let stand for at least 30 minutes, until cool, before unmolding.

5 No more than 3 hours before serving, arrange 2 cups of the berries closely together on top of the tart, completely covering the custard with fruit.

6 In a heavy saucepan, combine the remaining 1 cup berries with the cassis and sugar. Cook over moderate heat, stirring to mash the berries and dissolve the sugar, until slightly thickened, 3 to 5 minutes. Strain through a fine-mesh sieve, pressing on the solids to extract as much juice as possible. Stir the lemon juice into the glaze.

7 With a small pastry brush, paint the glaze all over the berries and the uppermost rim of the tart shell.

Serves 6 to 8
Recipe by Margaret Fox

Jigsaw Pears

Simple geometry – the zigzag cut makes these pears look like a work of art.

2 cups dry white wine
1 cup sugar
2 tablespoons almond extract
6 large pears
3 tablespoons finely chopped pecans

1 tablespoon finely chopped mint leaves
6 mint sprigs and 6 mint leaves, for garnish

1 Bring the wine, sugar, almond extract and 5 cups of water to a boil in a large, nonreactive saucepan. Reduce the heat to low and simmer for 10 minutes.

2 Meanwhile, peel the pears, leaving the stems intact. Place a pear upright on a work surface and insert a paring knife at an angle into its "equator"; cutting almost to the core in a zigzag fashion, work around the circumference. Repeat with the remaining pears. Secure the halves of each pear together by pushing toothpicks up through the base.

3 Using a slotted spoon, transfer the pears to the simmering liquid, cover and poach for 10 to 15 minutes, or until tender when pierced with a knife point. Transfer to a plate and set aside until cool enough to handle.

4 Meanwhile, reduce the poaching liquid over high heat to about 1½ cups, about 20 minutes. Remove the pan from the heat and let cool to room temperature.

5 Remove the toothpicks and gently separate the pear halves. Scoop out the cores in each base, but do not cut through to the blossom end.

6 Toss the pecans and chopped mint together in a small bowl. Fill each pear cavity with 2 teaspoons of the mixture and replace the|pear tops. Set the pears in shallow dessert bowls and spoon about ¼ cup of the syrup around each. To garnish, place a mint leaf near each stem and float a mint sprig in each bowl.

Serves 6
Recipe by Rosalee Harris

Baked Apples with Raspberry Vinegar

Oranges in Rosemary Syrup

The raspberry vinegar makes a sprightly addition to these homey baked apples.

3 large, firm baking apples, such as Rome Beauty or Pippin	1 tablespoon raspberry vinegar
2 tablespoons light brown sugar	2 tablespoons unsalted butter, melted

1 Preheat the oven to 375°. Wash and dry the apples. Cut in half crosswise and scoop out the seeds with a melon baller or teaspoon; do not dig through the apple. Place the apple halves, cut-side up, in a baking dish. Take care that they do not tip; trim a slice from the bottoms if necessary.
2 Fill each cavity with 1 teaspoon of the sugar and ½ teaspoon of the vinegar. Brush the cut surfaces with the melted butter.
3 Pour ½ cup of hot water into the bottom of the baking dish and bake for 30 to 45 minutes, until tender. Add additional water if water evaporates during baking.
4 Let cool until just warm and serve with whipped cream or a custard sauce.

Serves 6
Recipe by Chuck Williams

A stunning combination of flavors – you'll be surprised how well rosemary mixes with the sweet-tart orange.

½ cup sugar	4 navel oranges, peeled
2 tablespoons finely chopped fresh rosemary	Sprigs of fresh rosemary, for garnish

1 In a small saucepan, combine the sugar and chopped rosemary with 1 cup of water. Bring to a boil, reduce the heat and simmer for 5 minutes. Remove from the heat and let cool to room temperature.
2 Slice the oranges into ¼-inch thick rounds. Arrange the slices in a shallow serving dish or on a platter. Pour the syrup over the oranges and let stand at room temperature for 2 to 3 hours. Serve the oranges in the syrup, garnished with sprigs of rosemary.

Serves 6 to 8
Recipe by James and Helen Nassikas

Cold Lemon Soufflé

A cold tart soufflé that is a refreshing antidote to the dog days of summer.

2 envelopes unflavored gelatin	1 cup heavy cream
6 eggs, separated	2 tablespoons finely
1½ cups sugar	chopped pistachio nuts
3 tablespoons grated lemon zest	Candied Lemon Peel
(from about 4 medium lemons)	(optional; recipe follows)
¾ cup fresh lemon juice (from	Whipped cream (optional)
about 4 medium lemons)	

1 Wrap a 5-cup soufflé mold with a folded strip of heavy-duty aluminum foil or parchment paper to form a collar. Arrange the collar to extend about 3 inches above the rim of the dish and secure it with string or tape.

2 Sprinkle the gelatin over ⅓ cup of water in a small saucepan.

3 In a large bowl, beat the egg yolks with 1 cup of the sugar, the lemon zest and lemon juice until well blended. Place the bowl over a pan of gently simmering water and continue beating until the mixture is thick and creamy, about 15 minutes. Remove from the heat.

4 Warm the gelatin over low heat, stirring, until melted. Stir into the hot lemon mixture and continue to beat until cool.

5 In a large bowl, beat the egg whites until soft peaks form. Add the remaining ½ cup sugar and continue beating until stiff and glossy. Beat the cream until it forms stiff peaks.

6 Place the lemon-egg yolk mixture over a bowl of ice and water and stir until it begins to thicken and set. Gently fold in the whipped cream. Then fold in the beaten egg whites. Pour the mixture into the prepared soufflé dish. Smooth the top with a spatula.

7 Refrigerate for at least 3 hours, or until set. (The soufflé can be made to this point a day ahead, but the gelatin may toughen a bit under extended refrigeration.)

8 Before serving, remove the collar from the soufflé. Gently press the chopped pistachios onto the sides of the soufflé where it rises above the dish. Arrange the Candied Lemon Peel garnish on top and decorate with whipped cream, if desired.

Serves 8 to 10
Recipe by John Robert Massie

Candied Lemon Peel

In a larger quantity, this recipe serves as a wonderful confection, for nibbling with espresso or giving as a gift.

Zest of 2 lemons, cut into long,	2 cups sugar
thin julienne	

1 In a small saucepan, combine the lemon zest and 2 cups of water. Bring to a boil over high heat; cook for 1 minute, then drain. Repeat this process 3 more times to soften the zest and remove the bitterness.

2 In a small saucepan, combine the sugar with 2 cups of water. Bring to a boil. Reduce the heat to moderately low, add the zest and simmer gently for 2 to 3 hours, until the strips are translucent. Remove the candied peels with tongs and set aside on a lighty oiled rack to dry. Store airtight indefinitely.

Recipe by Diana Sturgis

Frozen Fresh Fruit Yogurt

Tropical Fruit Compote

No need to go to an ice cream store – make frozen yogurt yourself at home. This recipe is simple and low in calories at only 155 per serving.

1 pint low-fat vanilla yogurt
¾ cup pureed fresh fruit (such as strawberries, raspberries, banana or kiwi)
2 tablespoons liquid fructose*

¼ teaspoon vanilla extract
*Available at health food stores

In a large bowl, combine the yogurt, fruit puree, fructose and vanilla; whisk until blended. Freeze in an ice cream maker according to the manufacturer's instructions.

Serves 4
Recipe from Chez Eddy

This compote must macerate overnight to allow its flavors to develop, so plan accordingly.

1 bottle (25.4 ounces) sweet white wine, such as Sauternes or Muscat
1 cup sugar
1 vanilla bean
6 strips of orange zest, each about 2 inches long
4 ripe kiwi fruits, peeled and cut crosswise into ¼-inch slices
2 ripe papayas – peeled, seeded and cut into thin wedges

2 ripe pears – peeled, cored and cut crosswise into ⅛-inch slices
24 strawberries, halved lengthwise
1 orange, peeled and cut into sections
1 cup lightly packed fresh mint leaves, for garnish

1 In a large heavy skillet, combine the wine, sugar, vanilla bean and zest. Bring to a boil over moderately high heat and cook, stirring occasionally, until reduced by one-fourth, about 10 minutes.

2 Meanwhile, arrange the fruit decoratively in a shallow heat-proof dish.

3 Carefully strain the hot syrup over the fruit. Let stand until cool, then cover with plastic wrap and refrigerate overnight.

4 Garnish with mint leaves before serving.

Serves 6 to 8
Recipe by W. Peter Prestcott

Fresh Papaya Sorbet

Pure, cold papaya flavor that's simply delicious makes this rich
orange sorbet special. Garnish each serving with thin wedges of
fresh lime. Also shown are Pink Champagne, Pink Grapefruit
and Raspberry sorbets (recipes follow).

1 In a small saucepan, combine the sugar and ¾ cup of water. Cook
over moderate heat, stirring constantly to dissolve the sugar, then
bring just to a boil. Remove from the heat and let cool to room
temperature.
2 Pour the syrup into a bowl set over a larger bowl of ice and stir until
cool. Add the lime juice and pureed papaya. Scrape the mixture
into an ice cream maker and freeze according to the manufacturer's
instructions.

¾ cup sugar
¼ cup fresh lime juice
**2 cups pureed papaya (2 large
papayas, peeled)**

Makes about 3½ cups
Recipe by Anne Disrude

Sorbet de Champagne

Sweet yet astringent, this sorbet can stand alone as a light dessert after a big dinner. Serve with one last bottle of bubbly pink Champagne.

1¼ cups sugar	⅔ cup plus 1 tablespoon
½ cup fresh lemon juice	pink Champagne
(from about 3 lemons)	2 egg whites

1   In a heavy saucepan, dissolve 1 cup of the sugar in 1¼ cups of water. Bring to a boil and remove from the heat. Stir in the lemon juice and ⅔ cup of the Champagne. Strain through a fine sieve into a medium bowl; cover and refrigerate until chilled.

2   In a small saucepan, over moderate heat, dissolve the remaining ¼ cup sugar in 2 tablespoons of water. Bring to a boil and cook for 1 minute; remove from the heat.

3   Beat the egg whites with an electric mixer until foamy. Gradually beat in the hot sugar syrup in a thin, steady stream. Continue beating for 3 to 5 minutes, or until the egg whites are stiff.

4   Quickly stir the Champagne syrup into the egg whites – they will remain separated – and pour the mixture into the container of an ice-cream maker. Add the remaining 1 tablespoon Champagne. Freeze the sherbet in an ice cream maker, according to the manufacturer's instructions. Turn the sherbet, which will be soft, into a covered container and place in the freezer until firm, about 4 hours or overnight.

Serves 6 to 8
Recipe by Catherine and
Ghislain de Vogüé

Pink Grapefruit Ice

This ice may be served for dessert or as a mid-meal refresher course. Use the pinkest or reddest grapefruits you can find to add as much color as possible.

4 cups freshly squeezed pink	About ½ cup sugar
grapefruit juice, strained (from	
about 5 large pink grapefruits)	

1   In a large bowl, stir together the grapefruit juice and ½ cup sugar until the sugar dissolves. Taste and add more sugar if desired.

2   Pour the mixture into an ice cream maker and freeze according to the manufacturer's directions. Serve in chilled sherbet glasses.

Serves 8
Recipe by Diana Sturgis

Raspberry Sorbet

One of the finest ways to treat raspberries – a cool, tart/sweet finale to a summer or wintertime meal.

2 cups sugar   **Juice of 3 lemons**
4 cups fresh raspberries

1 In a nonreactive saucepan, combine the sugar and 2 cups of water. Bring almost to the boil over moderate heat. Reduce the heat and simmer, uncovered, for about 10 minutes. Allow the syrup to cool to room temperature.

2 Place the raspberries and lemon juice in a food processor or blender and puree. Push the puree through the finest blade of a food mill or a fine sieve; discard the seeds.

3 Combine the syrup with the raspberry puree in a large mixing bowl. Pour into an ice cream maker and freeze according to the manufacturer's instructions.

4 Spoon the sorbet into a bowl or decorative mold and freeze for about 4 hours.

Serves 8
Recipe from The Chanticleer Restaurant
Nantucket, Massachusetts

Concord Grape Ice

A light dessert ice that could help you enjoy a sweet dessert wine or a wedge of farmhouse cheddar from Vermont.

1 quart Concord grape juice   **½ cup sugar or to taste**
(see Note)

1 In a large bowl, combine the grape juice and sugar. Stir until the sugar dissolves. Cover and refrigerate until chilled.

2 Pour the cold syrup into the canister of an ice cream maker and freeze according to the manufacturer's instructions. Alternatively, pour the mixture into 2 metal ice cube trays and freeze until mushy. Then turn into a food processor and process briefly to break up the large ice crystals; freeze again in the trays. Repeat if necessary to reach the desired texture.

Note:

If freshly squeezed Concord grape juice is not available in your area, make it yourself. For 1 quart, puree 4 pounds of Concord grapes with 1 cup of water in 4 batches in a food processor fitted with the plastic blade. Strain and discard the solids.

Makes about 1 quart
Recipe by Diana Sturgis

Granita di Limone

A rough ice with smooth tart lemon flavor. Serve it after any meal – big or small.

2½ cups fresh lemon juice (from about 12 lemons)
1½ cups superfine sugar

¼ cup orange or tangerine liqueur
Frozen seedless grapes, for garnish

1 Combine the lemon juice and sugar in a large bowl and stir until the sugar is completely dissolved. Add 3¾ cups of cold water and the liqueur; stir to combine.
2 Pour the mixture into a shallow nonreactive pan and freeze for 5 hours, stirring every hour to break up the ice crystals that have formed. Pack the mixture into a decorative mold and freeze again.
3 To serve, unmold the granita onto a large platter. Garnish with the frozen grapes.

Serves 12
Recipe by W. Peter Prestcott

Cantaloupe Sorbet with Pepper and Port

In Italy this type of dish is called an intermezzo. We call it a palate-refresher and serve it between courses, but it works just as well as a light dessert.

2 small cantaloupes
¼ cup sugar
1 tablespoon fresh lemon juice

½ teaspoon freshly ground pepper
Pinch of salt
Ruby port, chilled

1 Working on a large platter to catch the juices, split and seed the cantaloupes, cut into chunks and remove the rind. Strain the reserved juices to remove the seeds.
2 Combine the cantaloupe juice with enough water to equal ¼ cup. Pour into a small heavy saucepan and add the sugar. Bring slowly to a boil, stirring to dissolve the sugar. Boil for 1 minute, remove from the heat and let cool.
3 Place the sugar syrup, melon, lemon juice, pepper and salt in a food processor. Puree until smooth. Strain through a sieve; to avoid any graininess, do not press on the solids.
4 Pour the puree into an ice cream maker and freeze according to the manufacturer's instructions. To serve, scoop into individual glasses and pour about 1 tablespoon of port on top of the sorbet.

Makes about 3½ cups
Recipe from Enoteca Pinchiorri

Granita di Espresso

An imposing structure of coffee-flavored ice that makes a light dessert to accompany espresso and coffee liqueurs.

1½ cups finely ground espresso coffee
4½ cups boiling water
¾ cup plus 2 teaspoons superfine sugar
¼ cup coffee liqueur, such as Tia Maria or Kahlúa

¾ cup heavy cream
1 tablespoon Cognac or brandy
Strips of lemon zest, for garnish

1   Brew the coffee using all of the boiling water.
2   Combine the hot coffee with ¾ cup of the sugar and the coffee liqueur. Stir until the sugar is dissolved. Let cool.
3   Pour into a shallow nonreactive pan and freeze for about 5 hours, stirring every hour to break up any large ice crystals that have formed. Pack into a decorative 6-cup mold and freeze again.
4   Before serving, whip the cream until it forms soft peaks. Add the remaining 2 teaspoons sugar and the Cognac; whip for 30 seconds more. Unmold the granita onto a large platter. Mound or pipe the whipped cream around it and garnish with strips of lemon zest.

Serves 12
Recipe by W. Peter Prestcott

Calvados Sorbet

If you like apples, the flavor of this sorbet is bound to please you. Serve it with a snifter of Calvados on the side.

1½ cups hard cider, preferably French
1 cup sugar
½ cup Calvados

2 tablespoons fresh lemon juice
½ cup heavy cream

1   In a medium nonreactive saucepan, combine the cider, sugar and ¾ cup of water. Bring to a boil over moderate heat, reduce the heat to low, cover and simmer gently, stirring occasionally, for 10 minutes. Let the syrup cool to room temperature and then refrigerate until quite cold.
2   Add the Calvados, lemon juice and cream. Freeze in an ice cream maker according to the manufacturer's instructions. Pack into a covered container and store in the freezer until ready to serve.

Makes about 1 quart
Recipe by Jean Anderson

Zabaglione al Champagne

Miniature Berry and Cherry Tartlets

This delicate zabaglione, made with Champagne instead of the traditional Madeira, is light and refreshing over fresh strawberries.

2 egg yolks, at room temperature　**2 tablespoons sugar**
⅓ cup plus 1 tablespoon
　Champagne

Combine the egg yolks, Champagne and sugar in the top of a double boiler set over simmering water. Whisk over low heat until the sauce is thick and smooth, about 10 minutes; do not overcook or the zabaglione will curdle. Remove from the heat and serve immediately.

Serves 4
Recipe from Gian Marino Restaurant,
New York City

Tiny two-bite tartlets provide a showcase for jewel-like height-of-the-season berries.

1 cup all-purpose flour　　**1 pint berries**
1 tablespoon sugar　　　　　**(strawberries,**
Pinch of salt　　　　　　　　**raspberries, blueberries,**
6 tablespoons cold unsalted　**fraises des bois or**
　butter, cut into pieces　　　**cherries)**
2 tablespoons ice water　　　**¼ cup apricot jam**

1 In a medium bowl, mix together the flour, sugar and salt. Cut in the butter until the mixture resembles coarse meal. Add the ice water while tossing with a fork and mix until the dough pulls away from the sides of the bowl. Form the dough into a ball, flatten into a 6-inch disk, cover with plastic wrap and refrigerate for at least 20 minutes.

2 On a lightly floured surface, roll out the dough ⅛ inch thick. Using a 3-inch biscuit cutter, cut out as many circles of dough as possible. Place a round of dough in each 2-inch tartlet mold and gently press it into shape.

3 Place the tartlet shells on a cookie sheet and refrigerate for 30 minutes.

4 Preheat the oven to 350°. Line each tartlet shell with foil and fill with pie weights or dried beans. Bake the tartlets for 10 to 12 minutes, until golden brown. Remove the foil and weights.

5 Let the shells cool to room temperature, then carefully remove from the molds. (The tartlet shells can be prepared up to 1 day ahead.)

6 Up to 1 hour before serving, decoratively arrange a few berries in each tartlet shell.

7 In a small saucepan, combine the apricot jam with 2 tablespoons of water and cook over moderately high heat, stirring, until the jam melts, 3 to 5 minutes. Spoon a small amount of warm glaze over the fruit in each tartlet.

Makes about 16 small tartlets
Recipe by Christopher Idone

Frozen Berry Yogurt With Cardinal Sauce

This fruited yogurt is berry berry good and wonderfully low in calories – only 190 per serving.

1 package (10 ounces) frozen raspberries in light syrup, partially thawed	6 tablespoons superfine sugar
	1 tablespoon Grand Marnier
1 package (10 ounces) frozen strawberries in light syrup, partially thawed	¼ teaspoon grated orange zest
	Cardinal Sauce (recipe follows)
	1 cup fresh red raspberries, for garnish
2 cups low-fat plain yogurt	6 mint sprigs, for garnish

1. In a food processor, puree the partially thawed raspberries and strawberries. (If you wish to remove the seeds, strain the puree through a fine-mesh sieve and return the puree to the food processor.) Add the yogurt, sugar, Grand Marnier and orange zest and process for 20 seconds. Scrape the sides down and process until absolutely smooth, 30 to 40 seconds longer.
2. Spoon the mixture into a 9-inch square baking dish or pan. Set in the freezer and freeze for 3 to 4 hours, or until soft-firm.
3. To serve the dessert, layer scoops of the berry yogurt and Cardinal Sauce alternately into 6 parfait glasses, ending with a drizzle of the sauce. Tuck a few raspberries in and around the final scoop of frozen yogurt and garnish each portion with a sprig of mint.

Serves 6
Recipe by Jean Anderson

Cardinal Sauce

1 package (10 ounces) frozen raspberries in light syrup, thawed	¼ cup low-sugar strawberry jam
	1 tablespoon superfine sugar
	1½ teaspoons cornstarch

1. Drain the thawed raspberries in a strainer set over a bowl; reserve the juices and set aside. In a food processor, process the drained raspberries and the strawberry jam until smooth, about 20 seconds. Strain the mixture through a fine-mesh sieve into a small bowl and set the puree aside.
2. Measure out the reserved raspberry juice and, if necessary, add cold water to measure ½ cup. In a small heavy saucepan, combine the sugar and cornstarch, pressing out all lumps. Add the raspberry juice and cook over low heat, stirring constantly, until the mixture bubbles up and turns clear, about 2 minutes. Remove from the heat and stir into the raspberry puree. Cover and refrigerate until ready to serve.

Makes about 1½ cups
Recipe by Jean Anderson

Oeufs à la Neige

Light-as-air meringue eggs float in a pond of creamy custard sauce. An interesting contrast in textures, Oeufs à la Neige can make a sweet finale to a warm wintertime supper.

1½ quarts milk
2½ cups sugar
3 tablespoons vanilla extract
Double recipe Swiss Meringue
   (recipe follows)
10 egg yolks

1 In a large shallow saucepan or enameled casserole, combine the milk, 1 cup of the sugar and the vanilla. Bring to a simmer over moderately high heat, stirring occasionally to dissolve the sugar. Adjust the heat so the liquid is just below a simmer; allow bubbles to form around the edge of the pan but not in the center, or when the meringues are added, they may break up.

2 Make the Swiss Meringue. Using two large serving spoons, scoop up an oval "egg" of meringue and slide it into the hot liquid. Add as many meringue eggs as will fit without crowding. Poach, turning once and adjusting the heat as necessary, for about 5 minutes, or until firm. Carefully remove with a large slotted spoon or strainer and drain on a cotton or linen towel. Repeat with the remaining meringue.

3 Measure 4 cups of the poaching milk into a heavy medium saucepan and bring to a boil; remove from the heat.

4 In a large bowl, whisk the egg yolks and 1 cup of sugar until light colored and thick enough to leave a quickly dissolving trail when the whisk is lifted. Whisking constantly, gradually beat the hot milk into the yolks in a thin, steady stream. Return the mixture to the saucepan and cook over moderate heat, stirring constantly, until the custard sauce thickens enough to heavily coat the back of a spoon, about 5 minutes.

Recipe continues on page 100

Oeufs à la Neige Continued

5 Set the pan over a bowl of ice and stir until the custard cools. Pour the chilled custard into a large shallow serving dish. Arrange the meringue eggs on top. Cover and refrigerate for up to 3 hours before serving.

6 Shortly before serving, place the remaining ½ cup sugar in a small heavy saucepan and add 2 tablespoons of water. Bring to a boil over moderately high heat and continue to cook, without stirring, until the syrup is a deep caramel color, about 3 minutes. Immediately remove from the heat and let cool for 3 minutes. Stir the caramel with a fork until it hardens enough to begin to string when you lift the fork. Using the fork, drizzle the caramel lightly over the meringue eggs.

Serves 8
Recipe by John Robert Massie

Swiss Meringue

4 egg whites, at room temperature

**Pinch of cream of tartar
1 cup sugar**

1 In a mixer bowl, beat the egg whites and cream of tartar at low speed. When the whites begin to foam, increase the speed to high and beat until soft peaks form.

2 Continuing to beat on high speed, gradually add ½ cup of the sugar, 1 tablespoon at a time, beating briefly between each addition to be sure the sugar dissolves. When the ½ cup of sugar is incorporated, turn off the mixer. The whites will be glossy and dense and will form stiff peaks.

3 Sprinkle the remaining ½ cup sugar over the beaten egg whites. Using a spatula, gently fold the sugar into the whites until thoroughly blended.

Makes about 4 cups
Recipe by John Robert Massie

Chocolate Silk

Dense, dark and delicious, this creamy dessert is a lightened version of a classic pots de crème au chocolate, weighing in at only 160 calories per serving. If you succumb and top it with the optional whipped cream and pistachios, it's still only 200 calories per serving.

**6 tablespoons sugar
¼ cup sifted unsweetened cocoa powder
2 tablespooons sifted cornstarch
1 teaspoon unflavored gelatin
1 cup half-and-half
1 cup evaporated skim milk
⅔ cup whole milk**

**2 jumbo egg yolks, lightly beaten
2 teaspoons vanilla extract**

**Optional Topping:
¼ cup heavy cream, whipped
1 tablespoon coarsely chopped blanched pistachio nuts or
6 candied violets**

1 In a large heavy saucepan, combine the sugar, cocoa, cornstarch and gelatin, pressing out all lumps. Add the half-and-half, evaporated skim milk and whole milk; whisk vigorously to blend. Set the pan over moderately low heat and cook, stirring constantly with a wooden spoon, until the mixture just boils and is thickened and smooth, about 10 minutes.

2 Blend a little of the hot mixture into the beaten egg yolks, then stir the warmed egg yolks back into the pan. Cook over moderately low heat, stirring constantly, for 3 to 4 minutes. The mixture must not boil or the eggs will scramble. Remove from the heat and stir in the vanilla. Set the saucepan on a rack to cool for 10 minutes, stirring frequently to prevent a skin from forming on the surface.

3 Ladle the mixture into 6 decorative 4-ounce pot de crème cups or white porcelain ramekins and let cool completely. Cover each cup with plastic wrap, then refrigerate at least 5 hours, or overnight.

4 Serve as is or top each serving with a little of the whipped cream and either a scattering of chopped pistachios or a single candied violet.

Serves 6
Recipe by Jean Anderson

Crystallized Lemon Tart

Amy Ho, who works with Barbara Tropp, makes this very pretty, simple tart from just three ingredients: lemons, sugar and eggs. Prepare the lemons 8 to 24 hours before baking.

2 medium-large lemons with thin, unmarked skin (7 ounces total)
1 teaspoon grated lemon zest
1¼ cups sugar

2 eggs
1 prebaked Standard Tart Shell (recipe follows)

1 Scrub the lemons under warm water until fragrant. Cut off the tip to expose the fruit, then cut crosswise into paper-thin slices. Cut the slices in half. Layer the sliced lemons, grated zest and sugar in a bowl. Toss and set aside for 30 to 60 minutes; toss again. Cover and let stand at room temperature for 8 hours or overnight, stirring once or twice.

2 Preheat the oven to 375°. Stir the lemon mixture gently and remove any seeds. Whisk the eggs until light colored and slightly thickened, 2 to 3 minutes. Add the lemons and fold in with a rubber spatula to mix well.

3 Set the prebaked shell on a baking sheet. Pour in the lemon filling, distributing the lemons evenly and unfolding any curled slices so that they lie flat.

4 Bake in the center of the oven until the filling is bubbling and almost set and the shell is golden, about 25 minutes. Remove the baking sheet from the oven and slide the tart onto a rack to cool before unmolding. The filling will firm as the tart cools.

5 Serve the tart slightly warm or at room temperature, cut into small slices. This tart keeps beautifully overnight. Let cool, wrap well and refrigerate; let return to room temperature before serving.

Serves 8 to 10
Recipe by Barbara Tropp

Standard Tart Shell

1½ cups all-purpose flour
1 tablespoon sugar
Pinch of salt

1¼ pounds chilled unsalted butter, cut into ½-inch cubes
¼ cup cold water

1 In a large bowl, combine the flour, sugar and salt. Cut in the butter until the mixture resembles coarse meal.

2 Add the water in a thin stream, tossing until the dough begins to mass together. Add a few more drops of water if necessary. Gather the dough into a ball; press into a 6-inch disk. Wrap tightly and refrigerate until cold but still malleable, 30 to 60 minutes.

3 Roll out the dough on a lightly floured surface to a round an even ⅛ inch thick. Fit into an 11-inch tart pan with a removable bottom, pressing the dough against the sides of the pan without stretching it. Trim the excess to leave about 1 inch all around. Fold the hem in and press against the pan to reinforce the sides. Neatly trim the crust even with the rim of the pan. Cover with plastic wrap and refrigerate for at least 30 minutes, or freeze, before filling and/or baking. (The unbaked shell can be refrigerated overnight or frozen.)

4 Preheat the oven to 375°. Set the chilled tart shell on a baking sheet. Line with aluminum foil and fill to the rim with aluminum pie weights or dried beans.

5 Bake the shell in the center of the oven for 20 to 25 minutes, or until the rim of the shell is dry when the foil is pulled back and the walls have shrunk slightly away from the pan. Remove the foil and weights. Return the shell to the oven and bake for 10 minutes, or until the crust is dry all over. Slide the tart pan off the baking sheet onto a rack and let the shell cool before filling.

Makes an 11-inch tart shell
Recipe by Barbara Tropp

Soufflé Omelet with Fresh Plum Sauce

Whether you serve it with plum sauce or another fruit accompaniment, this light dessert will be puffed and golden when you bring it to table.

3 eggs, separated
1 teaspoon almond extract
1½ tablespoons all-purpose flour
1 egg white
Pinch of salt
⅛ teaspoon cream of tartar

2 tablespoons granulated sugar
1 tablespoon minced toasted almonds
1 tablespoon confectioners' sugar
1 cup Fresh Plum Sauce (recipe at right), heated

1   Preheat the oven to 400°. In a medium bowl, whisk together the egg yolks and almond extract. Gradually whisk in the flour.

2   Beat the egg whites, salt and cream of tartar until soft peaks form. Sprinkle on the granulated sugar and beat until stiff but not dry.

3   Fold about ½ cup of the beaten egg whites into the egg yolk mixture to lighten it. Fold in the remaining egg whites just until blended.

4   Generously butter a shallow oval baking or gratin dish. Spoon the soufflé mixture into three mounds in the dish. Bake for 10 minutes, or until golden.

5   Sprinkle with the toasted almonds and confectioners' sugar. Serve the warm Plum Sauce on the side.

Serves 4
Recipe by W. Peter Prestcott

Fresh Plum Fool

Light and simple—nothing could be easier or better than this.

3 cups Fresh Plum Sauce (recipe follows)
1 cup sour cream
2 tablespoons blackberry brandy

1½ cups heavy cream, chilled
½ cup granulated sugar
½ cup packed brown sugar

1   In a medium bowl, stir together the plum sauce, sour cream and blackberry brandy. Set aside.

2   Whip the cream until soft peaks form. Beat in the granulated sugar. Fold in the plum mixture until partly blended, leaving streaks of color.

3   Turn the fool into a decorative bowl. Sprinkle the brown sugar on top. Chill for several hours before serving.

Serves 6
Recipe by W. Peter Prestcott

Fresh Plum Sauce

2 pounds sweet, ripe red plums, quartered and pitted
1 cup large pitted prunes (about 6 ounces), coarsely chopped

½ cup sugar
1 cup ruby port
2 tablespoons fresh lime juice
2 teaspoons Angostura bitters

1   In a medium nonreactive saucepan, combine the plums, prunes, sugar, port, lime juice and bitters. Cook over very low heat, stirring occasionally, until the sauce is thick, about 1 hour.

2   Remove from the heat, pour into a bowl and let cool. Store, tightly covered, in the refrigerator. (This recipe can be made at least 3 days ahead.)

Makes about 3 cups
Recipe by W. Peter Prestcott

Tuiles

The French cookie that is the epitome of sophistication – incredibly rich and incredibly thin.

1 recipe Basic Almond Cookie Batter (page 105)   **1 cup (3 ounces) sliced blanched almonds**

1 Preheat the oven to 425°. Butter a large heavy baking sheet. Place in the oven for 1 minute, until the sheet is warm and the butter is melted. Remove from the oven.

2 Using a tablespoon measure, spoon 4 separate half-filled tablespoons of the batter at least 5 inches apart onto the warm baking sheet. Using the back of a spoon, spread the batter into thin circles 3 inches in diameter, leaving at least 1 inch between circles to allow for spreading during baking. Sprinkle each cookie with 1 rounded teaspoon of the almonds.

3 Bake in the lower third of the oven for 5 to 6 minutes, until the cookies have a golden brown border ½ inch wide. Meanwhile, have ready 1 long or 2 shorter rolling pins or similar curved surfaces about 2 inches in diameter.

4 Remove the cookies from the oven. Working quickly, slide the back of a wide metal spatula under a cookie, pushing to separate the cookie from the sheet without tearing; the cookie will be soft and pliable. Drape the cookie, almond-side up, over the rolling pin and, with your hands, gently mold the cookie to the curve of the pin. Repeat with the remaining 3 cookies. Leave in place to cool and harden, about 2 minutes; set aside. If the cookies cool before they can be easily molded, return to the oven for 30 seconds to restore their pliability.

5 Scrape the baking sheet clean, wipe with a paper towel and lightly butter it. It is not necessary to rewarm the sheet. Repeat Steps 2 through 4 to form the remaining batter into tuiles. (Although better fresh, the recipe can be made to this point a few days ahead. Store the tuiles in an airtight tin or wrap them individually in plastic bags and store in the freezer. Let return to room temperature before serving.)

Makes about 20
Recipe by Diana Sturgis

Chocolate-Lace Almond Cookies

Drizzle chocolate over these cookies through a paper cone or just let it fall off the end of a spoon or straw.

1 recipe Basic Almond Cookie Batter (page 105)   **4 ounces semisweet chocolate**

1 Preheat the oven to 425°. Butter a large heavy baking sheet. Place in the oven for 1 minute, until the sheet is warm and the butter is melted. Remove from the oven.

2 Using a teaspoon measure, spoon 4 to 6 separate teaspoons of the batter at least 4 inches apart onto the warm baking sheet. With the back of a spoon, spread the batter into thin circles 2 to 2½ inches in diameter, leaving at least 1 inch between circles to allow for spreading during baking.

3 Bake in the lower third of the oven for 5 minutes, until the cookies have a golden-brown border ½ inch wide.

4 Remove the cookies from the oven. Slide the back of a wide metal spatula under each cookie, pushing to separate the cookie from the sheet without tearing. Transfer to a wire rack and let cool.

5 Scrape the baking sheet clean, wipe with a paper towel and lightly butter it. It is not necessary to rewarm the sheet. Repeat Steps 2 through 4 to form the remaining batter into cookies.

6 Melt the chocolate in a microwave oven or in a double boiler over hot – but not boiling – water. Scrape into a small pastry bag fitted with a plain ⅛-inch tip or into a small paper cone. Pipe decorative swirls onto the cooled cookies and let set. (Although better fresh, the recipe may be made a few days ahead. Store the cookies in an airtight tin or stack them with a sheet of waxed paper between each layer, wrap in plastic bags and store in the freezer. Unstack them while still frozen and let come to room temperature before serving.)

Makes about 60
Recipe by Diana Sturgis

Cigar Cookies

Serve these crunchy elegant cookies as an accompaniment to ice cream or espresso.

1 recipe Basic Almond Cookie Batter (page 105)

1 Follow the recipe for Tuiles through Step 2, omitting the almond topping.

2 Bake in the lower third of the oven for 5 to 6 minutes, until the cookies have a golden-brown border 1 inch wide. Have ready 4 long-handled wooden spoons or dowels ½ inch in diameter.

3 Remove the cookies from the oven. Working quickly, slide the back of a wide metal spatula under a cookie, pushing to separate the cookie from the sheet without tearing; the cookie will be soft and pliable. Wrap it around the handle of the spoon and slide down toward the bowl of the spoon. Repeat with the remaining 3 cookies on the other wooden spoons. Leave in place until cooled and set, about 2 minutes; slide off and set aside. If the cookies cool before they can be easily molded, return to the oven for 30 seconds to restore their pliability.

4 Scrape the baking sheet clean, wipe with a paper towel and lightly butter it. It is not necessary to rewarm the sheet. Repeat Steps 1 through 3 to form the remaining batter into "cigars." (The recipe may be prepared several days ahead. The cookies may be frozen, but will also keep well stored in an airtight tin.)

Makes about 30
Recipe by Diana Sturgis

Orange-Apricot Chiffon

Joan Scobey adapted this recipe from *Cooking With Michael Field,* a book she edited, but she lightened it up a bit to cut back on calories.

1 envelope (¼ ounce) unflavored gelatin	1 tablespoon minced orange zest
2 cans (17 ounces each) apricot halves or pitted apricots, drained	⅛ teaspoon salt
	¼ cup crushed amaretti cookies and 1 can (11 ounces) mandarin oranges, drained and patted dry, for garnish
4 eggs, separated	
4 tablespoons sugar	
½ cup fresh orange juice	

1 In a small bowl, sprinkle the gelatin over ¼ cup of cold water and let stand until softened. Meanwhile, puree the apricots in a blender or food processor.

2 In the top of a double boiler, off the heat, beat the egg yolks until frothy. Mix in 2 tablespoons of the sugar and continue beating until the mixture is thick and falls from the beaters in a ribbon, about 2 minutes. Blend in the orange juice, zest and salt.

3 Place the mixture over simmering water and cook, stirring constantly, until it thickens to the consistency of a hollandaise sauce, about 7 minutes. Stir in the softened gelatin until completely dissolved. Pour the mixture into a large bowl and blend in the apricot puree. Cover and refrigerate until thickened but not set, about 45 minutes.

4 Beat the egg whites just until foamy, add the remaining 2 tablespoons sugar and continue to beat until the whites form soft peaks. Gently fold into the apricot mixture until no streaks of white remain. Pour into a 2-quart serving bowl, cover and refrigerate until thoroughly chilled and set, at least 1 hour.

5 Just before serving, sprinkle the chiffon with crushed amaretti cookies and arrange mandarin orange sections over the top. Serve with a bowl of whipped cream and a basket of amaretti cookies, if desired.

Serves 8
Recipe by Joan Scobey

Summer Fruits with Sweet Cheese

Cooking teacher and cookbook author Lydie Marshall's favorite summer dessert is always very simple. She finds the best-looking fruits in the market and tops them with a tangy fresh cheese and a sprinkling of sugar. She chooses blueberries, strawberries and sour cherries in June; blackberries and red currants in July; and peaches and plums, poached in a simple sugar syrup, in August.

½ pound fresh cream cheese	About 1½ cups crème de cassis or crème de myrtilles
½ pound mascarpone, or 1 cup sour cream	1 pint blueberries
¼ cup sugar	1 pint strawberries
1 to 2 tablespoons heavy cream	½ pint fresh or frozen sour cherries (optional)

1 Beat the cream cheese and the mascarpone with a heavy-duty mixer until thick. Beat in the sugar and enough heavy cream to soften the cheese to the consistency of stiff whipped cream. Reserve in the refrigerator.

2 To serve, pour 2 to 3 tablespoons crème de cassis into each dish. Reserving enough berries and cherries for garnish, divide the rest among the serving dishes. Top with 2 spoonfuls of the cream cheese mixture and decorate with the reserved fruit. Pass a bowl of sugar on the side for guests to sprinkle as they please.

Serves 6 to 8
Recipe by Lydie Marshall

Ambrosia Mariposa

This ambrosia can be served in many ways–colorfully arranged on chilled plates, in tall stemmed glasses, in hollowed-out fruit cups, or even in a large glass bowl that lets the layers of color show through.

4 large navel oranges
1 large pink grapefruit
1 teaspoon granulated sugar
1 medium coconut
1 tablespoon confectioners' sugar
¼ teaspoon ground mace
3 tablespoons cream of coconut
1 tablespoon light rum

1 Preheat the oven to 400°. Peel and segment the oranges and grapefruit, making sure to remove all membrane, pith and seeds, if there are any.

2 Layer the orange segments on individual salad plates or in the bottom of a serving bowl. Layer the grapefruit sections over them. Sprinkle with the granulated sugar and set aside.

3 Place the coconut in a small baking pan and bake for 15 to 20 minutes, or until the shell cracks. Remove from the oven and let rest until cool enough to handle, about 5 minutes.

4 Place the coconut in a heavy plastic bag and hit it with a hammer several times to break it into several pieces. (Discard the liquid.) Rinse the coconut pieces and, using a small sharp knife, pry the meat out of the shell. Using either a sharp knife or a swivel-bladed vegetable peeler, remove the brown skin. Finely grate the coconut in a food processor or by hand. Measure out 1 cup grated coconut; reserve the remainder for another use.

5 Add the confectioners' sugar and the mace to the coconut. Mix well and set aside.

6 Drain any juices from the fruit segments and reserve them.

7 Combine the coconut cream, rum and 2 tablespoons of the reserved juice and pour over the fruit.

8 Top the fruit with the coconut mixture, cover and refrigerate for 3 hours or overnight. Serve cold.

Serves 6
Recipe by W. Peter Prestcott

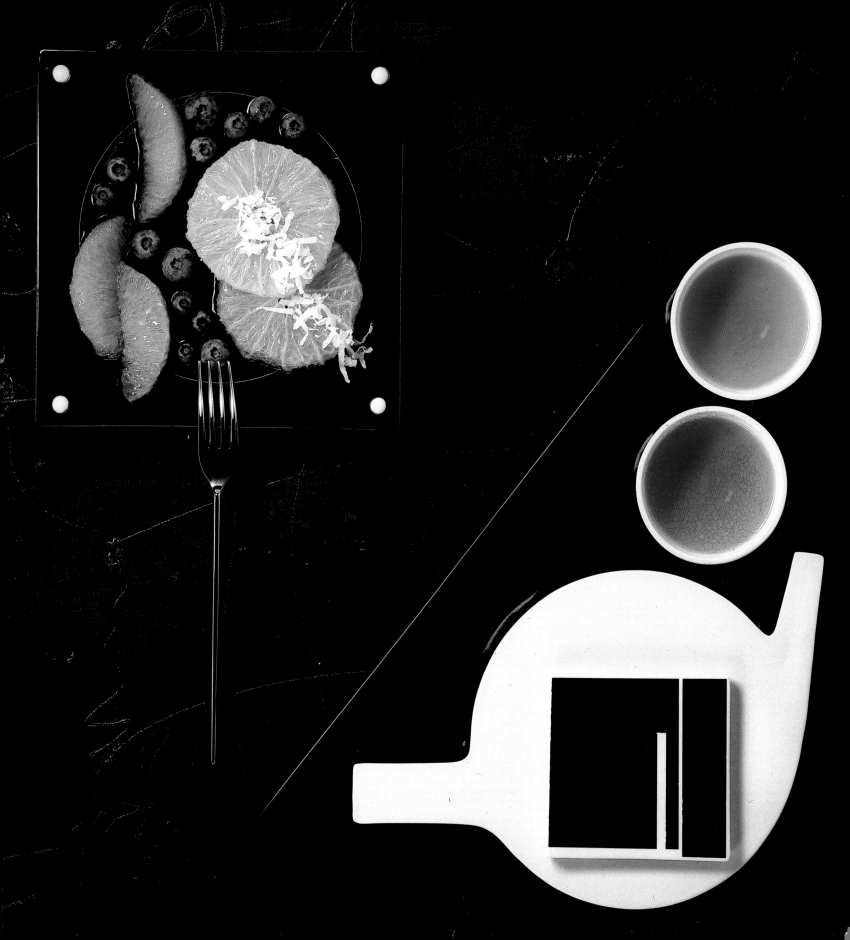

Celestial Lemon Roll

Light as air, long on flavor and low on calories (165 per serving) –
a flashy finish to follow lemon chicken.

Lemon Filling:
3 tablespoons cornstarch
⅓ cup granulated sugar
1 teaspoon grated lemon zest
⅓ cup fresh lemon juice
1 jumbo egg yolk
1 tablespoon unsalted butter

Angel Food Cake Roll:
**4 jumbo egg whites, at room
    temperature**

⅛ teaspoon salt
⅛ teaspoon cream of tartar
½ cup sifted superfine sugar
½ cup sifted cake flour
2 teaspoons fresh lemon juice
½ teaspoon vanilla extract
¼ teaspoon almond extract
3 tablespoons confectioners' sugar
**Lemon zest, sprigs of lemon
    verbena or lemon geranium,
    for garnish**

Make the lemon filling:

1 In a small heavy saucepan, combine the cornstarch and granulated
   sugar. Whisk in the lemon zest, lemon juice and ¾ cup of water.
   Cook, stirring, over moderate heat until the mixture boils and is
   thick and smooth, about 3 minutes. Blend a little of the hot mixture
   into the egg yolk and scrape the warmed yolk back into the pan.
   Cook over low heat, stirring constantly, for 1 minute. Remove from
   the heat and stir in the butter. Let cool to room temperature,
   stirring often to prevent a skin from forming, cover with plastic
   wrap placed directly on the surface and refrigerate. (The filling
   can be made a day ahead. Cover and refrigerate. Return to room
   temperature and stir to restore to a spreading consistency
   before proceeding.)

Make the cake roll:

2 Preheat the oven to 300°. Spray a 15-x-10-inch jelly-roll pan
   lightly with nonstick vegetable spray and line the bottom and sides
   of the pan with parchment or waxed paper. Oil the paper lightly
   with the nonstick spray.

3 In a large bowl, beat the egg whites with the salt and cream of tartar until the egg white bubbles are tiny and of even size and
   will mound when turned with a spatula, about 1 minute. Do not
   overbeat to soft peaks.

4 With a rubber spatula, gently fold in the superfine sugar, 2 tablespoons at a time. Sift the flour, about 2 tablespoons at a time,
   over the egg whites and fold in gently. When all of the flour is incorporated, fold in the lemon juice, vanilla and almond extract.

5 Spread the batter into the prepared pan, smoothing it evenly into the corners. Bake on the middle rack until springy to the
   touch, 20 to 25 minutes. The cake will be pale; do not overcook.

6 Meanwhile, spread a kitchen towel on the counter and sift
   the confectioners' sugar over it to cover an area approximately
   the size of the cake.

7 As soon as the cake is removed from the oven, invert it onto the
   sugared towel and peel off the paper at once. Using a knife
   with a serrated edge, cut off any crisp edges that might crack as the
   cake is rolled. With one of the short ends toward you, roll
   the cake up in the towel. Let the cake cool in the towel for about
   35 minutes.

8 Unroll the cake, spread it evenly with the filling, leaving ½-inch
   margins all around, then reroll, jelly-roll style and let stand,
   covered by the towel, 20 minutes longer. Remove the towel and sift
   any loose confectioners' sugar over the roll. Ease the roll onto
   a platter and garnish with lemon zest, sprigs of lemon verbena or
   lemon geranium.

Serves 8
Recipe by Jean Anderson

Pears Poached in Sauternes

Choose an affordable Sauternes for this recipe – you'll love the fragile flavor the wine gives the pears.

6 large pears, such as Anjou –
   peeled, cored and quartered
   (about 3¼ pounds)
2 tablespoons fresh lemon juice
1 bottle (25.4 ounces) Sauternes
   wine
3 tablespoons sugar
4 whole cloves

1 teaspoon pear brandy
   (optional)
Vanilla ice cream, for
   serving
Freshly ground black
   pepper
Freshly grated lime zest

1 In a medium bowl, toss the pears with lemon juice.
2 In a large, shallow, nonreactive pan, combine the Sauternes, sugar and cloves. Bring to a boil over moderately high heat. Add the pears. When the liquid returns to a simmer, reduce the heat to moderately low and cook until the pears are tender when pierced, 8 to 10 minutes. Remove the pears and set aside. Discard the cloves.
3 Boil the poaching liquid over moderate heat until reduced to ½ cup, 8 to 10 minutes. Remove from the heat and let cool. Stir in the pear brandy, if using. (The recipe can be prepared ahead to this point. Combine the pears and the syrup, cover and refrigerate.)
4 To serve, place 3 pear quarters and a scoop of ice cream on each plate. Sprinkle each serving with 1 tablespoon of the syrup and garnish with a light dusting of pepper and lime zest.

Serves 8
Recipe by W. Peter Prestcott

Ginger-Glazed Oranges

More adventuresome souls might want to drizzle this with Cointreau or another orange liqueur.

5 large navel oranges
½ cup bitter orange marmalade
1¼ teaspoons ground ginger

3 tablespoons chopped
   fresh mint
Mint sprigs, for garnish

1 Cut the peel and underlying membrane off the oranges in lengthwise strips, following the shape of the fruit. Slice the peeled oranges crosswise into thin rounds and arrange, overlapping, on a small serving platter.
2 In a small heavy saucepan, combine the marmalade with ¼ cup of water. Melt, stirring occasionally, over low heat. Stir in the ginger and bring the glaze to a boil. Remove from the heat and press through a sieve.
3 Brush the glaze over the sliced oranges. Scatter the chopped mint over the top and decorate with sprigs of mint.

Serves 6
Recipe by Anne Montgomery

Sauternes Macaroons with Strawberries

These macaroons are a delicious accompaniment to a dish of strawberries. Traditionally, the berries are served with an older Saint-Julien poured over them, though here, a glass of Sauternes will do nicely.

2 cups ground, blanched almonds (about 8 ounces)
3 egg whites
¼ cup sugar
4 tablespoons Sauternes
1½ pints strawberries, halved

1 Preheat the oven to 350°. Line a large heavy baking sheet with lightly buttered parchment or waxed paper.
2 In a mixing bowl, combine the ground almonds, egg whites, sugar and 2 tablespoons of the Sauternes. Beat with a wooden spoon until well blended. The mixture should be firm enough to hold its shape.
3 Spoon tablespoons of the batter at least 1 inch apart onto the prepared baking sheet. Leave the dough rough edged. Brush each cookie lightly with the remaining Sauternes.
4 Bake in the upper third of the oven for 25 to 30 minutes, until lightly browned. Transfer to a rack to cool.
5 Divide the strawberries among 6 dessert dishes and serve along with the macaroons.

Serves 6
Recipe by John Robert Massie

Peaches Poached in Raspberries and Red Wine

Peaches poached in this rich and robust raspberry wine syrup take on a new dimension – they're the perfect way to end a summer meal. Paula Wolfert often poaches small purple figs in the syrup and then tops them with caramelized orange peel. You may also want to try substituting pears when peaches are out of season (see Note).

1 pint fresh raspberries
1 cup sugar
Juice of ½ lemon
1 bottle (25.4 ounces) full-bodied red wine with at least 12½
percent alcohol content, such as a Zinfandel, Bordeaux, or Pinot Noir
12 small whole peaches, peeled
Whole fresh raspberries, for garnish

1 Combine the raspberries, ⅓ cup of the sugar and the lemon juice in a food processor or blender and process until pureed, about 2 minutes. Rub the mixture through a fine sieve and discard the seeds. Transfer the puree to a large nonreactive saucepan and add the wine and the remaining ⅔ cup of sugar. Bring to a boil, reduce the heat to low and keep the liquid at a steady simmer.
2 Add the peaches and poach for 4 minutes. Remove to a bowl with a slotted spoon.
3 Bring the poaching liquid to a full boil and boil until reduced to a syrup (about 1½ cups). Pour the syrup over the fruit, cover, and refrigerate until thoroughly chilled, at least 3 hours or overnight. Occasionally spoon some of the syrup over the fruit as it chills. Serve cold, garnished with a few whole fresh raspberries.

Note:
If you use pears, poach them for 5 to 6 minutes and garnish the finished fruit dish with candied violets.

Serves 6
Recipe by Paula Wolfert

Strawberries Romanoff

Rich orange ice cream offset by Grand Marnier-soaked straw-berries—this is the stuff of which 3-star Michelin recipes are made.

2 quarts strawberries, halved or quartered if large
¼ cup plus 1 tablespoon confectioners' sugar
¼ cup plus 1 tablespoon Grand Marnier

1 cup heavy cream, chilled
1 quart Orange Ice Cream (recipe follows)
1 navel orange—peel and white pith removed, sectioned

1 In a large bowl, combine the strawberries with ¼ cup of the confectioners' sugar and ¼ cup of the Grand Marnier; toss well. Cover and refrigerate for 1 hour.

2 In a chilled bowl, beat the cream until soft peaks form. Beat in the remaining 1 tablespoon sugar and Grand Marnier; refrigerate for up to 2 hours.

3 To serve, scoop the ice cream into 6 chilled dessert dishes or wine goblets. Spoon the strawberries around the ice cream. Drizzle some of the strawberry juices over the top and garnish with the whipped cream and orange sections.

Serves 6
Recipe from l'Auberge de l'Ill
Illhaeusern, Alsace

Orange Ice Cream

3 navel oranges
¾ cup granulated sugar
3 cups heavy cream
1 cup milk

1 teaspoon vanilla extract
4 egg yolks, at room temperature
¼ cup Grand Marnier

1 Using a vegetable peeler, strip the zest from the oranges. (Save the oranges for another use.) In a food processor, combine the sugar with one-third of the zest. Process until the zest is minced, about 1 minute.

2 Scrape the orange sugar into a medium saucepan. Add the cream, milk, vanilla and the remaining zest. Bring to a boil over moderate heat, stirring occasionally to dissolve the sugar. Set aside to steep for 10 minutes.

3 In a medium bowl, beat the egg yolks until thick and light. Whisk in the orange cream until well blended.

4 Pour the mixture back into the saucepan and cook over moderate heat, stirring constantly, until the custard thickens enough to coat the back of a spoon, about 4 minutes. Stir in the Grand Marnier.

5 Strain the custard into a stainless steel bowl set over a larger bowl of ice and water. Stir until cool. Pour the custard into an ice cream maker and freeze according to the manufacturer's instructions.

Makes about 1 quart
Recipe from l'Auberge de l'Ill
Illhaeusern, Alsace

Cafe Renni's Honeydew Granite

Light and only a bit sweet, this rough melon ice is a lighthearted conclusion to a major meal.

1 medium honeydew melon
2 tablespoons light corn syrup

1 teaspoon fresh lemon juice
Fresh mint sprigs, for garnish

1 Halve and seed the melon. Working over a sieve to catch the juices, scoop out the flesh. Reserve the juice.
2 Puree the flesh in a food processor or blender. Strain through a fine-mesh sieve, pressing lightly so that no pulp is forced through. Combine with the reserved melon juice.
3 Stir the corn syrup and lemon juice into the melon juice. Place in an ice cream maker and freeze according to the manufacturer's instructions.
4 Serve in chilled glasses, garnished with a sprig of mint.

Serves 4
Recipe by Chef Mark Carrozza
Cafe Renni, Lambertville, New Jersey

Lemon-Orange Sherbet

A refreshing, light dessert, tangy with the flavor of citrus. It can be made with or without an ice cream maker. Serve in tiny scoops (made with a melon baller) piled high in a Champagne flute or parfait glass.

6 lemons
1 navel orange
1½ cups sugar

¼ teaspoon salt
2 quarts milk

1 Finely grate the zest from the lemons and the orange; set aside. Squeeze the juice from the lemons and the orange.
2 In a large, heavy nonreactive saucepan, combine the fruit juices and the sugar. Cook, stirring, over low heat until the sugar dissolves. Stir in the lemon and orange zests, the salt and the milk, which will curdle. Remove from the heat and let cool to room temperature.
3 Freeze the sherbet mixture in an ice cream maker following the manufacturer's instructions or pour the mixture into a large shallow dish and place in the freezer. When the sherbet is semi-frozen (about 4 hours), remove from the freezer, scrape into a large mixer bowl and beat to break up the large ice crystals. Place the bowl in the freezer again until the sherbet is completely frozen.
4 Before serving, remove from the freezer and allow to stand for 5 to 10 minutes, until slightly softened. If made by hand, beat until smooth before scooping into dessert dishes.

Makes about 2½ quarts
Recipe by Mary Bacas

Glazed Pineapple with Macadamia Nut Crunch

Hawaii's most flavorful exports—pineapples and macadamia nuts—combine here for an easy-to-assemble dessert that's not overly threatening to your figure.

1 large ripe pineapple – ends trimmed, skin and eyes removed
1 cup coarsely chopped macadamia nuts
⅓ cup (packed) light brown sugar
Pinch of salt
4 tablespoons unsalted butter, melted

1 Preheat the boiler. Cut the pineapple into 8 slices, each about 1 inch thick. For a decorative presentation you might want to cut notched grooves 1 inch apart on the top of each slice to suggest the grooves in a scallop shell.
2 In a small bowl, combine the nuts, brown sugar and salt. Add the butter and stir until well blended.
3 Place the pineapple slices on a baking sheet lined with foil. Sprinkle with a few tablespoons of the nut mixture or arrange in a graphic pattern over each pineapple slice.
4 Broil the pineapple slices about 6 inches from the heat until the filling starts to caramelize, about 1½ minutes. Serve hot.

Serves 8
Recipe by Anne Disrude

Orange Custard

Smooth creamy orange custard that's offset at serving time by a touch of maple syrup.

1 whole egg
½ cup egg substitute, such as Egg Beaters
1 tablespoon liquid fructose*
2 cups evaporated milk
¼ teaspoon orange extract
1 navel orange
Fresh mint sprigs, for garnish
2½ teaspoons maple syrup
*Available at health food stores

1 Preheat the oven to 300°. Lightly oil five ½-cup custard cups and set aside on a baking sheet.
2 Press the egg and egg substitute through a fine mesh sieve into a medium bowl. Add the fructose, evaporated milk and orange extract and whisk to combine.
3 With a fine grater, remove the zest from the orange and add to the custard mixture. Reserve the orange.
4 Divide the custard mixture among the prepared cups. Cover with aluminum foil. Bake for 25 to 30 minutes, until about two-thirds of the custard is set; the center will remain loose, but will set as it cools. Let cool to room temperature; then refrigerate until thoroughly chilled, at least 1 hour.
5 With a sharp paring knife, remove the white pith and membrane from the orange and divide the fruit into sections. Unmold the custards onto small plates. Garnish each with the orange sections and mint sprigs. Drizzle ½ teaspoon of maple syrup over each custard.

Serves 5
Recipe from Chez Eddy

Works of Art

Works of Art

■ **For centuries, artists have been using food in their art — painterly still-lifes of perfect pears and apples, of citrus fruits in rough-hewn wooden bowls. For almost**

as long, imaginative cooks have been acting like artists, creating food that looks like art. Whether the beauty of a particular dessert is due to its elaborate design or to its still-life simplicity, there's no question that inspired arrangement can add greatly to the enjoyment of a food.

This chapter is devoted to highlighting delicious desserts that look exquisite as well. Here's to those presentation-oriented chefs who are not content with food that merely tastes great, but who create a recipe that is a feast for the eyes as well as the stomach. Don't think your talents are too meager; some of these recipes will test your mettle in the kitchen, but others could be assembled by a child.

Food as art works best when it is well planned. And it functions especially well as a show-stopper ending to an otherwise "normal" meal. A solid dinner of rare roast beef, roasted new potatoes and asparagus can be made unforgettable if it's followed by our Vesuvius, a volcano of ice cream flowing with rivers of fiery rum. It may be plain ice cream, but this flaming dessert is a real event.

Or fill several dozen tiny cream puffs and stack them like a tall Christmas tree, using hot liquid caramel as glue to construct a true edifice of food – the Croquembouche. For another drop-dead dessert, you can spin a fragile golden cage from long strands of caramel and use it as a dome over a cake. Decorate it with edible gold dust and you'll have Zauber Torte, a fantastic creation that earns its magical name.

A basic chocolate cake can be transformed into Chocolate Leaf Cake, a work of art, if it's laden with a tangle of glistening, intricately patterned chocolate leaves. Serve it after any meal or no meal at all – no one will be thinking about dinner.

The possibilities for food as art are virtually endless. Take, for example, Jane and Ben Thompson's Ice Cream and Fruit Sherbet Bombe, a colorful, multilayered dessert. To make it, you can use an ornately shaped antique ice cream mold or a plain square or round. The artfulness comes in how you layer the different colors of ice cream and what sensibilities of design and form you bring to bear on the interplay of shapes and colors. The mold can be striped in contrasting colors or filled with waves of similar shades. It can even be polka-dotted if you take the time to make it that way. Whether you go at it as though you were Jackson Pollock, M.C. Escher or Carl Fabergé is up to you.

Who can deny the beautiful simplicity of Georges Blanc's Bresse Farmhouse Chocolate Cake, albeit only a half inch high. Though this cake is simple to execute (as are the Pear Brandy Tart and Grand Marnier Crème Caramel), the visual payoff resides in the care with which the ingredients are shaped or arranged.

Though some think that the true and proper appreciation of fine art requires knowledge, training and an experienced eye, the opposite is true with the fine art of food. Its execution might demand technique and practice, but its appreciation requires only our senses and our ability to enjoy. Let the table be your gallery; go ahead and have a feast. ■

Zauber Torte

This is the stuff that dreams are made of. Glistening strands of golden caramel will set the atmosphere in a darkened dining room. Make sure that tall tapers offer the only illumination.

Golden Génoise:
¾ cup cake flour
⅓ cup cornstarch
12 egg yolks, at room temperature
1 cup superfine sugar
1 teaspoon vanilla extract
6½ tablespoons clarified butter, slightly warm

Apricot Buttercream:
1 cup (6 ounces) dried apricots, preferably unsulphured from California
1 tablespoon Barack Palinka (apricot eau-de-vie) or apricot brandy
3 egg yolks
¼ cup plus 2 tablespoons granulated sugar
¼ cup light corn syrup
½ pound unsalted butter, at room temperature

Assembly:
2 tablespoons Barack Palinka (apricot eau-de-vie) or apricot brandy
Caramel Cage and Gold Dust (recipe follows)

Make the génoise:

1 Preheat the oven to 350°. Grease and flour a 9-cup (9-inch) kugel-hopf pan. Sift together the flour and cornstarch.

2 Place the egg yolks and superfine sugar in a large mixing bowl and set over a saucepan filled with an inch or two of simmering water; do not let the water touch the bowl. Whisk constantly until the mixture is almost hot, about 5 minutes. Remove from the heat.

3 With an electric mixer, beat on high speed until the mixture is very thick and pale and the bowl is cold, about 6 minutes. Reduce the speed and quickly beat in the vanilla and ¼ cup water.

4 Sift one-half of the flour and cornstarch mixture over the batter and gently fold in with a balloon whisk or a perforated skimmer. Repeat with the remaining flour and cornstarch. Adding one-half at a time, gently and quickly fold in the butter until just blended.

5 Immediately pour the batter into the prepared pan and bake for 35 minutes, or until the cake is golden brown and a cake tester inserted in the center comes out clean. Immediately unmold the cake by inverting onto a greased wire rack; let cool. (The cake can be made a day ahead. When cool, wrap well in plastic wrap to prevent drying out and store at room temperature.)

Recipe continues on page 124

Zauber Torte Continued

Make the buttercream:

6 Place the apricots in a small saucepan with ¾ cup of water. Let soften at room temperature for at least 2 hours or overnight. Cover the pan and bring to a boil. Reduce the heat to low and simmer for 10 to 20 minutes, until the apricots are completely soft. Puree the apricots and their liquid in a food processor or blender; press through a sieve. Stir in the Barack Palinka. Set the apricot puree aside.

7 With an electric mixer, beat the egg yolks on medium-high speed until thick and light in color, about 10 minutes. In a small heavy saucepan, combine the granulated sugar and corn syrup. Bring to a rolling boil over moderate heat, stirring constantly.

8 With the mixer at medium-high speed, beat the hot syrup into the egg yolks in a thin steady stream. Continue beating until the mixture is cool. On low speed, beat in the butter, 1 tablespoon at a time. Beat in the apricot puree.

Assemble the torte:

9 With a serrated knife, split the cake in half horizontally to make 2 layers. Sprinkle each cut side with 1 tablespoon of the Barack Palinka. Sandwich the layers together with about ⅓ cup of the apricot buttercream. Spread the remaining buttercream evenly over the outside of the cake; refrigerate until serving time. The cake can be served as is, simply frosted, or finished with the gold dust and cage as follows.

10 Using a small strainer, sift the gold dust over the buttercream, tilting the cake to get an even coating. Place the cake on a large flat platter and cover it with the caramel cage. (If the caramel cage breaks when assembling the cake, use the broken pieces as decoration right on the frosting.)

11 To serve, lift off the cage and break it into pieces. Serve some of the caramel with each slice of cake.

Serves 12 to 16
Recipe by Rose Levy Beranbaum

Caramel Cage and Gold Dust

1 cup granulated sugar
⅛ teaspoon cream of tartar

Candied violets (optional)

1 Cover the outside of a 9-cup (9-inch) kugelhopf pan with a sheet of lightweight aluminum foil, fitting it as smoothly as possible to the pan. Do not tuck the edges under. Trim, leaving a ½-inch edge to support the base of the cage. Lightly oil the foil or spray it with vegetable spray.

2 In a small heavy saucepan, combine the sugar and cream of tartar with ⅓ cup of water. Cook over moderately low heat, stirring to dissolve the sugar. Wash down any sugar particles from the sides of the pan with a wet brush. Increase the heat to moderately high and boil, without stirring, until the caramel turns pale amber, about 10 minutes.

Vesuvius (Flaming Ice Cream)

3 Quickly place the saucepan in a larger pan of boiling water to stabi-
  lize the heat of the caramel. Let stand until the caramel cools
  to about 240° on a candy thermometer and falls from a fork in fairly thick strands.

4 Working next to the stove, use a wooden spoon to drizzle a thin
  stream of hot caramel back and forth over the covered cake
  pan. The strands should be as thick as spaghettini and should be
  spaced to create a lacy covering. Work quickly, reheating
  the caramel when necessary over moderately low heat to keep it
  fluid. Make extra loops at the bottom of the cage for added
  strength. If desired, affix crystallized violets onto the cage or around
  the bottom with small dabs of caramel. Reserve a thin layer
  of caramel in the pan for the gold dust.

5 Allow the cage to cool for about 10 minutes, then carefully lift the
  cage and the foil from the pan. Beginning at the side farthest
  away from you, gently pull the foil away from the cage, gathering
  the foil into a ball as you go. (The cage may be returned to a
  well-oiled kugelhopf pan and stored in an airtight container for
  several weeks.)

6 Reheat the reserved caramel and pour it onto a greased baking sheet.
  Let stand until completely hardened. Break up the hard caramel and pulverize it in a food processor. You will need 3 to 4 tablespoons of this gold dust to sprinkle on the cake. (The gold dust
  may be made ahead and stored airtight for several weeks.)

Recipe by Rose Levy Beranbaum

Be sure to dim the lights before serving this flaming mountain of
a dessert.

1 quart rich vanilla ice cream (page 72)	**½ cup raisins**
	½ cup 151-proof rum

1 At least 1 hour before serving, scoop the ice cream into 6 shallow
  dessert dishes, preferably made of metal, ceramic or heavy glass.
  Press a deep indentation (the crater of the "volcano") into each ball
  of ice cream. Place the dishes in the coldest part of the freezer; the
  ice cream should be very firm when served.

2 An hour before serving, place the raisins in a small bowl and let
  macerate in ¼ cup of the rum.

3 Just before serving, press a few of the macerated raisins into the
  sides of each portion of ice cream and spoon a few into the crater at
  the top. Fill the craters with the remaining rum. At the table,
  ignite each "crater," using a long match, and also touch the match to
  any rum that runs down the sides of the volcanoes into the dishes.

Serves 6
Recipe from Pen & Pencil
Restaurant, New York City

Chocolate Leaf Cake

For a big-deal conclusion to an otherwise simple meal, bring out this very chocolate cake, covered with a cascade of as many chocolate leaves as you deem fitting.

6 ounces semisweet chocolate, coarsely chopped
½ cup safflower oil
1½ cups (6 ounces) walnuts or walnut pieces, toasted and cooled (see Note, next page)
¾ cup granulated sugar
½ teaspoon ground cinnamon
2 cups fresh bread crumbs (made from about 6 slices of firm-textured white bread)
6 eggs, separated and at room temperature
⅓ cup Cognac or brandy
Mocha-Walnut Buttercream (recipe follows)
Chocolate Glaze (recipe follows)
Chocolate Leaves (technique follows) or chopped walnuts, for garnish

1 Preheat the oven to 350°. Grease an 8-inch springform pan. Dust with flour; tap out any excess.

2 In a microwave oven or small heavy saucepan, melt the chocolate with the safflower oil over low heat until just warm. Stir to blend and let cool to room temperature.

3 In a food processor, combine the walnuts and 2 tablespoons of the sugar. Process briefly until just ground, 10 to 12 seconds. In a large bowl, combine the ground nuts, cinnamon and bread crumbs; toss well to combine.

4 In another bowl, beat the egg yolks lightly. Gradually whisk in ½ cup of the sugar, beating until the mixture is pale and thick, about 5 minutes.

5 In a large bowl, beat the egg whites until soft peaks form. Gradually add the remaining 2 tablespoons sugar and continue to beat until stiff, glossy peaks form.

Recipe continues on the next page

Chocolate Leaf Cake Continued

6 Fold the cooled chocolate mixture and the Cognac into the beaten egg yolks. Pour over the bread crumb mixture and fold together until blended. Stir one-third of the beaten whites into the mixture to lighten it. Fold in all of the remaining egg whites until no white streaks remain.

7 Quickly scrape the batter into the prepared cake pan and bake in the middle of the oven for 45 to 50 minutes, or until the surface is covered with small cracks and a cake tester inserted in the center comes out clean.

8 Transfer the cake to a wire rack and let cool for 10 minutes. Remove the sides of the pan and let cool completely. (The cake can be made to this point up to a day ahead. Wrap well.)

9 Invert the cake and carefully remove the springform bottom. With a long serrated knife, split the cake horizontally into 2 or 3 equal layers. Spread the Mocha-Walnut Buttercream between the layers and sandwich the cake together again.

10 Place the cake, flat-side up, on a rack over a jelly-roll pan. Pour the warm Chocolate Glaze over the cake. Using a metal spatula, spread it evenly over the top and sides. Refrigerate until the glaze sets, about 30 minutes.

11 Using a metal spatula (your fingers may melt the chocolate), arrange the leaves decoratively on top of the cake.

Note:

To toast walnuts, place them on a baking sheet and bake in a 350° oven until fragrant, about 10 minutes.

Serves 12
Recipe by Diana Sturgis

Mocha-Walnut Buttercream

1 tablespoon powdered instant coffee
1 ounce semisweet chocolate, coarsely chopped
¼ pound unsalted butter, at room temperature

1 cup confectioners' sugar
1 egg yolk
½ cup toasted walnuts, cooled and chopped (see Note at left)

1 In a small bowl, dissolve the coffee in 2 teaspoons water.

2 In a microwave oven or small heavy saucepan, melt the chocolate with the coffee over very low heat, stirring until smooth. Remove from the heat and let cool to room temperature.

3 In a food processor, combine the butter, confectioners' sugar, egg yolk and cooled chocolate mixture. Process until smooth, about 30 seconds. Turn the mixture into a small bowl and stir in the nuts. (The buttercream can be made one day in advance. Cover and refrigerate. Let return to room temperature before spreading.)

Makes about 1¼ cups
Recipe by Diana Sturgis

Poires Belle Hélène

Chocolate Glaze

4 ounces semisweet chocolate, coarsely chopped   **3 tablespoons unsalted butter**

In a microwave oven or small heavy saucepan, melt the chocolate and the butter over low heat. Stir until smooth and use the glaze while it's still warm.

Makes about ⅔ cup
Recipe by Diana Sturgis

Chocolate Leaves

Bittersweet, semisweet or milk chocolate, melted and tempered   **Nontoxic leaves with a fairly pronounced vein pattern, such as lemon leaves, washed and patted dry**

1 Using a small pastry brush, brush the underside of the leaf with a thin coat of chocolate. As soon as it begins to set, repeat with a second thin coat. Refrigerate until firm, about 10 minutes.
2 Beginning at the stem end, fold back and peel off the real leaf.

Recipe by Diana Sturgis

Choose shapely stemmed coupes that show off this simple-to-make food "sculpture."

3 cups plus 1 tablespoon sugar
2 teaspoons vanilla extract
4 Bartlett or Bosc pears, peeled
4 ounces dark chocolate (semisweet, bittersweet or sweet), coarsely chopped
3 tablespoons unsalted butter
¾ cup heavy cream
1 pint vanilla ice cream, slightly softened
Candied violets, for decoration

1 In a medium saucepan, cook 3 cups of the sugar and 3 cups of water over moderate heat, stirring until the sugar dissolves. Increase the heat to high and boil for 2 minutes. Reduce the heat to moderately low. Add 1 teaspoon of the vanilla and the pears. Cover and poach for 20 to 30 minutes, until the pears are tender but still slightly resistant to a fork.
2 Remove the pears from the syrup and let cool to room temperature. Refrigerate the syrup until chilled.
3 Remove the cores from the cooled pears from the bottom, leaving the tops intact. Return to the syrup and refrigerate, covered, until ready to use.
4 In a small heavy saucepan, combine the chocolate, butter, ¼ cup of the cream, the remaining 1 tablespoon sugar and ¼ cup of water. Bring to a boil over low heat. Simmer until the sauce is thick and smooth, about 5 minutes. Add the remaining 1 teaspoon vanilla and remove from the heat.
5 To assemble, divide the ice cream among 4 chilled dessert dishes. Place the pears on top of the ice cream (hold in the freezer up to 15 minutes at this point if necessary).
6 Beat the remaining ½ cup cream until stiff peaks form. Using a pastry bag with a star tip, pipe the whipped cream around the base of the pears. Decorate with candied violets.
7 Rewarm the chocolate sauce slightly if it has cooled and pass separately or drizzle over the pears just before serving.

Serves 4
Recipe by Diana Sturgis

Bresse Farmhouse Chocolate Cake

This humbly named but very sophisticated thin chocolate cake is the creation of Georges Blanc, the youngest chef ever awarded a three-star rating from the *Guide Michelin.*

7 ounces bittersweet or semisweet chocolate, broken into small pieces
¼ pound plus 1 teaspoon unsalted butter
¼ cup cake flour
½ cup plus 1 tablespoon superfine sugar

3 eggs
¾ cup heavy cream, reduced by half (see Note)
1 tablespoon unsweetened cocoa powder

1 Preheat the oven to 400°. Lightly butter an 8-inch springform pan.
2 In a double boiler, melt 4 ounces of the chocolate with ¼ pound of the butter, cut into small pieces.
3 In a medium bowl, blend the flour and ½ cup of the sugar. Add the eggs and mix well.
4 Add the melted chocolate and butter to the bowl and, with an electric mixer, beat at high speed for about 5 minutes, until the batter is smooth and forms a ribbon when the beaters are lifted.
5 Pour the batter into the prepared pan (it will be about 1 inch deep) and bake for 15 to 20 minutes, until the cake is set and a toothpick inserted in the center comes out dry.
6 Unmold the cake onto a rack and let cool; it will fall to about half its original height.
7 Meanwhile, in a double boiler, melt the remaining 3 ounces chocolate with the remaining 1 teaspoon butter.
8 In a small heavy saucepan, bring the reduced cream to a boil, then whisk it vigorously into the chocolate. Continue whisking until smooth and glossy.
9 Place sheets of waxed paper under the cake and cooling rack. Pour the frosting over the top of the cake, using a metal spatula to spread the frosting evenly over the top and sides.
10 After the frosting has hardened slightly, about 5 minutes, use a long straight knife to mark the top in a crisscross pattern. Mix the cocoa with the remaining 1 tablespoon sugar and sprinkle it decoratively over the cake before serving.
Note:
Simmer the cream until reduced by half, about 20 minutes.

Serves 6
Recipe by Georges Blanc
La Mère Blanc, Vonnas, France

Mocha Cream-Filled Profiteroles

The cream puffs for these profiteroles can be made ahead of time and kept refrigerated, or they can be made up to 3 months ahead and stored, tightly wrapped, in the freezer. Don't fill the profiteroles until just before serving, or they will become soggy.

Cream Puffs:
4 tablespoons unsalted butter
¾ cup all-purpose flour
2 teaspoons sugar
Pinch of salt
3 eggs, at room temperature

Mocha Filling:
1 cup heavy cream, chilled
1 tablespoon powdered instant coffee
1 tablespoon dark rum
2 ounces semisweet chocolate, finely chopped
Strawberries, for garnish

Make the cream puffs:

1 Preheat the oven to 400°. Butter and flour 1 or 2 baking sheets. Place ¾ cup water and the butter in a medium saucepan. Bring to a boil and cook until the butter melts, about 1 minute.

2 In a small bowl, combine the flour, sugar and salt. Remove the pan from the heat and add the flour mixture all at once. Stir until well blended. Return to moderate heat and cook, stirring, until the mixture pulls away from the sides of the pan, 1 to 2 minutes. Remove from the heat.

3 Break one egg into the hot dough and beat vigorously with a wooden spoon until the egg is completely incorporated and the paste is no longer slippery. One at a time, add the remaining 2 eggs.

4 Spoon the mixture into a pastry bag fitted with a ½-inch plain tip and pipe 1-inch mounds 2 inches apart on the prepared baking sheet. The pastry can also be dropped from teaspoons.

5 Bake for 10 minutes. Reduce the oven temperature to 350° and bake for 20 minutes longer, or until the pastry puffs are golden and firm to the touch. Remove from the oven and turn off the heat. Pierce each puff with the tip of a small sharp knife and return to the oven. Leave the oven door ajar and let the puffs dry out in the warm oven for 10 minutes. Let cool on a wire rack. (The cream puffs can be made up to 3 months ahead and frozen. Reheat frozen puffs in a 325° oven until warmed through, about 10 minutes. Let cool before filling.)

Meanwhile, make the mocha filling:

6 Whip the cream until soft peaks form. Add the instant coffee and rum and beat until stiff.

7 In a microwave oven or small saucepan, melt the chocolate over very low heat, stirring until smooth. Remove from the heat.

8 Make a slit in each cream puff about one-third of the way down from the top, making sure not to cut all the way through. Spoon the mocha cream into a pastry bag fitted with a ½-inch plain round tip. Pipe the cream into the puffs.

9 Place 4 filled puffs on each plate and stack a fifth puff on top. Drizzle each portion with a little of the melted chocolate. Serve garnished with whole strawberries if desired.

Serves 4
Recipe by W. Peter Prestcott

Frozen Ginger Soufflé

A soufflé that can't fall – a cool and creamy sure thing after a cold-weather curry.

2 envelopes (¼ ounce each)
   unflavored gelatin
1 cup sake (Japanese rice wine)
8 eggs, separated and at room
   temperature
⅔ cup superfine sugar
½ teaspoon ground mace
½ teaspoon ground ginger

1 cup heavy cream, chilled
¼ cup finely diced
   crystallized ginger
Slivered almonds,
   crystallized ginger and
   whipped cream, for
   garnish (optional)

1 Fasten a parchment paper collar around a 6-cup soufflé dish with tape or string. Take care that the collar extends the height of the dish by at least 3 inches.

2 In a small bowl, sprinkle the gelatin over the sake and set aside until softened. Place the bowl in a pan of hot water and stir occasionally until the gelatin dissolves, about 3 minutes. Set aside and keep warm in the hot water.

3 In a double boiler, beat the egg yolks, sugar, mace and ginger over barely simmering water until the mixture is light-colored, creamy and warm to the touch, about 5 minutes. Remove from the heat and continue to beat until the mixture cools, thickens and forms a ribbon when the beater is lifted, about 3 minutes. Scrape into a large bowl and set aside.

4 Beat the cream until it doubles in volume and forms soft peaks. Beat the egg whites until they form soft peaks.

5 Stir the dissolved gelatin mixture and the crystallized ginger into the beaten egg yolks. Place the bowl in a larger bowl half-filled with ice and water and stir with a rubber spatula until the mixture begins to thicken and mound, 2 to 4 minues, depending on the type of bowl used (metal chills faster than glass or ceramic).

6 Immediately remove from the ice water and fold in the whipped cream. One-third at a time, fold in the egg whites until no streaks of white remain; do not overmix. Turn into the prepared soufflé dish, cover loosely with waxed paper and freeze until firm, at least 6 hours.

7 Before serving, remove the paper collar. Decorate the sides with slivered almonds and the top with crystallized ginger and whipped cream, if desired. Serve frozen.

Serves 8 to 10
Recipe by Diana Sturgis

Almond Cookies

This basic almond cookie batter produces cookies that, while still warm, are pliable enough to coax into a number of different plain or fancy shapes; the four recipes that follow make the shapes shown here. Of course, you can also stop short of the shaping directions to produce delicious and crisp wafers.

Basic Almond Cookie Batter:
⅔ **cup sugar**
½ **cup all-purpose flour**
½ **cup finely chopped blanched almonds**
1 **whole egg, lightly beaten**
2 **egg whites**
½ **teaspoon vanilla extract**
4 **tablespoons unsalted butter, melted**

1 In a medium bowl, mix the sugar, flour and almonds. Add the whole egg, egg whites and vanilla and beat with a wooden spoon until well incorporated. Stir in the butter and 1 tablespoon of water; the batter will be thin and slightly granular. (The batter may be made 1 day ahead and refrigerated, tightly covered. Stir before using and add up to 1 tablespoon additional water, if necessary, to restore the consistency.)

2 Follow the directions for making Chocolate-Painted Tulip Cups with Raspberries and Whipped Cream, Tuiles, Cigar or Chocolate-Lace Almond Cookies.

Makes about 20 4½-inch or
60 2-inch cookies
Recipe by Diana Sturgis

Chocolate-Painted Tulip Cups with Raspberries and Whipped Cream

These tulip cups can be painted with chocolate, filled with fresh fruit, mounded with cream or mousse or served as is. They require a small investment in time for a big payoff in presentation.

1 recipe Basic Almond Cookie
    Batter (on previous page)
2 ounces semisweet chocolate
1 cup heavy cream, chilled
2 teaspoons sugar

½ teaspoon vanilla extract
1 cup raspberries
Chocolate shavings, for
    garnish

1 Preheat the oven to 425°. Butter a large heavy baking sheet. Place in the oven for 1 minute, until the sheet is warm and the butter is melted. Remove from the oven.

2 Using a tablespoon measure, drop 4 separate tablespoons of the batter at least 5 inches apart onto the warm baking sheet. Using the back of a spoon, spread the batter into thin circles 4 inches in diameter, leaving at least 1 inch between circles to allow for spreading during baking.

3 Bake in the lower third of the oven for 6 to 8 minutes, until the cookies have a golden-brown border 1 inch wide. Meanwhile, cut 4 pieces of aluminum foil into 4-inch squares and set out 4 narrow glass jars (such as store-bought spice jars or other cylindrical containers 1½ to 2 inches in diameter) bottom-side up on the work surface.

4 Remove the cookies from the oven. Working quickly, slide the back of a wide metal spatula under a cookie, pushing to separate the cookie from the sheet without tearing; the cookie will be soft and pliable. Invert the cookie and drape it over the spice jar. Place a square of foil on top to protect your fingers and with your hands, gently mold the cookie around the jar into a tulip shape. Repeat with the remaining 3 cookies on the other spice jars. Leave in place until cooled and set, about 2 minutes; set aside. If the cookies cool before they are molded, return to the oven for 30 seconds to restore their pliability.

5 Scrape the baking sheet clean, wipe with a paper towel and lightly butter it. It is not necessary to rewarm the sheet. Repeat Steps 2 to 5 to form the remaining batter into tulip cups. (Although better fresh, the recipe can be made to this point a few days ahead. Store tulip cups in an airtight tin or wrap them individually in plastic bags and store in the freezer. Let the tulip cups come to room temperature before using them.)

6 Melt the chocolate in a microwave oven or in a double boiler over hot – but not boiling – water. With a dry pastry brush, lightly paint the inside of each tulip cup with melted chocolate and let set.

7 In a medium bowl, beat the cream until soft peaks form. Add the sugar and vanilla and continue to beat until stiff peaks form.

8 Up to an hour before serving, spoon or decoratively pipe the whipped cream into the tulip cups. Dot with the raspberries and sprinkle chocolate shavings on top.

Makes about 20
Recipe by Diana Sturgis

Fruit Loaf with Raspberry Sauce

No matter how ornate the mold, colorful fresh fruit—caught in a

sweet, smooth custard—can't fail to star in this dessert.

Raspberry Sauce:
1 pint fresh raspberries (see Note, next page)
About ¼ cup sugar, or to taste, depending on the sweetness of the berries
About 1 tablespoon fresh lemon juice

Fruit Loaf:
5 teaspoons unflavored gelatin
1½ cups milk
1 large or 2 small vanilla beans, split
1 cup plus 2 tablespoons sugar
4 egg yolks
1 cup heavy cream, chilled
2 cups cubed, peeled ripe peaches
½ pint fresh raspberries
¾ cup strawberries, preferably small
¾ cup blackberries

Make the sauce:

1 Sprinkle the fresh raspberries with the sugar, cover and refrigerate overnight. Puree the raspberries in a food processor or blender; strain to remove the seeds. Adjust the flavor with the lemon juice and more sugar if necessary. Cover and refrigerate until serving time.

Make the loaf:

2 Line a 7-cup loaf pan or decorative mold with plastic wrap; lightly oil the wrap. Gently work out as many air bubbles and wrinkles as possible. Set aside.

3 In a small saucepan, sprinkle the gelatin over ½ cup of the milk and set aside to soften.

4 Meanwhile, in a heavy nonreactive saucepan, combine the remaining 1 cup milk with the vanilla bean and ⅓ cup of the sugar. Bring to a simmer over moderate heat, stirring to dissolve the sugar. Remove from the heat.

5 In a medium bowl, whisk the egg yolks and the remaining sugar until thick and lemon colored.

6 Gradually whisk in ¼ cup of the hot milk to warm the yolks. Slowly add the mixture to the remaining milk and cook over moderately low heat, stirring constantly with a wooden spoon, until the custard is thick enough to coat the back of the spoon, 5 to 8 minutes; do not allow the mixture to boil or it will curdle. Remove from the heat and continue to stir for about 1 minute, to cool the custard slightly and help stop the cooking.

Recipe continues on the next page

Fruit Loaf with Raspberry Sauce Continued

7 Place the saucepan of softened gelatin over low heat and warm gently, stirring frequently, until completely dissolved, 3 to 4 minutes. Stir the dissolved gelatin into the custard, mixing well. Strain into a stainless-steel bowl and let cool to room temperature; then cover and refrigerate, stirring every 5 or 10 minutes, until the mixture is thick enough to mound but is not set.

8 Beat the cream, preferably in a chilled bowl with chilled beaters, over ice and water, until stiff and doubled in volume. (The whipped cream and custard should be at the same temperature when you combine them.) Using a large spatula, gently fold the whipped cream into the thickened custard.

9 Immediately fold in the fruits, taking care not to crush them. Spoon the mixture into the prepared mold. Tap gently to settle, cover and chill for at least 8 hours or overnight, until completely set.

10 Before serving, invert the mold onto a chilled platter and peel off the plastic wrap. Using a thin, sharp knife dipped in hot water and wiped dry, cut into even slices, about ¾ inch thick. Place on individual serving dishes in a pool of the Raspberry Sauce.

Note:

For the sauce, 2 packages (10 ounces each) of frozen raspberries may be substituted for the pint of fresh berries, but the ¼ cup of sugar should be omitted. However, to create the lovely mosaic of the fruit loaf, firm fresh berries are necessary. If fresh raspberries are unavailable or prohibitively expensive, substitute additional strawberries. Out of season, drained canned peaches and blackberries or fresh blueberries may be used.

Serves 8 to 10
Recipe by Paula Wolfert

Ilona Torte

Although this cake is at its best the day it is baked, it will keep in the refrigerator for up to two days. Our version of this classic cake comes from George Lang, who offers it as one of the centerpieces of the dessert table at his New York restaurant, Café des Artistes.

1 cup sugar
5 ounces semisweet chocolate, cut into small pieces
6 tablespoons unsalted butter, at room temperature
8 eggs, separated

1¾ cups plus ⅓ cup coarsely ground walnuts
2 tablespoons fresh bread crumbs
Pinch of salt
Mocha Buttercream (recipe follows)
Walnut halves, for garnish

1 Preheat the oven to 375°. Butter a 10-inch round, 2½-inch-deep springform pan. Line with a round of waxed paper. Butter and flour the paper and the sides of the pan; tap out any excess.

2 In a saucepan, combine the sugar and ¼ cup of water and cook over moderate heat, stirring occasionally, until the sugar dissolves, about 5 minutes.

3 Add the chocolate, remove from the heat and stir until the chocolate melts. Set aside to cool for 15 minutes.

4 In a medium bowl, beat the butter with an electric mixer at medium speed until light. Beat in the egg yolks, one at a time, beating until each is incorporated before adding another. On low speed,

add half the chocolate syrup, then 1¾ cups of the ground walnuts, then the remaining syrup and the bread crumbs, mixing just enough to blend after each addition.

5 In a large bowl, beat the egg whites with the salt until stiff peaks form. Stir one-third of the whites into the chocolate-nut mixture to lighten it, then pour the chocolate mixture into the egg whites, letting it run down one side of the bowl. Fold the two together until thoroughly blended; do not overmix. Gently pour the batter into the prepared pan.

6 Bake in the center of the oven for 35 to 40 minutes, or until the center feels set when pressed.

7 Let the torte cool in the pan for 15 minutes. Release the sides of the springform and invert the torte onto a rack covered with a paper towel. Remove the pan bottom and the waxed paper, and let cool completely, for at least 2 hours, before frosting.

8 Split the torte in half horizontally. Place the top half, top-side down, on a round platter. Reserving 1 cup of the buttercream for decoration, cover the cake with ¾ cup of the remaining buttercream (see Note).

9 Place the second layer on top of the filling, smooth-side up. Frost the top and the sides of the cake with the remaining buttercream.

10 Press the remaining ⅓ cup nuts into the frosting on the sides of the cake. Using a pastry bag with a star or shell tip, decorate the top edges and the base of the cake with the reserved 1 cup buttercream. Garnish the top with walnut halves. Refrigerate until serving time.

Note:

If you prefer not to decorate the cake with a pastry bag, use 1¾ cups of the buttercream to fill the cake and the remainder to frost it.

Serves 14 to 16
Recipe from George Lang
Café des Artistes, New York City

Mocha Buttercream

6 ounces semisweet chocolate, cut into small pieces
2 teaspoons powdered instant espresso coffee

½ pound plus 2 tablespoons unsalted butter, at room temperature
3 egg yolks
⅔ cup confectioners' sugar

1 In a heavy saucepan or in a microwave oven, combine the chocolate, ⅓ cup of water and the instant espresso. Stir over low heat until the chocolate is completely melted. Scrape into a bowl and set aside to cool completely.

2 Using an electric mixer, cream the butter until light and fluffy. One at a time, beat in the egg yolks, beating until each is incorporated before adding another. Gradually add the confectioners' sugar. Scrape in the cooled chocolate mixture and blend thoroughly.

Makes about 3 cups
Recipe from George Lang
Café des Artistes, New York City

Ice Cream and Fruit Sherbet Bombe

Whether you construct an edifice of colorful layers in a plain pan or in an antique mold, this artful dessert is sure to please your guests. If you do a layer or two a day, it takes little time or effort to construct. Choose the flavors and colors that please you.

1 pint rich vanilla ice cream, softened
3 tablespoons Armagnac or Cognac
1 pint boysenberry sherbet
1 teaspoon fresh lemon juice
3 tablespoons kirsch
1 pint pear sherbet, softened
3 tablespoons pear brandy or Cognac
1 pint strawberry ice cream
3 tablespoons raspberry brandy or kirsch
1 pint orange sherbet
3 tablespoons Pernod or Ricard
1 pint chocolate ice cream, softened
1½ tablespoons dark rum
1½ tablespoons coffee liqueur
1 cup (4 ounces) grated bittersweet or semisweet chocolate (optional)

1 Mix the vanilla ice cream with the Armagnac until smooth. Pour the mixture into a 3½-quart bombe mold or a deep bowl and freeze for 10 minutes.

2 Remove from the freezer and, using a spatula, coat the sides of the mold about halfway up with the partially frozen ice cream. Return to the freezer for 2 hours, or until the ice cream is solid.

3 Mix the boysenberry sherbet with the lemon juice and kirsch, pour over the vanilla ice cream and freeze for 10 minutes. Using a spatula, work the boysenberry mixture halfway up the sides of the mold to coat the inside of the vanilla layer; return to the freezer and freeze for 1 hour, or until firm.

4 Repeat the procedure three more times using the pear sherbet and pear brandy, the strawberry ice cream and raspberry brandy, and the orange sherbet and Pernod, freezing the mold for 1 hour after the addition of each layer.

Recipe continues on page 138

Ice Cream and Fruit Sherbet Bombe Continued

5 Blend chocolate ice cream with the rum and coffee liqueur until smooth. Blend in ⅓ cup of the grated chocolate. Pour this into the center of the bombe; it will fill the center and form another layer on top of the other flavors. Smooth the surface with a spatula. Sprinkle another ⅓ of the grated chocolate evenly over the chocolate surface. Freeze until firm, about 2 hours or overnight.

6 To serve, invert the mold onto a plate and wrap around it a towel that has been dipped in hot water and wrung out. Lift the mold off the bombe, sprinkle the bombe with the remaining ⅓ cup chocolate and cut in thin wedges to serve.

Serves 20
Recipe by Jane and Ben Thompson

Marjolaine

This spectacular multi-layered creation of the late chef Fernand Point needs to be refrigerated overnight, so plan accordingly.

1⅓ cups whole hazelnuts	15 ounces semisweet chocolate, broken into small pieces
1¼ cups whole blanched almonds	10 ounces crème fraîche (1 cup plus 2 tablespoons)
1½ cups sugar	
¼ cup all-purpose flour	Vanilla Buttercream (recipe follows)
8 egg whites, at room temperature	Chocolate curls, for garnish
½ teaspoon fresh lemon juice	

1 Preheat the oven to 350°. Butter the bottom of a 15- x 10-inch jelly roll pan. Line the bottom with parchment paper; butter and flour the paper and sides of the pan. Tap to remove excess flour.

2 On two separate baking sheets, roast the hazelnuts and almonds for about 10 minutes, until lightly browned. Rub the hazelnuts in a towel to remove as much of the brown skin as possible. Reduce the oven temperature to 300°.

3 In a blender or food processor, working in batches if necessary, combine 1 cup plus 1½ tablespoons of the hazelnuts, all of the almonds, 1¼ cups of the sugar and the flour. Grind the mixture to a powder, 15 to 20 seconds for each batch. Set aside in a medium bowl.

4 In a large bowl, beat the egg whites until stiff. One-fourth at a time, gradually fold the nut mixture into the whites.

5 Pour the batter into the pan and spread evenly with a spatula. Bake for 45 minutes, or until the top is light golden and slightly crisp. Loosen the edges with a knife, invert onto a cooling rack and peel off the paper. Let cool thoroughly.

6 Butter a small metal cake or pie pan and set aside. In a small heavy saucepan, combine the remaining ¼ cup sugar and the lemon juice. Cook over moderate heat without stirring until the sugar dissolves and the syrup is golden. Pour in the remaining hazelnuts and stir with a wooden spoon to coat the nuts. Immediately pour into the buttered pan. Let cool to room temperature. When thoroughly cooled, break the praline into pieces and grind to a powder in a blender.

7 In a double boiler or microwave oven, melt the chocolate. Remove from the heat and stir in the crème fraîche. Scrape the chocolate cream into a bowl and set aside to cool.

8 To assemble, place the cake on a flat surface and, with a large serrated knife, cut crosswise into four equal strips (about 10½ by 3½ inches). Line them up, side by side. Measure out 1 cup of the chocolate cream and spread it evenly onto one of the strips; reserve the remaining cream for coating.

9 Spread 1 cup of the Vanilla Buttercream onto the second strip of cake.

10 Combine the remaining buttercream with the praline powder and spread 1 cup of it onto the third strip of cake. (You may have a little left over.)

11 Place the chocolate-covered layer on a serving platter, top with the plain buttercream layer and then the praline buttercream layer. Top with the fourth cake strip and press lightly.

12 Spread the reserved chocolate cream in a thin layer over the top and sides of the cake. Comb the sides with a fork to decorate. With a vegetable peeler, shave curls of chocolate directly onto the top of the cake. Refrigerate overnight before slicing.

Serves 20
Recipe adapted by *Food & Wine*

Vanilla Buttercream

3 egg whites, at room temperature
Pinch of cream of tartar
½ cup sugar

¼ pound plus 4 tablespoons unsalted butter, at room temperature
1½ teaspoons vanilla extract

1 In a large mixer bowl, beat the egg whites and cream of tartar until soft peaks form.

2 In a small saucepan, combine the sugar with ¼ cup of water. Bring to a boil over high heat and cook until the syrup reaches the soft-ball stage, 240° on a candy thermometer.

3 Immediately remove the syrup from the heat and, at high speed, beat it into the egg whites in a thin steady stream. Continue to beat the mixture until tepid, about 8 minutes.

4 Gradually beat in the butter, 2 tablespoons at a time. Beat in the vanilla. Refrigerate, covered, until ready to use.

Makes about 2 cups
Recipe adapted by *Food & Wine*

La Tulipe's Golden Delicious Apple Tart

Sally Darr, chef/co-owner with her husband, of New York's La Tulipe restaurant makes this – the best of the best apple tarts. The recipe is flawless.

Pastry:
1 cup all-purpose flour
1 tablespoon sugar
Pinch of salt
¼ pound unsalted butter, chilled and cut into small bits
About 3 tablespoons ice water

Filling and Glaze:
4 Golden Delicious apples, as small as possible
¼ cup sugar
4 tablespoons unsalted butter, thinly sliced
¼ cup apricot preserves
1 tablespoon rum

Make the pastry:

1 Mix the flour, sugar and salt in a bowl. Cut in the butter until the mixture resembles flakes of oatmeal. Drizzle in the ice water while tossing the flour mixture with a fork, adding just enough water to form the dough into a rough ball. On a lightly floured surface, press away a few tablespoons of the dough at a time with the heel of your hand, pushing quickly to form a smear about 6 inches long. Scrape together into a ball.

2 Continuing on a lightly floured surface, shape the dough into a rough rectangle about 4 inches wide and 6 inches long. Fold up the bottom third, then fold the top third over that, as you would a letter. Rotate the dough a quarter-turn counterclockwise, so that it looks like a book you are about to open. Roll out to form an even rectangle about ¼ inch thick. Fold into thirds again, wrap in plastic and refrigerate for about 1 hour.

3 Pound the chilled dough with a rolling pin to flatten slightly and let soften briefly so that it can be rolled. On a lightly floured surface, roll out the dough to form a circle 12 to 13 inches in diameter. Loosely fit the pastry into a 9½-inch tart pan with a removable bottom. Roll the pin across the top to cut off excess pastry. Press the pastry firmly into the pan. Prick the bottom at 1-inch intervals with a fork. Chill for about 1 hour.

Make the filling:

4 Preheat the oven to 450°. Using an apple corer, neatly cut the cores from the apples. Peel, then halve each apple. Place one apple half, flat-side down, on your work surface and cut crosswise into very thin slices, retaining the shape of the apple by keeping the slices together. (Do not slice lengthwise, from stem to blossom.) Repeat with the remaining apple halves. Set one apple half in the pastry with the wider, stem end against the edge. Fan the slices very slightly apart, tipping toward the center of the pie. Do the same with five more halves, leaving the center of the pastry uncovered. Arrange the remaining 2 apple halves in a rough flower shape in the center, fanning out the overlapping slices. Sprinkle with the sugar and evenly distribute the butter over the top.

5 Set the tart on the lowest rack of the oven and bake until the apples are lightly browned and somewhat caramelized and the crust is a rich brown, about 40 minutes.

6 Remove the side of the tart pan and, using the largest spatula available, gently slide the tart from the base onto a rack.

7 In a small pan, heat the preserves with the rum, stirring until smooth. If the mixture is too thick to pour, add 1 tablespoon of water. Strain through a fine sieve and brush the warm glaze evenly over the warm tart. Serve immediately or within a few hours. Rewarm the tart if it becomes completely cool.

Serves 8
Recipe by Sally Darr
La Tulipe Restaurant, New York City

Grand Marnier Crème Caramel

Shimmering in a coat of golden caramel, this soothing custard makes a dramatic display on a domed crystal cake stand.

2¼ cups granulated sugar	¼ cup plus 2 tablespoons
5 whole eggs	**Grand Marnier**
1 egg yolk	1 cup heavy cream, chilled
3¼ cups milk	2 tablespoons confectioners' sugar

1 In a heavy medium saucepan, combine 1½ cups of the granulated sugar with ½ cup of water. Cook over moderate heat, stirring once or twice to dissolve the sugar, until the mixture turns a rich golden brown and begins to caramelize, about 12 minutes. Immediately remove from the heat and pour the caramel into a 6- to 7-cup metal ring mold. Using pot holders to protect your hands (the caramel makes the mold extremely hot), quickly swirl the caramel up and around to coat the mold.

2 Preheat the oven to 325°. In a large bowl, whisk the whole eggs and the additional egg yolk with the remaining ¾ cup granulated sugar until well blended but not frothy. Stir in the milk and ¼ cup of the Grand Marnier. Pour this mixture into the caramel-coated mold.

3 Place the mold in a roasting pan on the middle shelf of the oven and add enough simmering water to reach halfway up the sides of the mold. Bake until a knife inserted in the middle of the custard comes out clean, about 1 hour 30 minutes.

4 Remove the mold from the roasting pan and set on a rack to cool to room temperature, about 2 hours. Cover and refrigerate for at least 2 hours, or until well chilled.

5 Run a knife around the edges of the mold to loosen the custard. Invert to unmold onto a platter; refrigerate, covered, if not serving immediately. Most of the solid caramel will remain in the mold. If you have used a lightweight aluminum mold, you can crack and release the caramel by slightly twisting the mold the way you remove ice cubes from a plastic tray. With a heavier mold, it's best to rap the mold several times sharply on a flat surface and then dig out the pieces with a heavy spoon; do not use a knife. Place the chunks of caramel in a sturdy plastic bag and crush into small bits with a rolling pin.

6 Beat the cream until soft peaks form. Add the confectioners' sugar and beat until stiff. Stir in the remaining 2 tablespoons Grand Marnier.

7 Just before serving, mound the whipped cream in the center of the custard and garnish the top with the bits of cracked caramel.

Serves 8 to 10
Recipe from Peter Sussman
The Phoenix Restaurant
Warren, Vermont

Coeur à la Crème

Sweetened cream cheese molded into the shape of a heart and
surrounded with an intense fruit puree makes an impressive
presentation for any occasion. It's a seductive way to capture the
heart of someone you love.

Coeurs:
**1 large package (8 ounces) cream
   cheese, at room temperature**
⅔ cup sifted confectioners' sugar
1¼ cups heavy cream
1 teaspoon vanilla extract
1 teaspoon fresh lemon juice
**1 teaspoon Grand Marnier,
   framboise or kirsch**

Sauce:
**2 pints raspberries or
   strawberries, hulled and
   washed, or 2 cups peeled, sliced
   peaches**
½ cup granulated sugar
1 tablespoon fruit-flavored brandy
1 teaspoon fresh lemon juice

Presentation:
Whole berries or peach slices

Make the coeurs:

1 In a food processor or with an electric mixer, beat the cream cheese
   until smooth and fluffy. Gradually add the confectioners' sugar
   and beat, scraping down the sides of the bowl.

2 Beat the cream until stiff. Gently fold half of the whipped cream into the cream cheese mixture. Add the vanilla, lemon juice and
   liqueur and gently fold in the remaining whipped cream.

3 Line six ½-cup coeur à la crème molds, one 3-cup mold or a closely
   woven basket with a double thickness of dampened cheesecloth.
   Spoon the mixture into the molds and fold the cheesecloth over the
   top. Place the molds in a large shallow baking pan and refrigerate overnight.

Make the sauce:

4 In a blender or food processor, puree the berries or peaches, sugar,
   liqueur and lemon juice. Strain through a fine sieve.

5 To serve, unfold the cheesecloth and invert the mold(s) on a chilled
   plate. Arrange berries or peach slices around base and off-
   center on the coeur, if desired. Spoon some of the sauce around the
   heart(s) and serve cold.

Serves 6
Recipe by Chef Patrick O'Connell
The Inn at Little Washington

Papillote of Pears with Orange and Vanilla

Surprise a special guest by serving this beautiful dessert, which comes out of the oven in a heart-shaped toasted paper pocket.

1 tablespoon clarified or melted butter
1 ripe pear – peeled, halved lengthwise and cored
2 teaspoons fresh lemon juice
½ vanilla bean
1 tablespoon plus 1 teaspoon crème fraîche
2 teaspoons sugar
4 strips of orange zest, each about 2 by ½ inch
2 small scoops of vanilla ice cream

1 Preheat the oven to 400°. Fold two 15- x 10-inch sheets of butcher's paper, parchment or aluminum foil in half crosswise to make 15- x 10-inch rectangles. Using scissors, cut each rectangle into a heart shape with the fold running vertically down the center. Open up the hearts and brush each with ½ tablespoon of the butter.

2 Brush the pear halves with the lemon juice to prevent discoloration. Cut each half lengthwise into 6 long crescent slices and place on half of each heart. Fan out slightly.

3 Scrape the seeds from the vanilla bean and mix them with the crème fraîche and sugar. Spoon over the pears. Place 2 strips of orange zest on top of each pear half and top with a piece of the scraped vanilla bean.

4 Fold the paper over the pears and beginning at the top of each heart, make a series of tight overlapping folds to seal the papillotes.

5 Place the papillotes on a cookie sheet and bake for 12 minutes. Open at table and serve immediately, topped with a scoop of ice cream.

Serves 2
Recipe by Anne Disrude

Croquembouche

A veritable tower of cream puffs and pastry cream held together with delicious caramel glue. The Croquembouche will provide a glorious edible centerpiece for the dessert table.

Cream Puff Shells (recipe follows)
Vanilla Pastry Cream (recipe follows)
3 cups sugar
Candied violets, for garnish (optional)

1 Make 2 recipes of the Cream Puff Shells. Do not try to make a double recipe at one time.

2 Make the Vanilla Pastry Cream.

Fill the shells with the cream:

3 Spoon the pastry cream into a pastry bag fitted with a narrow plain tip. Insert the tip into the small hole in each puff and squeeze to fill.

Make the caramel:

4 In a heavy medium saucepan, combine the sugar with 1 cup water. Bring to a boil over high heat, stirring to dissolve the sugar. Cook without stirring until the caramel turns light golden brown, 350° on a candy thermometer, 8 to 10 minutes. During the cooking process, wash down any crystals of sugar from the sides of the pan with a small pastry brush. Remove from the heat and set the pan in a larger pan of simmering water to keep the caramel at a working consistency.

Assemble the croquembouche:

5 One by one, pick up the filled cream puff shells with tongs and dip the tops about halfway into the hot caramel; try to keep the tongs clean. As they are dipped, arrange a single layer of puffs, caramel side out, in an 8-inch circle on a flat platter. Continue dipping and stacking to build up a pyramid of the filled puffs, indenting each succeeding layer slightly and angling the outside puffs top-side out. The finished croquembouche should be 12 to 14 inches high. (An oiled croquembouche mold facilitates this task, but is not necessary.) Decorate with candied violets if desired.

Serves 16 to 20
Recipe by John Robert Massie

Cream Puff Shells

If energy flags, forget building a Croquembouche and serve these puffs alone. They're a classic on their own.

¼ **pound unsalted butter**	**1 cup all-purpose flour**
¼ **teaspoon salt**	**5 eggs**

1 Preheat the oven to 400°. Lightly butter and flour two heavy baking sheets.

2 In a medium saucepan, combine the butter with 1 cup water and bring to a boil over moderately high heat. Immediately add the salt and flour all at once and cook, stirring constantly with a wooden spoon, until the dough masses together and a crust forms on the inside of the pan, 2 to 3 minutes.

3 Off the heat, add 1 egg and beat with a wooden spoon until smooth and glossy. One at a time, add 3 of the remaining eggs, beating well after each addition.

4 Spoon the mixture into a pastry bag fitted with a ½-inch (#6) plain tip. Pipe 1½-inch mounds of the batter onto the prepared baking sheets, spacing them about 2 inches apart.

5 In a small bowl, beat the remaining egg with 1 tablespoon water to make an egg wash. With a small pastry brush dipped in the egg wash, gently smooth the top of each pastry mound, flattening any peaks that stick up and evenly coating the top of each one. Avoid letting the egg wash drip down the sides onto the baking sheet; it will retard rising.

6 Bake for 35 minutes, or until golden. Remove from the oven. As soon as the puffs are cool enough to handle, punch a small hole in the bottom of each with a narrow pastry tip or small knife. Return the puffs to the baking sheet punctured-sides up. Return to the still-warm oven, with the heat off, and let them dry out for 1 hour. Let cool completely before filling.

Makes about 3 dozen small puffs
Recipe by John Robert Massie

Vanilla Pastry Cream

This recipe makes a creamy filling for cakes or pastries, too.

3 cups milk	**1 cup sugar**
1 vanilla bean, split	**6 tablespoons all-purpose**
9 egg yolks, at room temperature	**flour**

1 In a saucepan, bring the milk and vanilla bean to the boiling point. Remove from the heat. Remove the vanilla bean and place a round of buttered waxed paper on the surface to prevent a skin from forming.

2 In a large bowl, beat the egg yolks and sugar until pale and thick. One tablespoon at a time, gradually beat in the flour.

3 Gradually whisk in the hot milk. Pour into a clean heavy saucepan and bring to a boil over moderately low heat, whisking constantly. Reduce the heat to low and cook, stirring, for 3 to 5 minutes, or until the custard is thick enough to coat a spoon heavily and has completely lost any raw flour taste.

4 Scrape the custard into a bowl and cover the surface with a round of buttered waxed paper. Let cool to room temperature and refrigerate, covered, for up to 3 days before using.

Makes about 3¾ cups
Recipe by John Robert Massie

Simple Pleasures

Simple Pleasures

■ **Remember the time you shared a big pot of homemade chili with the neighbor across the hall and really regretted having nothing besides badly battered Lorna Doone's for** after-dinner treats? You wanted something good, yet simple. Well, in a mere ten minutes, you could have whipped up some of Bette Duke's Frozen Coffee Cream, a perfect solution to that last-minute need for a stir-and-serve-it dessert. Next time an impromptu gathering assembles at your house, think fast and make something easy – one of the recipes from our collection of Simple Pleasures.

The choice of a simple dessert needn't always arise from a need for making something from nothing; on occasion, the appetizer and entrée may be so elaborate that only something simple could follow. Other times, you have to work all day, pick up the car, go get a haircut, choose six lively lobsters, stop for some wine, and still be ready to receive guests at eight o'clock. After all that rigmarole, only the easiest dessert will do.

These Simple Pleasures are the goodies you can stir up in a flash. Some – like the Tennessee Whiskey Cream Pie – will require some time in the freezer, while others – the Mace-Scented Carrot Torte, for example – require some baking and/or cooling time, but not one of them is at all complex. You won't use every bowl, saucepan and spoon in the kitchen and you won't need any special equipment. Some recipes, such as the Summer Pudding or Brownie Pie, might require a smidgen of fore-thought (you'll need to have some chocolate or fresh fruit on hand), but none of them calls for exotic ingredients. Some of the simplest of our pleasures, in fact, can use ingredients that are store-bought. A scoop of Häagen-Dazs, for example, will look and taste just terrific when it's presented the way Peter Prestcott suggests in his Coupe Jamaica.

Keep in mind that a simple dessert need not look all that simple. It's a rare dessert that is easier to prepare than Cantaloupe with Port Wine and Cracked Black Pepper. Almost absurdly uncomplicated, given its elegance and sophistication, this delicately accented fruit is fit for the finest, ceremonial big-deal dinners. Or, take Margaret Romagnoli's Tira Mi Su recipe: It couldn't be quicker to fix – all you do is layer the ingredients one atop the other – but it looks downright complicated. Likewise, Katharine Hepburn's Brownies are stirred up in a saucepan, the ingredients beaten together with a wooden spoon. You'll have to decide whether it's worth waiting for them to cool, or if you'd rather go at them still warm, right out of the oven.

Making the chocolate-dipped strawberries couldn't be simpler to do, and since they should not be stored, there's no need whatever to bother with tempering the chocolate. The short-cut chocolate truffle recipe included here can be whipped up in a food processor in five minutes or less. The secret of these morsels' success lies in the quality of the chocolate or cocoa you use. Don't stint on these ingredients; buy good chocolate and let its complex richness shine through.

It is the wise cook who plans for the future. Next time you're making pie pastry or cookie-crumb crusts, make extra pie shells and freeze them. If that crucial part of a recipe is ready to go, chilled or baked pies will be a cinch. If you're in the mood for caramel sauce on your ice cream, make lots and keep the extra in a jar in the refrigerator. Sugar is a preservative; things that are sweet usually have a fairly long shelf-life if properly stored. If you're well prepared, you'll be able to meet the next dessert challenge with a simply smashing success. ■

Sparkling Spiced Strawberries and
The Easiest Creamy Chocolate Truffles

Strawberries in white wine – a refreshing, largely liquid dessert that
marries the sweet fruitiness of berries with the complexities of
balsamic vinegar. Absolutely delicious. It works wonderfully with
chocolate truffles (recipe on page 152).

2 pints strawberries, hulled
   and sliced
2 tablespoons sugar
Pinch of ground cinnamon
2 teaspoons balsamic vinegar,
   preferably well aged
1 bottle (about 3 cups) dry
   or semisweet sparkling
   white wine

1 Place the strawberries in a bowl. Sprinkle them with the sugar and
   cinnamon and toss gently. Let the strawberries stand at room
   temperature for 30 minutes, tossing 2 or 3 times.
2 Sprinkle on the vinegar, toss and refrigerate, covered, until serving
   time.
3 Divide the strawberries among 6 large goblets or dessert bowls.
   Pour about ½ cup of wine into each goblet and serve.

Serves 6
Recipe by Vincenzo Buonassisi

The Easiest Creamy Chocolate Truffles

The better the chocolate you use, the more delicious these truffles will be. And they could hardly be quicker to fix.

Truffles:
8 ounces semisweet chocolate
¾ cup heavy cream
2 tablespoons unsalted butter, at room temperature

1 tablespoon liquor or flavored liqueur (optional)
⅔ cup unsweetened cocoa powder

Coating:
1½ to 2 cups unsweetened cocoa powder

Make the truffle mixture:

1 Place the chocolate in the bowl of a food processor and pulse repeatedly, 6 or more times, until the chocolate is finely chopped – it will resemble tiny round pellets.

2 In a small saucepan, warm the heavy cream over moderately low heat just until it is very hot. Do not let the cream come to a simmer.

3 Pour the cream over the chopped chocolate and process for 15 to 20 seconds, until blended. Scrape down the sides of the bowl and process for 5 seconds more. Add the butter and liquor if you are using it and process briefly, until combined. Add the cocoa powder and pulse to blend. Scrape down the sides of the bowl and process again.

4 Cover a baking sheet with waxed paper. Drop the truffle mixture by spoonfuls onto the waxed paper. Chill in the freezer until firm, at least 30 minutes.

Coat the truffles:

5 Place the cocoa powder on a shallow plate or pie pan. Working with a spoonful at a time, roll the truffles between your palms until smooth and evenly rounded. Work as quickly as possible since the mixture will warm with handling. Roll each truffle in the cocoa to coat lightly and evenly. Place each truffle in a candy cup and refrigerate before serving. Serve the truffles at room temperature.

Makes 2 to 3 dozen
Recipe by Mardee Haidin Regan

Frozen Coffee Cream

Instead of a demitasse of espresso, try this smooth and creamy Italian semi-freddo al caffè.

4 egg yolks
½ cup sugar
2 cups heavy cream, chilled

2 tablespoons powdered instant espresso coffee
Whipped cream and grated sweet chocolate, for garnish

1 In a medium mixer bowl, beat the egg yolks on high speed until smooth. Slowly add the sugar and beat until thick and pale, 2 to 3 minutes.

2 In a large mixer bowl, beat the cream until soft peaks form.

3 Sprinkle the coffee over the cream and fold in gently, just until mixed.

4 Stir one-quarter of the beaten cream into the egg mixture to lighten it. Fold in the remaining cream until incorporated. Spoon the coffee cream into individual ½-cup ramekins or stemmed glasses. Cover lightly with plastic wrap and place in the freezer until firm but not hard, 1 to 1½ hours. Serve garnished with whipped cream and grated chocolate.

Serves 8
Recipe by Bette Duke

Tennessee Whiskey Cream Pie

Sour mash fans will be pleased to find yet another way to enjoy their favorite liquor – this time it's a creamy filling inside a chocolate cookie crust.

1¼ cups finely crushed chocolate wafer cookie crumbs (about 5 ounces)	¼ cup Tennessee sour mash (such as Jack Daniel's) or bourbon
¾ cup plus 2 tablespoons sugar	¼ cup crème de cacao
6 tablespoons unsalted butter, melted	2 cups heavy cream, chilled
1 envelope unflavored gelatin	Grated bittersweet chocolate, for garnish
6 egg yolks, at room temperature	

1. Preheat the oven to 325°. In a medium bowl, combine the chocolate cookie crumbs, ¼ cup of the sugar and the melted butter until evenly mixed. Scrape into a 9-inch pie pan and pat into a firm, even crust.
2. Bake for 10 minutes, until slightly crisp. Let cool on a wire rack for 5 minutes, then refrigerate, uncovered, for 30 minutes to cool completely.
3. Place ½ cup of cold water in a small saucepan and sprinkle on the gelatin.
4. In a medium bowl, beat the egg yolks with ½ cup of the sugar until thick and light colored, about 1 minute. Beat in the liquor and crème de cacao.
5. Warm the gelatin mixture over low heat, stirring occasionally, until dissolved. Gradually add to the egg mixture, beating until smooth.
6. Beat the heavy cream until soft peaks form. Add the remaining 2 tablespoons sugar and beat until stiff peaks form. Stir about one-quarter of the cream into the egg mixture to lighten it. Fold in the remaining cream until well combined. Spread evenly over the cooled pie crust and sprinkle with the grated chocolate. Freeze until firm, about 4 hours.

Serves 8
Recipe by Diana Dalsass

Katharine Hepburn's Brownies

Liz Smith, well-known syndicated entertainment columnist, scooped Katharine Hepburn's personal brownie recipe several years ago. You'll find that a little bit of batter goes a long way to produce these flat, dense, nutty bites. So, pin up your hair, stand up straight, suck in your cheeks and get cooking.

2 ounces unsweetened chocolate	¼ cup all-purpose flour
¼ pound unsalted butter	¼ teaspoon salt
1 cup sugar	1 cup coarsely chopped walnuts
2 eggs	
½ teaspoon vanilla extract	

1. Preheat the oven to 325°. Butter an 8-inch square baking pan. In a heavy saucepan, melt the chocolate with the butter over low heat, stirring until completely melted. Remove from the heat and stir in the sugar. Add the eggs and vanilla and "beat it all like mad." Stir in the flour, salt and walnuts and mix well.
2. Spoon the batter into the prepared pan and bake for 40 minutes. "Take it out; let it cool; cut into squares and go crazy."

Makes 1 dozen
Recipe by Katharine Hepburn

Cantaloupe with Port Wine and Cracked Pepper

A fruit still life that you can eat. Serve this with additional port for

sipping after a light summer lunch or dinner.

1 Halve the cantaloupe lengthwise and discard the seeds. Cut each
half into 6 long thin crescents.

2 Arrange 3 slices of the melon, standing up or overlapping slightly,
on each of 4 salad plates. Drizzle each serving with about 2 tablespoons of the port and sprinkle with a generous quantity of cracked
black pepper.

Serves 4
Recipe by Jim Fobel

1 ripe cantaloupe
8 tablespoons port wine
Freshly cracked black pepper

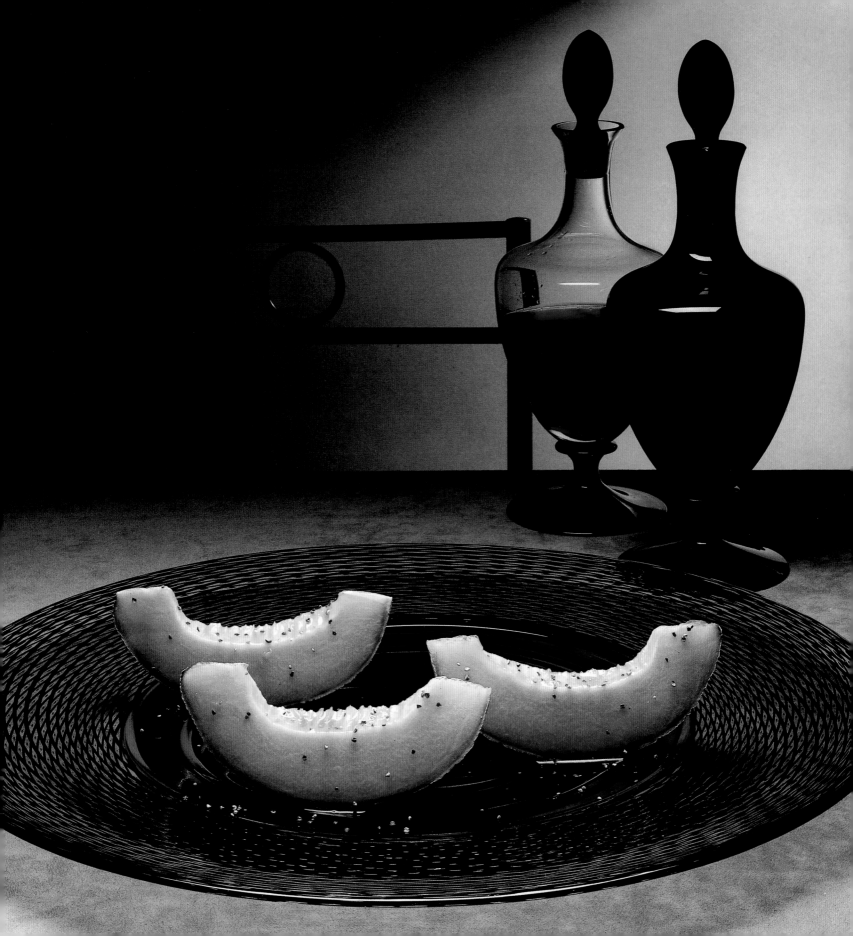

Frozen Chocolate Bananas on Sticks

Ice-cold bananas coated with chocolate make a fabulous sweet treat.

4 ripe but firm bananas
8 ounces semisweet or milk
  chocolate

¾ cup finely chopped walnuts

1 Peel the bananas and insert a wooden skewer or ice cream stick through one of the ends, reaching halfway into each. Wrap in plastic wrap and freeze until solid, preferably overnight.

2 Melt the chocolate in the top of a double boiler set over simmering water or in a microwave oven. Scrape the chocolate into a shallow plate. Place the chopped nuts on a plate.

3 Remove the plastic from one frozen banana and dip it into the chocolate, spooning chocolate over the entire banana until it is evenly coated. Quickly roll in the nuts. Rewrap in plastic wrap and keep in the freezer until ready to serve. Repeat with the remaining bananas.

Serves 4
Recipe by Jim Fobel

Rummy Pineapple with Vanilla Ice Cream

An intoxicating group of flavors that mingle as well here as they do in a drink.

1 ripe medium pineapple – peeled,
  cored and sliced into eight
  ½-inch rings
6 tablespoons unsalted butter, cut
  into tablespoons

½ cup plus 1 tablespoon
  light brown sugar
¼ cup white rum
8 scoops of vanilla ice cream

1 Cut slits halfway into the pineapple rings at 1-inch intervals, leaving the rings attached at the center.

2 Scatter the butter over the bottom of a large skillet, preferably nonstick. Sprinkle ½ cup of the brown sugar evenly over the butter and place a single layer of pineapple slices on top. Cook over moderate heat for 5 minutes after the butter and sugar begin to bubble. Turn and cook for 5 minutes longer. Transfer the rings to a platter. Add the remaining slices to the skillet and cook in the same manner; transfer to the platter.

3 Pour the accumulated juices from the platter back into the skillet and add the remaining 1 tablespoon brown sugar. Bring to a boil over high heat and cook until the liquid is reduced to a syrupy caramel, 3 to 5 minutes. Remove from the heat and let cool to lukewarm. Stir in the rum.

4 To serve, place a pineapple ring in each of 8 dessert dishes. Top each with a scoop of vanilla ice cream and spoon the sauce over all, dividing evenly.

Serves 8
Recipe by Diana Sturgis

Croûte of Fruit

Caramel Apples with Rum and Coffee Ice Cream

A great spur-of-the-moment dessert that uses whatever fruit is on hand – even those that may be a bit past their prime. Top with a dollop of crème fraîche, sour cream, ice cream or a sprinkling of brown sugar.

4 tablespoons unsalted butter, at room temperature
8 slices pound cake, brioche or sponge cake, cut ½ inch thick
2 ripe medium peaches, peeled and sliced
2 large plums, sliced
1 banana, sliced
2 tablespoons plus 2 teaspoons sugar
Sour cream (optional)

1 Spread about ½ teaspoon of butter on one side of each cake slice. Arrange the slices, buttered-side up, close together on a baking sheet, leaving no space between them.
2 Starting from the edges and working toward the center, arrange the peaches and plums on the cake slices to simulate a flower. Place the banana slices in the center. Be sure to cover the cake completely to prevent burning. Sprinkle 1 teaspoon of sugar over the fruit on each slice and dot each with 1 teaspoon of the remaining butter, cut into little bits.
3 Broil about 6 inches from the heat or bake in a 500° oven for about 10 minutes, until the top is slightly caramelized. Serve hot or warm, with sour cream if desired.

Serves 8
Recipe by Jacques Pépin

Serve the apples as soon as they're cooked and get ready to make a second batch – friends will love this easy recipe.

¼ pound plus 4 tablespoons unsalted butter
⅔ cup sugar
1 teaspoon fresh lemon juice
1½ tablespoons dark rum
6 small or 4 large apples – peeled, cored and cut into thin slices
1½ pints coffee ice cream

1 In a large skillet, combine the butter, sugar, lemon juice and ¼ cup of water. Stir together over moderate heat until the sugar dissolves. Simmer over low heat until thickened and caramel colored, about 10 minutes. Stir in the rum.
2 Add the apples. Toss to coat with the sauce. Cook, turning, until slightly softened, about 2 minutes.
3 Scoop the ice cream into 6 dessert dishes. Top with the apples and sauce and serve at once.

Serves 6
Recipe from Jimmy's Place
Chicago, Illinois

Fresh Apple Fritters

Bet you can't remember the last time you had hot apple fritters. If it's been that long, try these right away.

1 egg, beaten	**About 2 quarts peanut oil,**
1 cup milk	**for deep frying**
4 tablespoons unsalted butter,	**3 cups sifted all-purpose**
melted	**flour**
1 teaspoon vanilla extract	**½ cup granulated sugar**
1 large navel orange	**1 tablespoon baking powder**
1 large tart apple, peeled, cored	**½ teaspoon salt**
and chopped	**Confectioners' sugar**

1 In a medium bowl, whisk together the egg, milk, butter and vanilla.

2 Finely grate the zest from the orange into the egg mixture. Squeeze the juice and add to the egg mixture; stir in the apple.

3 In a deep-fryer or heavy deep saucepan, heat 1¾ inches of oil to 350°.

4 In a large bowl, sift together the flour, granulated sugar, baking powder and salt. Make a well in the center. Gradually pour the egg-apple mixture into the well while stirring in the flour from around the edge to make a thick batter.

5 Fry level tablespoons of the batter in batches without crowding until the fritters are brown and crisp, about 5 minutes. Drain on paper towels. Dust with confectioners' sugar and serve hot.

Makes 40 to 50 small fritters
Recipe from Stephenson's Restaurant
Kansas City, Missouri

Coupe Jamaica

A simple coupe with all the right flavors. Try making a huge sundae in one big bowl and going at it with long-handled spoons.

1 cup moist shredded coconut,	**1 tablespoon melted**
preferably freshly grated	**unsalted butter**
¼ cup (packed) brown sugar	**3 tablespoons dark rum**
	1 quart coffee or vanilla ice cream

1 Preheat the oven to 375°. Mix the coconut, sugar, and butter in a shallow baking dish. Bake, stirring every few minutes, until golden.

2 Add the rum and mix well.

3 Scoop the ice cream into one big "community" bowl or 6 individual dishes and spoon the warm coconut mixture over the top.

Serves 6
Recipe by W. Peter Prestcott

Icy Fresh Cranberry Pie

A cranberry ice cream pie that's tart and refreshing and at the same time creamy and smooth.

Graham Cracker Crust:
1½ cups graham cracker crumbs
¼ cup confectioners' sugar, sifted
6 tablespoons melted unsalted butter
½ teaspoon ground cinnamon

Filling:
2 navel oranges, rinsed and dried
2 cups (about ½ pound) cranberries, picked over

½ cup granulated sugar
1 tablespoon fresh lemon juice
1 pint vanilla ice cream, softened

Assembly:
1 cup heavy cream, chilled
1 cup cranberries, picked over
2 egg whites, beaten until frothy
About 1 cup granulated sugar

Prepare the crust:

1 Preheat the oven to 350°. In a bowl or in a food processor, combine the graham cracker crumbs with the confectioners' sugar, melted butter, and cinnamon until moistened. Press the mixture evenly into a 9-inch pie pan. Bake for 10 minutes and allow to cool completely.

Prepare the filling:

2 Cut the oranges up coarsely, including the peel. Using a food chopper or food processor, coarsely chop the cranberries and oranges together. Stir in the granulated sugar and lemon juice.

3 Fold the cranberry-orange mixture into the softened ice cream until well blended. Spoon the mixture into the cooled pie shell and freeze until firm.

To assemble:

4 About 30 minutes before serving, transfer the pie to the refrigerator to soften slightly. Whip the cream until stiff peaks form, and spread the whipped cream over the pie. A few at a time, dip the cranberries into the beaten egg whites and transfer to the sugar with tongs or a slotted spoon. Roll the berries in the sugar to coat lightly. Arrange the sugared cranberries around the edge of the pie and serve at once.

Serves 8
Recipe by Pearl Byrd Foster

Chocolate Marvel Pie

A chocolate pie that easily could become a family favorite for those who love cookie-crumb crusts and chocolate.

1½ cups finely crushed chocolate wafer crumbs
5 tablespoons sugar
5 tablespoons plus 1 teaspoon unsalted butter, melted

6 ounces semisweet chocolate, broken into ½-inch pieces
3 tablespoons milk
4 eggs, separated and at room temperature
1 teaspoon vanilla extract

1 Preheat the oven to 350°. In a medium bowl, combine the crumbs with 3 tablespoons of the sugar. Pour in the melted butter and toss with a fork until the crumbs are moistened. Press the mixture evenly against the bottom and sides of a 9-inch pie plate.

2 Bake in the center of the oven for 8 minutes. Remove from the oven and let cool to room temperature on a wire rack.

3 Meanwhile, in a double boiler over barely simmering water, melt the chocolate with the milk and the remaining 2 tablespoons sugar, stirring constantly, until smooth. Let cool to room temperature.

4 When cooled, add the egg yolks, one at a time, beating well after each addition. Add the vanilla.

5 Beat the egg whites until stiff but not dry. Fold gently into the chocolate mixture. Pour into the cooled pie shell and refrigerate for at least 3 hours before serving.

Serves 8
Recipe from The Fork Shop
Restaurant, Brookfield, Vermont

Tira Mi Su

In Italy, this dessert – which literally means "pick me up," probably because it is so tempting – is always made with fresh mascarpone cheese, a light, nonsalty cream cheese. Margaret Romagnoli has devised a simple substitute – a mixture of ricotta and cream cheese – that approximates the richness of the original.

**1 pound fresh mascarpone, or
    8 ounces each of whole-milk
    ricotta and fresh cream cheese**
¼ cup sugar
2 tablespoons rum
**31 biscotti all'uovo* or champagne
    biscuits**
**1 cup freshly brewed espresso
    coffee, cooled**
Zabaglione (recipe, next page)
**2 tablespoons unsweetened
    cocoa powder**
Strawberries, for garnish
***Available in Italian and specialty
    food stores**

1 In a food processor, blend the mascarpone (or the ricotta and cream cheese), the sugar and the rum until smooth.

2 On a serving plate, arrange 7 biscuits, flat-side up, side by side. Moisten lightly with ⅓ cup of the espresso. Spread one-third of the cheese mixture over the biscuits. Repeat 2 more times, finishing with the cheese.

3 Halve the 10 remaining biscuits crosswise and make a fence around the layered cheese. Pour the zabaglione over the top layer of the dessert. Sprinkle the cocoa over the top. Decorate with strawberries.

Serves 6 to 8
Recipe by Margaret Romagnoli

No-Roll Sugar Cookies

Zabaglione

4 egg yolks   **6 tablespoons Marsala**
¼ cup superfine sugar

1 Whisk the yolks and the sugar together in the top of a double boiler until pale yellow and fluffy.
2 Place over hot but not boiling water. Beat, adding the Marsala 1 tablespoon at a time, until the mixture is hot and thickened to the consistency of a light, fluffy batter.
3 Immediately remove from the heat and beat for 3 minutes longer.
4 Pour over the Tira Mi Su or serve as is, spooned atop fresh berries.

Serves 14
Recipe by Margaret Romagnoli

Crisp, light and easy to make, these cookies have a lovely melt-in-the-mouth texture. The recipe can easily be doubled.

2¼ cups all-purpose flour   **½ cup granulated sugar**
½ teaspoon baking soda   **½ cup confectioners' sugar**
½ teaspoon cream of tartar   **1 egg**
½ teaspoon salt   **½ cup flavorless vegetable oil**
¼ pound unsalted butter,   **½ teaspoon vanilla extract**
**   at room temperature**   **Granulated sugar, for dipping**

1 In a large bowl, sift together the flour, baking soda, cream of tartar and salt.
2 In a large mixing bowl, cream the butter, granulated sugar and confectioners' sugar until pale and fluffy. Beat in the egg and oil until well blended. Beat in the vanilla.
3 One-third at a time, add the dry ingredients, beating until blended after each addition. Cover with plastic wrap and refrigerate until firm, several hours or overnight.
4 Preheat the oven to 375°. Divide the dough into 8 sections. Working with 1 section at a time and keeping the remaining dough in the refrigerator, pinch off about 2 teaspoons of dough at a time and roll between your palms to form 1-inch balls. Place the balls 2 inches apart on ungreased cookie sheets.
5 Moisten the bottom of a 2½-inch glass with water and dip it in granulated sugar. Flatten each ball of dough with the sugar-coated glass, dipping the bottom of the glass in sugar before flattening each cookie.
6 Bake the cookies for about 8 minutes, until light golden around the edges. Let cool on a rack. Store in an airtight tin.

Makes about 4 dozen
Recipe by Leona Foote

Mace-Scented Carrot Torte

Go easy on yourself – use a food processor to grind the nuts and mince the carrots for this quick and easy torte.

1 cup pecans (4 ounces), ground	⅔ cup granulated sugar
2 tablespoons all-purpose flour	2 tablespoons fresh lemon juice
2 teaspoons baking powder	⅔ cup minced carrots (about 2
½ teaspoon ground mace	medium)
4 eggs, separated	Confectioners' sugar, for garnish

1 Preheat the oven to 350°. Butter an 8-inch springform pan. Line the bottom with parchment or waxed paper and butter the paper. Dust the pan with flour; tap out any excess. In a small bowl, combine the pecans, flour, baking powder and mace.

2 In a large bowl, whisk together the egg yolks and granulated sugar until pale. Add the lemon juice, carrots and pecan-flour mixture. Stir until blended.

3 Beat the egg whites until they form stiff peaks. Fold into the carrot mixture; do not overmix. Turn the batter into the prepared pan and smooth the top.

4 Bake in the center of the oven for 60 to 65 minutes, until golden. This type of torte will naturally sink slightly in the center. Let cool on a rack for 10 minutes. Run a blunt knife around the sides of the pan and unmold the cake. Turn right-side up and let cool completely on a rack. Slide onto a platter and garnish with a sprinkling of confectioners' sugar before serving.

Serves 8
Recipe by Dorie Greenspan

Baked Marmalade Pancake

A baked-in-the-oven pancake that makes a superlative dessert. If marmalade isn't to your taste, substitute a homemade fruit chutney.

2 eggs	¼ pound unsalted butter
½ cup all-purpose flour	6 tablespoons orange marmalade
½ cup milk	or any other citrus marmalade
¼ teaspoon almond or vanilla	2 tablespoons confectioners' sugar
extract	

1 Preheat the oven to 400°. In a medium bowl, whisk the eggs, flour, milk and almond extract until blended.

2 Melt the butter in a large ovenproof skillet over moderate heat. Remove the skillet from the heat and pour in the batter, tilting to cover the bottom of the pan evenly. Immediately place in the oven and bake for 15 minutes, or until puffed and golden brown.

3 Transfer to a serving plate, spread with the marmalade and dust with the sugar; serve immediately.

Serves 4
Recipe by Jim Brown

Brownie Pie

Snuggle up in your bed, turn on the late movie and dig into a
wedge of this chocolate-crusted brownie pie.

Chocolate Crust:
1 cup all-purpose flour
¼ cup sugar
¼ teaspoon salt
6 tablespoons cold unsalted
   butter, cut into 12 pieces
3 tablespoons unsweetened
   cocoa powder, preferably
   Dutch process
½ teaspoon vanilla extract
2 to 3 tablespoons ice water

Filling:
4 ounces unsweetened chocolate
¼ pound unsalted butter
3 eggs
1 cup sugar
¼ teaspoon salt
1 teaspoon vanilla extract
⅔ cup all-purpose flour
½ teaspoon baking powder
1 cup walnuts, coarsely chopped
   (optional)

Topping:
1 cup heavy cream

Prepare the chocolate crust:

1 Preheat the oven to 325°. In a mixing bowl or a food processor,
blend together the flour, sugar and salt. Add the butter and blend
until crumbly. Lightly stir in the cocoa and vanilla extract. Using
a fork to toss and mix, add just enough of the ice water to
make a dough that holds together when pressed between your fingers – it should still be slightly crumbly. Gather the dough into a ball
and set it aside.

2 Lightly coat a 9-inch pie pan with soft butter. Press the dough evenly into the pan to form a smooth crust. Trim the edges evenly and
chill the crust while you prepare the filling.

Prepare the filling:

3 Melt the chocolate and butter together in a microwave oven or a
small heavy saucepan over low heat. Stir to blend and allow to
cool slightly.

4 In a mixing bowl, beat the eggs until fluffy, about 2 minutes. Gradually beat in the sugar. Beat in the salt, the vanilla, and then
the melted chocolate mixture.

5 Sift the flour with the baking powder and gently mix the dry ingredients into the chocolate mixture, stirring by hand – do not overmix.
Stir in the chopped nuts. Pour the filling into the chocolate crust.

6 Bake the pie in the center of the oven for 20 minutes, or until the
edges of the filling are set while the center is still slightly
moist. Cool on a rack.

7 Just before serving, whip the cream until just stiff and spread gently
over the top of the pie.

Serves 8
Recipe by Helen Fioratti

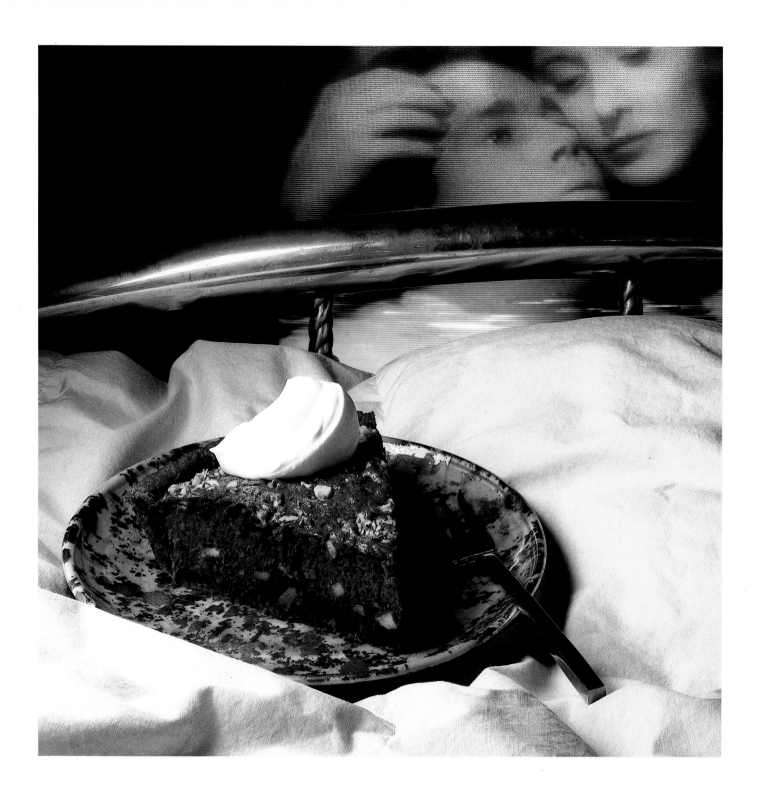

Potted Chocolate

Double the recipe, triple it or stir in nuts or chopped chocolate –
these little pots of chocolate aim to please.

2 ounces semisweet chocolate
1 tablespoon unsalted butter
1 tablespoon brewed strong coffee
5 chocolate wafers, coarsely
** crushed (about ¼ cup crumbs)**

1 egg white
1 tablespoon sugar
Whipped cream, for garnish

1 In a medium saucepan, combine the chocolate, butter and coffee.
   Cook over low heat, stirring frequently, until melted and
   smooth, about 4 minutes. Remove from the heat and scrape the
   mixture into a medium bowl; let cool completely. Stir in the
   cookie crumbs.

2 Meanwhile, beat the egg white until frothy. Add the sugar and continue beating until stiff but not dry. Fold the beaten white into
   the chocolate.

3 Spoon the chocolate mixture into two 3-ounce ramekins and refrigerate for at least 2 hours, until set, before serving. Garnish the
   potted chocolate with a dollop of whipped cream or decoratively
   pipe rosettes of the cream over the top.

Serves 2
Recipe by Molly O'Neill

French Bread and Peanut Butter Pudding

Peanut butter fans will find this creamy, custardy pudding irresistible. Serve it warm, dusted with confectioners' sugar, or pair it with
vanilla ice cream for a delicious warm/cold combination.

1 quart milk
2 cups heavy cream
2 tablespoons unsalted butter,
** softened**
16 slices of French bread, cut ½ to
** ¾ inch thick, crusts removed**

1 cup crunchy peanut butter
5 whole eggs
4 egg yolks
1 cup sugar
⅛ teaspoon salt
2 tablespoons vanilla extract

1 Preheat the oven to 350°. Lightly grease a deep 4-quart casserole.

2 In a large heavy saucepan, scald the milk and cream over moderate heat. Remove from the heat and set aside.

3 Meanwhile, lightly butter one side of each slice of bread. Thickly
   spread the peanut butter over the butter. Arrange the slices in the
   casserole, peanut butter side up, overlapping slightly if necessary.

4 In a large bowl, beat the whole eggs, egg yolks, sugar and salt until
   well blended. Gradually whisk in the milk-cream mixture in
   a thin stream until well mixed. Whisk in the vanilla. Slowly pour
   the custard mixture evenly over the bread slices, which will
   float to the top.

5 Place the casserole in a roasting pan and place in the center of the
   oven. Pour boiling water into the roasting pan to reach halfway up
   the sides of the casserole. Bake for 1 hour, or until the pudding is
   not quite set in the center.

6 Transfer to a wire rack and let cool for at least 30 minutes before
   serving.

Serves 12
Recipe by Maggie Waldron

German Sour-Cream Coffee Cake

The advantage here is clear: what doesn't get eaten for dessert tonight is perfect for breakfast tomorrow. The ideal recipe for weekend hosts and hostesses.

Filling:
½ cup chopped walnuts (2 ounces)
1 teaspoon ground cinnamon
½ cup sugar
Pinch of salt

Batter:
3 cups all-purpose flour
½ teaspoon salt
1 tablespoon baking powder
1 teaspoon baking soda
½ pound unsalted butter, at room temperature
1 cup sugar
3 eggs
1 teaspoon vanilla extract
1 cup sour cream

Prepare the filling:

1 In a small bowl, combine the walnuts, cinnamon, sugar and salt; set aside.

Prepare the batter:

2 Preheat the oven to 350°. Lightly butter a 10-inch angel-food-cake or tube pan, preferably one with a removable bottom, and set aside. In a medium bowl, sift together the flour, salt, baking powder and baking soda; set aside.

3 In a large bowl, cream the butter with the sugar until light and fluffy. One at a time, add the eggs, beating well after each addition. Add the flour mixture in small amounts, mixing thoroughly after each addition. Beat in the vanilla and sour cream.

Assemble and bake the cake:

4 Pour half the batter into the prepared pan and tap the pan on a hard surface several times to level the batter. Sprinkle half the filling evenly over the top. Add the remaining batter and tap the pan as before. Sprinkle the remaining filling evenly over the top. Bake the cake in the center of the oven for about 50 minutes, or until a toothpick inserted in the center comes out clean. Cool on a rack for 30 minutes and serve warm or at room temperature.

Serves 12 to 14
Recipe by Ruth Spear

Coffee Mascarpone with Rum

Very Italian and very good, this mascarpone is flavored with coffee and lightly sweetened with sugar and rum.

1½ tablespoons sugar
1 teaspoon powdered instant coffee or espresso
2 to 3 tablespoons dark rum
1 cup fresh mascarpone
1 package of slightly sweet biscuits, such as Petit Beurre

1 In a small bowl, mix together the sugar, coffee and rum and stir to dissolve the sugar and coffee.

2 Place the mascarpone in a medium bowl and stir in the coffee mixture until thoroughly blended.

3 Spoon the sweetened cheese into a crock or bowl and serve as a spread with the biscuits.

Serves 4
Recipe by Dario Mariotti

Summer Pudding

Soothe your parched summer palate with a cooling English summer pudding, traditionally made with fresh raspberries and red currants. If either of these is unobtainable, use blackberries, blueberries or even frozen berries, in whatever combination you like.

1 Line the bottom and sides of a 2-quart mixing bowl, soufflé dish or other round mold with the bread slices, overlapping the pieces slightly. (You may wish to cut the bread slices in half for a more decorative effect.) Reserve enough bread to cover the top of the pudding.

2 In a heavy nonreactive saucepan, combine the raspberries, currants and granulated sugar with 1 tablespoon of water. Cook the mixture for 2 minutes, remove from heat, and let cool completely.

3 Pour the fruit mixture into the bread-lined mold, and cover completely with the reserved bread slices, cut to fit. Cover the top of the pudding with a plate that fits snugly within the top of the mold, and weigh down the plate with a can or a bowl of water so the pudding is compressed. Refrigerate overnight or for up to 18 hours.

4 To serve, unmold the pudding onto a serving platter. Beat the heavy cream with the confectioners' sugar until very thick but not stiff and serve on top of or alongside the pudding.

Serves 6 to 8
Recipe by Maurice Moore-Betty

10 to 14 slices firm-textured white sandwich bread, crusts trimmed
4 cups raspberries, rinsed and drained
4 cups red currants, stemmed and washed
1 cup granulated sugar
1 cup heavy cream
¼ cup confectioners' sugar

Chocolate-Dipped Strawberries

Everyone loves chocolate-dipped strawberries but people seldom make them at home. We don't know why – it couldn't be simpler. Dipped strawberries should be refrigerated just long enough to set the chocolate; they should not be stored in the refrigerator.

3 ounces semisweet chocolate
1 tablespoon unsalted butter
1 teaspoon Cognac or brandy

12 large strawberries with stems attached, if possible

1 In a double boiler, combine the chocolate, butter and Cognac over moderate heat. Melt the mixture, stirring frequently, until smooth, about 5 minutes. Remove from the heat. Alternatively, melt the chocolate with the butter and Cognac in a microwave oven, stirring every 15 seconds until melted and smooth.

2 Cover a small platter or large flat plate with a sheet of waxed paper. Holding on to the stem or the hull, dip a strawberry halfway into the chocolate and place it on the prepared platter. Repeat with the remaining berries and chocolate. Refrigerate until set, about 10 minutes. Store the dipped berries in a cool place for up to 1 day.

Makes 12
Recipe by Molly O'Neill

Bananas in Caramel Cream

These bananas can be served by themselves or sliced and served over ice cream. They make a marvelous last-minute dessert.

4 tablespoons unsalted butter
3 tablespoons brown sugar
1 tablespoon minced orange zest
½ cup fresh orange juice
3 tablespoons fresh lemon juice
Pinch of freshly grated nutmeg
6 bananas, peeled

2 tablespoons banana liqueur
2 tablespoons Cointreau
2 tablespoons Cognac
¼ cup golden raisins, coarsely chopped
1 cup heavy cream

1 In a large nonreactive skillet, melt the butter over low heat. Add the brown sugar and cook, stirring frequently, until the sugar melts, 2 to 3 minutes. Stir in the orange zest, orange juice, lemon juice and nutmeg.

2 Place the bananas in the skillet and cook, turning once, for 2 to 3 minutes, until just heated through. Do not overcook or the bananas will become soft. With a slotted spatula or spoon, transfer the bananas to a platter.

3 Increase the heat to moderately high and boil the liquid in the skillet until it is syrupy and coats a spoon. Stir in the banana liqueur, Cointreau and Cognac and add the raisins. Boil until the liquid is reduced by half. Pour in the cream and boil until the sauce is reduced by one-third; there should be about 1 cup. Pour the sauce over the bananas and serve.

Serves 6
Recipe by Perla Meyers

Pecan-Raisin Clusters

So good, so sweet and chewy – these clusters will take you back to Christmas candy-making days of childhood.

8 ounces semisweet or milk chocolate	**1 cup (about 5 ounces) coarsely chopped pecans**
	½ cup golden raisins

1 Melt the chocolate and temper it by stirring or by working back and forth with a spatula, trowel or putty knife on a marble or Formica surface until the chocolate feels distinctly cool but is still semiliquid.

2 Toss the pecans and raisins in a medium bowl. Scrape the tempered chocolate into the bowl. Stir and fold with a rubber spatula to coat the fruit and nuts completely.

3 Drop heaping teaspoonfuls of the mixture onto waxed paper. Allow the clusters to harden at room temperature until firm, about 1 hour, or refrigerate just until set. Store, tightly wrapped, at cool room temperature.

Makes about 2½ dozen
Recipe by Diana Sturgis

Flambéed Maple-Rum Bananas

Use tiny finger bananas, if you can find them in your market, for they work beautifully in this dish. However, don't forget you'll need a total of 10, split lengthwise only.

¼ pound unsalted butter	**½ cup dark rum**
½ cup pure maple syrup	**1 quart vanilla ice cream**
5 bananas, halved crosswise, then split lengthwise	**⅓ cup chopped toasted pecans**

1 In a large skillet, melt the butter over moderately high heat. Stir in the maple syrup and bring to a simmer.

2 Add the halved bananas and cook, basting with the hot syrup in the pan, until hot, about 2 minutes.

3 Pour in the rum and ignite with a match. Ladle the sauce over the bananas as it flames.

4 To serve, place a scoop of ice cream in each dessert dish. Add 2 pieces of banana and a generous spoonful of the sauce. Garnish with the pecans.

Serves 10
Recipe by John Robert Massie

Hambleton Hall's Scotch Shortbread

The rich buttery flavor of this shortbread is sure to make a lasting impression. Serve it at teatime, after a leisurely luncheon or after a typical Sunday night supper.

1 In a large bowl, beat 1 cup of the sugar with the butter until light and fluffy.

2 Sift together the flour and cornstarch and gradually mix into the creamed butter. Gather the dough into a ball and flatten into a disk. Wrap in waxed paper and refrigerate for 1 hour.

3 Preheat the oven to 225°. Trace a 12-inch circle on a large baking sheet. Pat out the chilled dough to fit the circle, taking care that the top is even and smooth. Score the top of the pastry into 8 equal wedges. Press decorative designs into the edges, if desired.

4 Bake the shortbread in the upper middle of the oven for 35 minutes; do not allow to color. Remove from the oven, sprinkle with the remaining 2 tablespoons sugar and let cool on the sheet. Break into wedges before serving.

1 cup plus 2 tablespoons sugar
¾ pound unsalted butter, at room temperature
3¼ cups sifted all-purpose flour
⅔ cup sifted cornstarch

Serves 8
Recipe by Chef Nicholas Gill
Hambleton Hall, Hambleton, England

Caramel Sauce

Everybody pours caramel sauce over a sundae – try making a parfait with it so that there's caramel at the bottom, in the middle and on the top.

¾ cup light brown sugar
½ cup light corn syrup

4¼ tablespoons unsalted butter
½ cup heavy cream

1 In a medium saucepan, combine the brown sugar, corn syrup and butter. Bring to a boil, stirring, over high heat. Boil undisturbed until the mixture reaches the soft-ball stage, 234° to 240° on a candy thermometer.
2 Remove from the heat and immediately stir in the cream. (The sauce can be made ahead to this point, covered and refrigerated.) Just before serving, warm, stirring, over moderate heat or in a microwave oven until hot to the touch.

Makes about 1 cup
Recipe by Sarah Kelly

Bittersweet Double Chocolate Sauce

Connoisseur-quality chocolate sauce that should become a staple in your household.

¼ pound plus 4 tablespoons unsalted butter, cut into pieces
6 ounces bittersweet or semisweet chocolate, coarsely chopped
¾ cup plus 2 tablespoons sugar
¾ cup (firmly packed) unsweetened cocoa powder, sifted

1 teaspoon freeze-dried instant coffee
½ teaspoon ground cinnamon
½ cup light corn syrup
1¼ cups heavy cream
1 teaspoon vanilla extract

1 In a heavy saucepan, melt the butter and chocolate together over low heat, stirring occasionally, until smooth.
2 Stir in the sugar. Sift in the cocoa and stir well. Add the instant coffee, cinnamon and corn syrup. Slowly whisk in the heavy cream. Bring just to a boil, reduce the heat immediately and simmer for 5 minutes, stirring once or twice and scraping down the sides of the pan with a rubber spatula.
3 Remove from the heat, stir in the vanilla and pour immediately into a heatproof storage container. Let cool to room temperature, cover and refrigerate. (The sauce will keep well, refrigerated, for several weeks.)
4 To serve, remove the desired amount of sauce from the container and reheat in a double boiler or microwave oven, stirring, until hot.

Makes about 1 quart
Recipe by Michael McLaughlin

Hot Fudge Sauce

The definitive hot fudge – the more you eat, the more you want.

2 teaspoons instant coffee powder
2 teaspoons boiling water
7 ounces bittersweet chocolate,
   broken into pieces

1 tablespoon coffee liqueur,
   such as Kahlúa or
   Tia Maria
¼ pound plus 6 tablespoons
   unsalted butter, cut into
   small pieces

1 In a double boiler, combine the coffee and boiling water, stirring to dissolve the coffee granules over simmering water. Add the chocolate, coffee liqueur and butter.

2 Cook, stirring over simmering water, just until small pieces of chocolate remain. Remove from the heat and continue stirring until the sauce is smooth and the chocolate completely melted. Serve warm or at room temperature.

Makes 1½ cups
Recipe by Anne Disrude

Butterscotch Sauce

Soothing and creamy and really at its best if served warm.

¼ pound unsalted butter
1 cup (packed) light brown sugar
⅓ cup light corn syrup
1½ cups heavy cream

1 tablespoon vanilla extract
1 teaspoon fresh lemon juice,
   strained

1 In a heavy medium saucepan, melt the butter and brown sugar over moderate heat. Stir in the corn syrup. Whisk in the cream, increase the heat and bring just to a boil. Reduce the heat and simmer, stirring occasionally until slightly thickened, 15 to 20 minutes.

2 Remove from the heat, stir in the vanilla and lemon juice and pour immediately into a heatproof storage container. Let cool to room temperature, cover and refrigerate. (The sauce will keep well, refrigerated, for several weeks.)

3 To use, let return to room temperature or reheat gently.

Makes about 2½ cups
Recipe by Michael McLaughlin

Perfect
Partners

Perfect Partners

**■ Ever since Adam and Eve and the days of Noah, people
and things have been paired. And just like Barnum
and Bailey or Ginger and Fred, certain foods seem to fit**

together in a distinctive and memorable way. They're so perfect –
like pie and ice cream or cookies and milk – or so uncommonly
appealing – like pears and port – that we remember them.

What we offer here are flavor combinations that not only
work splendidly together, but manifest an unusual twist that takes
them an inventive step beyond the predictable dessert pairings.
Consider pineapple sauce over a banana-pecan waffle or bread pudding made with chocolate in it. These partnerships are exciting
new combinations that will thrill the palate and the eye.

If you doubt that any truly top-notch dessert combina-
tions could remain undiscovered, look at Arthur Gold and Robert
Fizdale's Cappuccino Ice Cream Cake with Hot Chocolate Sauce.
It's a dessert fancier's dream: three big crunchy oatmeal disks

layered with easy-to-make, cinnamon-spiked cappuccino ice cream and served up with hot chocolate sauce to spoon on top. The crunch of the oatmeal faced up against the silkiness of the ice cream is what makes this combo tick.

For a classic dessert with a pure, simple appeal, look no further than Grandma Walstrom's Pineapple-Buttermilk Sherbet paired with Aunt Irma's Sugar Cookies. These "receipts" are simplicity personified, their quality and honesty unrivaled. A chewy cookie wouldn't do for this soothing sweet sherbet; but a delicate and crisp one makes this alliance just right.

If it's time-tested masterpieces you seek, page to Simone Beck's exemplary Pommes Grand'mère de Hilo. Here, she combines a traditionally styled molded apple custard with one of her favorite flavors on earth – macadamia nuts. As an added fillip, she cooks the nuts into a brittle that's out of this world.

To be honest, the combination of Pineapple Spice Cake coated with Maple Buttercream and served with Pineapple Pecan Ice Cream and Pineapple Poached in Syrup may sound less than wonderful. But try it before you form opinions. Created by two of the talented chefs at San Francisco's Stanford Court Hotel, this three-part dessert illustrates how appealingly these flavors can mingle.

So, let the nay-sayers taste before they speak another word. Let the eager and experimental types use our partnerships as a springboard to try even more adventuresome combinations. But don't miss these new great teams of our time – clever, pleasing and surprising combinations. ∎

Cappuccino Ice Cream Cake with Hot Chocolate Sauce

Arthur Gold and Robert Fizdale serve this delicate three-tiered oatmeal cake layered with cappuccino ice cream (easy to make and easy to spread) and drizzled with hot chocolate sauce. Everything – cake layers, ice cream and sauce – can be made ahead. A real boon for the nervous host or hostess.

¾ cup quick-cooking oats
⅔ cup granulated sugar
1 tablespoon all-purpose flour
1 teaspoon baking powder
7 tablespoons unsalted butter, melted
1 egg, at room temperature, lightly beaten
Cappuccino Ice Cream (recipe follows)
2 tablespoons confectioners' sugar
Hot Chocolate Sauce (recipe follows)

1 Preheat the oven to 375°. Line 3 baking sheets with parchment paper. Draw an 8-inch circle in the center of each sheet.
2 In a bowl, combine the oats, granulated sugar, flour and baking powder. Stir in the melted butter until well blended. Stir in the lightly beaten egg.
3 Spoon about one-third of the batter onto each circle on the baking sheets and spread to cover thinly and evenly with a spatula or the back of a spoon. Bake for about 8 minutes, or until lightly browned. (You may want to form and bake these one at a time, as they must be watched carefully so that they do not burn.) Remove at once and slide the parchment with the cake onto a rack to cool. Repeat with the remaining batter. When the cakes are cool, peel off the parchment. Chill the cake layers before assembling.
4 To assemble, put one cake, flat-side down, on a chilled round platter. Working quickly, spoon half the ice cream over the cake. Spread into an even layer. Cover with the second cake and the remaining ice cream. Top with the third cake, flat-side up. Wrap the cake carefully in foil and put in the freezer immediately.
5 Transfer the cake from the freezer to the refrigerator 10 to 15 minutes before serving time to let the ice cream soften. Sprinkle with the confectioners' sugar, cut into wedges and serve with hot chocolate sauce on the side.

Serves 8
Recipe by Arthur Gold
and Robert Fizdale

Cappuccino Ice Cream

3 cups heavy cream
¾ cup superfine sugar
3 egg yolks
2 tablespoons powdered instant expresso coffee
1 teaspoon unsweetened cocoa powder
½ teaspoon ground cinnamon
1 teaspoon coffee liqueur, such as Kahlúa or Tia Maria

1 In a large bowl, beat the cream until it begins to mound. Gradually beat in half the sugar and beat until soft peaks form.
2 In another bowl, beat the egg yolks with the remaining sugar until light in color. Stir in the powdered espresso, cocoa, cinnamon and coffee liqueur. Fold in the whipped cream.
3 Scrape the mixture into an ice cream maker and freeze according to the manufacturer's instructions. Place in the freezer for 20 to 30 minutes to firm up before assembling the cake. (The ice cream can be prepared and frozen a day ahead. Soften slightly in the refrigerator, if necessary, before assembling.)

Makes about 1 quart
Recipe by Arthur Gold
and Robert Fizdale

Hot Chocolate Sauce

5 ounces semisweet chocolate, coarsely chopped
1⅓ cups milk
1 cup sugar
¼ cup corn syrup
2 tablespoons powdered instant espresso coffee
2 tablespoons unsalted butter, cut into small pieces
Pinch of salt
1 tablespoon brandy

1 In a heavy medium saucepan, combine the chocolate, milk, sugar, corn syrup, espresso powder, butter and salt. Cook over low heat, stirring frequently, until the chocolate and butter melt.
2 Increase the heat to high and bring the mixture to a boil. Cover and boil for 2 minutes. Remove the cover and continue to boil until the temperature reaches 230°, about 3 minutes. Remove from the heat and place the pan in a bowl of cold water to stop the cooking.
3 Beat the chocolate for 1 minute. Let cool for 3 minutes, then beat in the brandy. Reheat in a double boiler or microwave oven before serving.

Makes about 1½ cups
Recipe by Arthur Gold
and Robert Fizdale

Chocolate Bread Pudding with Custard Sauce

Quick, easy and foolproof, this rich pudding has a chocolate lover's bitter edge, which is nicely set off by its partner, a velvety custard sauce. Neither heavy nor sweet, the pudding resembles a chocolate mousse cake when chilled.

⅔ cup plus 1 tablespoon sugar
1 cup heavy cream
8 ounces semisweet chocolate, coarsely chopped
5 eggs, separated
¼ pound unsalted butter, cut into pieces
1 tablespoon vanilla extract

2 cups fresh bread crumbs, made from about 5 slices of firm-textured white bread
Custard Sauce (recipe follows) or lightly sweetened whipped cream

1 Preheat the oven to 350°. Butter an 8-inch square baking pan or 8-by-3-inch soufflé dish or cake pan and dust with 1 tablespoon of the sugar.

2 In a medium saucepan, bring the cream to a simmer. Meanwhile, place the chocolate in a food processor and chop finely, 15 to 20 seconds.

3 With the machine on, pour in the hot cream. As soon as the mixture is smooth, add ⅓ cup of the sugar and the egg yolks, one at a time. Add the butter and vanilla. Process just until smooth.

4 In a large bowl, combine the bread crumbs and the chocolate mixture. Stir until well blended.

5 Beat the egg whites until soft peaks form. Gradually beat in the remaining ⅓ cup sugar and continue to beat until the whites are glossy and stand in stiff peaks.

6 Stir one-third of the egg whites into the chocolate mixture to lighten it. Fold in the remaining whites until no white streaks remain. Turn into the prepared baking pan.

7 Place the baking pan in a roasting pan and add enough warm water to reach halfway up the sides of the baking pan. Bake in the center of the oven for 45 to 50 minutes, or until the pudding is set and a cake tester inserted in the center emerges with only a few crumbs clinging to it. Remove and let cool on a rack for 10 minutes, then invert onto a serving platter. Serve warm, with custard sauce.

Serves 12
Recipe by Diana Sturgis

Custard Sauce

6 egg yolks
⅔ cup sugar
2½ cups milk

1½ tablespoons brandy
1 teaspoon vanilla extract

1 In a large bowl, combine the egg yolks and ⅓ cup of the sugar. Beat until the sugar dissolves and the mixture is light colored, about 3 minutes.

2 In a heavy medium saucepan, combine the remaining ⅓ cup sugar and the milk. Bring to a boil. Gradually whisk the milk into the egg yolk mixture in a thin stream.

3 Return the custard to the saucepan. Cook over moderately low heat, stirring constantly, until the custard is thick enough to coat the back of a wooden spoon, about 10 minutes. It should register 180° on an instant-reading thermometer; do not let the custard boil or the eggs will curdle.

4 Remove from the heat and strain into a bowl. Stir in the brandy and vanilla. Serve warm, at room temperature or chilled. (The sauce can be made a day ahead. Refrigerate, covered.)

Makes about 3 cups
Recipe by Diana Sturgis

Banana-Pecan Waffle Ice Cream Sundae with Pineapple Sauce

A two-part dessert of opposing tastes, textures and temperatures: sweet and tart, creamy and crunchy, hot and cold.

½ cup all-purpose flour
¼ teaspoon ground cinnamon
Pinch of freshly grated nutmeg
¼ teaspoon baking soda
¾ teaspoon baking powder
Pinch of salt
1 teaspoon sugar
1 egg, separated
¼ cup sour cream
¼ cup plus 2 tablespoons milk

3 tablespoons plus 2 teaspoons unsalted butter, melted and cooled
½ ripe banana, mashed
6 tablespoons chopped toasted pecans
½ gallon vanilla ice cream
Chunky Pineapple Sauce (recipe follows)

1 In a medium bowl, sift together the flour, cinnamon, nutmeg, baking soda, baking powder, salt and sugar.

2 In another medium bowl, beat together the egg yolk, sour cream, milk, butter and banana. Stir in the pecans and the sifted dry ingredients and blend well.

3 Beat the egg white until stiff but not dry. Fold into the banana mixture until no white streaks remain.

4 Bake the batter in a preheated waffle iron according to the manufacturer's instructions. To serve, top each waffle with a scoop of ice cream and a large spoonful of pineapple sauce.

Serves 10 to 12
Recipe by Margaret Fox

Chunky Pineapple Sauce

1 ripe medium pineapple
½ cup sugar

1 tablespoon fresh lemon juice

1 Cut off the top and bottom of the pineapple. Stand the pineapple upright and slice off a ¼-inch layer all around to remove the rind and all of the eyes. Cut out and discard the tough core. Coarsely chop half the pineapple and set aside. Cut the other half into chunks and puree in a food processor.

2 In a medium nonreactive saucepan, bring the sugar and ¼ cup of water to a boil over high heat. Boil without stirring until the sugar dissolves, about 1 minute. Remove from the heat.

3 Add the pineapple puree, the reserved chopped pineapple and the lemon juice. Taste and adjust, if necessary. Gently warm the sauce over moderately low heat before serving.

Makes about 2½ cups
Recipe by Margaret Fox

Frozen Orange Truffle Soufflés

Here's a duet for the grownup who loved Hostess cupcakes as a kid because they had a surprise in the center. These small, frozen soufflés contain a more sophisticated treat – a creamy, homemade chocolate truffle.

1 envelope unflavored gelatin	**3 tablespoons orange liqueur,**
½ cup fresh orange juice	**such as Grand Marnier or**
5 eggs, separated and at room	**Orange Curaçao**
temperature	**1 cup heavy cream, chilled**
½ cup superfine sugar	**6 Chocolate Truffles**
1 teaspoon grated orange zest	**(recipe follows)**
	Strips of orange zest and whipped
	cream, for garnish (optional)

1 Wrap parchment paper or aluminum foil collars around six ⅔-cup soufflé dishes and fasten with tape or string.

2 In a small bowl, sprinkle the gelatin over the orange juice and set aside until softened. Place the bowl in a pan of hot water and stir occasionally until the gelatin dissolves, about 3 minutes. Set aside in the hot water.

3 In a double boiler, beat the egg yolks and sugar over barely simmering water until the mixture is light-colored, creamy and warm to the touch, about 5 minutes. Remove from the heat and continue to beat until the mixture cools, thickens and forms a ribbon when the beater is lifted, about 3 minutes. Stir in the orange zest and liqueur. Scrape into a large bowl and set aside.

4 Beat the cream until it is doubled in volume and forms soft peaks.

5 Beat the egg whites until they form soft peaks.

6 Stir the gelatin mixture into the beaten egg yolks. Place the bowl in a larger bowl half-filled with ice and water and stir with a rubber spatula until the mixture begins to thicken and mound, 2 to 4 minutes, depending on the type of bowl used (metal chills faster than glass or ceramic).

7 Immediately remove from the ice water and fold in the whipped cream. About one-third at a time, fold in the egg whites until no streaks of white remain; do not overmix.

8 Spoon ½ cup of the mousse mixture into each soufflé dish and place a truffle in the center. Divide the remaining mousse among the dishes to bury the truffles. Smooth the tops, cover loosely with waxed paper and place on a tray in the refrigerator until set and chilled, about 2½ hours.

9 Before serving, remove the paper collars. Decorate the tops with whipped cream and strips of orange zest, if desired. Serve chilled.

Serves 6
Recipe by Diana Sturgis

Chocolate Truffles

6 ounces semisweet chocolate,	**2 egg yolks, lightly beaten**
coarsely chopped	**3 to 4 tablespoons**
4 tablespoons unsalted butter, cut	**unsweetened cocoa powder**
into small pieces	
½ teaspoon vanilla extract	

1 In a double boiler, melt the chocolate and butter over simmering water. Remove from the heat and stir in the vanilla.

2 In a small bowl, gradually whisk the warm chocolate mixture into the egg yolks. Cover and refrigerate until firm, about 1 hour.

3 Shape level tablespoons of the chocolate mixture into balls and then roll them in the cocoa. Refrigerate the truffles.

Makes 16
Recipe by Diana Sturgis

Pineapple Spice Cake
with Pineapple Pecan Ice Cream

A stunning trio of desserts – cake, ice cream and poached pineapple – that can each stand alone but are far more exciting
when presented as a group. You'll be surprised at how tasty the
combination of pineapple and maple can be. Recipes for the
ice cream and poached pineapple follow.

**2½ cups sifted cake flour
1 tablespoon baking powder
½ teaspoon salt
1 teaspoon ground cinnamon
1 teaspoon ground allspice
½ teaspoon freshly grated nutmeg
½ teaspoon ground cloves
¼ pound unsalted butter, softened
½ cup sugar
¾ cup pure maple syrup
3 eggs, separated
1 teaspoon vanilla extract
⅓ cup milk
Maple Buttercream
   (recipe follows)
Pineapple Poached in Maple Syrup
   (recipe follows), prepared
   through Step 2
Pineapple Pecan Ice Cream
   (recipe follows)**

1 Preheat the oven to 350°. Grease and lightly flour a 9-x-2-inch round cake pan. Line the bottom with a circle of parchment or waxed paper.

2 In a medium bowl, combine the flour, baking powder, salt, cinnamon, allspice, nutmeg and cloves.

3 In a large mixer bowl, beat the butter on high speed until pale and fluffy, 3 to 4 minutes. Add the sugar and continue beating, stopping occasionally to scrape down the sides of the bowl, until well combined. Add the maple syrup and continue beating until thoroughly mixed. Scrape down the sides of the bowl again. Add the egg yolks and vanilla and beat on medium speed until incorporated.

4 Alternately add the dry ingredients and the milk in three stages, beating after each addition only until just combined and scraping the sides of the bowl twice.

Recipe continues on the next page

Pineapple Spice Cake
with Pineapple Pecan Ice Cream Continued

5　In another bowl, beat the egg whites until stiff but not dry. Stir one-third of the beaten whites into the batter to lighten the mixture. Fold the remaining whites into the batter. Pour the batter into the prepared baking pan.

6　Bake the cake for 50 to 60 minutes, or until the top is a deep golden brown and a cake tester inserted in the center comes out clean. Transfer to a wire rack and let cool for about 15 minutes. As soon as the pan is cool enough to handle, loosen the edges with a small knife and invert to unmold the cake onto the rack. Let cool completely before removing the paper.

7　To assemble, split the cake in half horizontally with a long serrated knife. Spread ⅓ to ½ cup of the buttercream in a thin layer over the bottom layer of the cake. Arrange the well-drained pineapple wedges on top of the buttercream, covering the entire top surface. Cover the pineapple with another thin layer of buttercream. Put the top of the cake, cut-side down, over the filling. Frost the top and sides of the cake with the remaining buttercream.

Serves 8 to 10
Recipe by Jim Dodge and
Gayle Henderson Wilson

Maple Buttercream

2 whole eggs
1⅓ cups maple syrup reserved
　from Pineapple Poached in
　Maple Syrup (recipe follows),
　prepared through Step 2

¾ pound unsalted butter,
　cut into 1-inch chunks and
　at room temperature

1　In a large bowl, beat the eggs until blended.

2　In a large heavy saucepan, bring the maple syrup poaching liquid to a boil over high heat. Continue to boil until the syrup reaches the soft-ball stage, 238° on a candy thermometer.

3　Beating constantly with an electric mixer, pour the boiling liquid into the eggs in a slow steady stream. Continue to beat until the mixture is cooled to room temperature and thick, about 5 minutes.

4　Add the butter in 4 stages, beating until well blended between each stage. Continue to beat until the frosting is fluffy and smooth.

Makes about 3 cups
Recipe by Jim Dodge and
Gayle Henderson Wilson

Pineapple Poached in Maple Syrup

1 ripe pineapple
2 cups pure maple syrup
1 cup plain yogurt, at room
    temperature
3 tablespoons heavy cream

1 Cut off the top and bottom of the pineapple. Stand the pineapple upright and slice off about a ¼-inch layer all around to remove the
   skin and "eyes." Cut the pineapple lengthwise into quarters. Cut out
   the tough woody core of each quarter and discard. Cut each quarter crosswise into ½-inch slices; then cut each slice into 2 wedges.

2 In a heavy medium saucepan, bring the maple syrup to a boil
   over high heat, being careful to keep the syrup from boiling over.
   Immediately turn off the heat and add the pineapple chunks.
   With a large spoon, push the chunks down into the hot liquid. Let
   the fruit steep off the heat, pressing down occasionally, until
   it is tender when pierced with a fork and the syrup is lightly warm
   to the touch, about 25 minutes. Drain the pineapple through a
   sieve, reserving the maple syrup. (The recipe can be prepared ahead
   to this point. Refrigerate the pineapple and maple syrup separately.)

3 If there is liquid on top of the yogurt, pour it off. Put the yogurt
   in a small bowl and whisk in the cream, 1 tablespoon at a time, until
   the mixture is the consistency of crème fraîche or slightly beaten
   whipped cream.

4 To serve, place the pineapple in shallow dessert bowls. Add 2 tablespoons of the maple syrup and top each with about 2 tablespoons
   of the yogurt-cream sauce.

Serves 4 to 6
Recipe by Jim Dodge and
Gayle Henderson Wilson

Pineapple Pecan Ice Cream

½ cup coarsely chopped pecans
2 cups heavy cream
1 cup milk
1¼ cups maple syrup
    poaching liquid (from
    preceding recipe), chilled

2 cups Pineapple Poached in
    Maple Syrup (preceding
    recipe), prepared
    through Step 2

1 Preheat the oven to 325°. Scatter the pecans in a small baking pan
   and bake for 10 to 15 minutes, shaking the pan once or twice, until
   the nuts are toasted. Transfer to a plate and let cool.

2 In a large bowl, combine the cream, milk and maple syrup poaching
   liquid. Blend well. Cover and refrigerate.

3 Working in two batches if necessary, pour the maple cream into the
   canister of an ice cream maker and freeze according to the manufacturer's instructions until the mixture is almost firm. Add the
   pineapple and toasted pecans and process briefly in the ice
   cream maker to blend thoroughly. Transfer the ice cream to a container with a tight-fitting lid and place in the freezer for about
   3 hours, or until firm.

Makes about 2 quarts
Recipe by Jim Dodge and
Gayle Henderson Wilson

Aunt Irma's Sugar Cookies

This partnership is all in the family: a delectable wedding of Jim Fobel's Aunt Irma's sugar cookies and his Grandma Wahlstrom's sherbet (recipe follows). Do heed Aunt Irma's advice: "You must knead this cookie dough by hand for at least 15 minutes or the cookies won't come out right."

1 cup granulated sugar	1 teaspoon cream of tartar
½ pound unsalted butter, chilled and cut into thin slices	¼ teaspoon salt
	Granulated sugar, for coating
2 eggs	the cookies
1 teaspoon vanilla extract	1 cup sifted confectioners' sugar
About 3 cups all-purpose flour	2 tablespoons milk
1 teaspoon baking soda	

1 Place the granulated sugar in a large bowl and cut in the butter until the mixture resembles oatmeal. Using a wooden spoon, beat in the eggs and vanilla.

2 In another large bowl, sift together 3 cups of the flour, the baking soda, cream of tartar and salt. Add the flour mixture to the butter mixture and beat with a wooden spoon until blended.

3 Preheat the oven to 350°. Lightly butter two or three cookie sheets. Knead the cookie dough for 15 to 20 minutes, adding just a little more flour if necessary to prevent the dough from sticking.

4 Using your hands, roll the cookie dough into walnut-size balls. Roll the balls in granulated sugar to coat completely. Place the balls on the prepared cookie sheets.

5 Using the bottom of a glass dipped in granulated sugar, flatten each ball of dough until it is about ¼ inch thick. Bake the cookies for 12 to 15 minutes, until light brown. Using a spatula, carefully transfer the cookies to a rack.

6 Meanwhile, in a medium bowl, whisk together the confectioners' sugar and milk until smooth. While the cookies are still hot, brush them with just enough of the icing to glaze them lightly. Let cool before serving.

Makes about 5 dozen
Recipe by Jim Fobel

Grandma Wahlstrom's Pineapple-Buttermilk Sherbet

If you have an ice cream maker, by all means, use it – it'll drastically cut down the preparation time.

1 quart buttermilk	1 cup sugar
1 can (20 ounces) crushed pineapple in heavy syrup	

1 Combine the buttermilk, the pineapple with its syrup and the sugar in a large bowl; stir to dissolve the sugar.

2 Pour the mixture into two standard ice cube trays (without ice cube dividers), filling them to within ¼ inch of the top. Place the trays in the freezer until partially frozen, about 45 minutes, then stir to break up the ice crystals. Return the trays to the freezer, stirring every 30 minutes, until completely frozen. If you are not serving the sherbet the same day, transfer it to a freezer container with a tight-fitting lid. Serve with Aunt Irma's Sugar Cookies.

Makes about 1½ quarts
Recipe by Jim Fobel

The Quilted Giraffe's Chocolate Soufflé with Coffee Ice Cream

How to succeed in entertaining with just a bit of an effort: whip up this exemplary combination – chocolate soufflé and homemade coffee ice cream.

1 cup sugar
¼ pound plus 2 tablespoons unsalted butter, cut into small pieces
8 ounces bittersweet chocolate, coarsely chopped
5 whole eggs, separated and at room temperature
½ cup lukewarm water
5 egg whites, at room temperature
Pinch of salt
Coffee Ice Cream (recipe follows)
Whipped cream, for garnish

1 Preheat the oven to 425°. Lightly coat the inside of twelve 1-cup soufflé dishes with butter. Dust the dishes using a total of ½ cup of the sugar; tap out any excess.

2 Melt the butter and chocolate in a double boiler over hot, but not boiling, water, stirring occasionally. Scrape into a large bowl.

3 Meanwhile, in a mixer bowl, beat the egg yolks with the lukewarm water at high speed until light and fluffy, about 10 minutes. Fold into the chocolate.

4 Beat the 10 egg whites with the salt until soft peaks start to form. Slowly sprinkle in the remaining ½ cup sugar and continue beating until stiff and glossy. One-third at a time, gently fold into the chocolate mixture.

5 Divide the soufflé base among the prepared soufflé dishes, filling up to the rim. Bake in the lower third of the oven until puffed, about 10 minutes. Place a small scoop of coffee ice cream in the center of each soufflé, which will collapse and enfold the ice cream. Top with a dollop of whipped cream and serve at once.

Serves 12
Recipe by Barry Wine
The Quilted Giraffe, New York City

Quilted Giraffe's Coffee Ice Cream

This is an eggy, custardy coffee ice cream that can handle a big ladle of Hot Fudge Sauce (page 175) or a drizzle of Bailey's Irish Cream liqueur.

2 cups heavy cream
1 cup milk
½ cup finely ground coffee beans
6 egg yolks
²/₃ cup sugar
¼ teaspoon salt

1 In a large heavy saucepan, bring the cream and milk to a simmer over moderately high heat. Remove from the heat and stir in the coffee. Let stand for 20 minutes, stirring occasionally.

2 Meanwhile, beat the egg yolks with the sugar until light in color and thick enough to fall in ribbons from the whisk.

3 Strain the coffee grounds from the cream through a fine sieve lined with several layers of dampened cheesecloth. Return the cream to the saucepan and gently heat but do not boil.

4 Gradually whisk 1 cup of the hot cream into the egg yolks. Whisk the mixture back into the saucepan. Cook over moderate heat, stirring constantly, until the custard thickens enough to coat the back of a spoon. Do not let boil or the custard will curdle.

5 Strain the custard into a metal bowl. Cool quickly by setting in a larger bowl of ice and water and stirring. Add the salt and freeze in an ice cream maker according to the manufacturer's instructions.

Makes about 1 quart
Recipe by Barry Wine
The Quilted Giraffe, New York City

Pommes Grand'mère de Hilo

Simone Beck – known to all as Simca – is a remarkably outspoken

fan of the macadamia nut. This recipe for molded apple custard

with macadamia nut brittle proves she has a true affinity for great

ways of using them.

Brittle:
3 ounces (about ⅔ cup)
    macadamia nuts
⅓ cup sugar
1 teaspoon fresh lemon juice
¼ teaspoon baking powder

Apple Custard:
3 pounds (6 or 7) apples, Granny
    Smith or Golden Delicious
    peeled, cored and cut into
    ⅛-inch slices
6 tablespoons unsalted butter
1 tablespoon ground cinnamon
2 thin slices stale bread
4 eggs
⅓ cup sugar
Pinch of salt
¼ cup heavy cream
2 tablespoons Calvados or Cognac
¼ cup raspberry jam

Make the brittle:

1 Preheat the oven to 350°. If you are using salted macadamia nuts, rinse them of their salt, then pat dry. Toast the nuts in a baking pan for 8 to 10 minutes, until lightly golden. Remove the nuts, but leave the oven on.

2 While the nuts are still warm, combine the sugar, lemon juice and 1 tablespoon of water in a small saucepan and bring the mixture to a boil over high heat. Swirl the pan occasionally, until the mixture turns medium gold in color. Remove the pan from the heat and stir in the toasted nuts. Add the baking powder, which will make the caramel froth and turn creamy. Pour the caramel onto a well buttered baking sheet and let cool completely.

Make the apple custard:

3 Increase the oven temperature to 375°. Butter another large baking sheet and spread the apple slices on it in a single layer. Dot with the butter and sprinkle with the cinnamon. Bake the apples for 20 to 30 minutes, stirring them once or twice, until very tender. Set aside to cool. Leave the oven at 375°.

Recipe continues on page 194

Pommes Grand'mère de Hilo Continued

4 When the macadamia brittle is cold, remove it from the baking sheet with a metal spatula, and chop coarsely with a knife or in a food processor, switching the motor on and off rapidly and repeatedly. Chop until the pieces are the size of corn kernels; do not over-process. Reserve.

5 Crush the stale bread into coarse crumbs with a rolling pin or in the food processor. Line the bottom of a 6-cup baking dish, such as a charlotte mold or soufflé dish (or 6 individual 1-cup molds or eight 6-ounce molds) with waxed paper cut to fit. Butter the paper and the sides of the mold(s), then coat the mold(s) with as many of the bread crumbs as will adhere. Combine the remaining crumbs with the macadamia brittle.

Assemble the dessert:

6 In a large bowl, beat the eggs with the sugar, salt, cream and Calvados. Stir in the cooled apples. If using one large mold, spoon one-third of the apple-custard mixture into the mold, then sprinkle on half of the brittle mixture. Add half of the remaining apple mixture and then the remaining brittle. Finally, spoon in the remaining apples. If using individual molds, layer apples, brittle and more apples to fill. (The filled molds may hold for an hour at room temperature if necessary.)

7 Bake the mold(s) for 30 minutes, or until puffed very slightly and the sides are set. Remove to a rack and cool for 30 minutes before unmolding.

8 While the custard is cooling, melt the raspberry jam in a small saucepan over low heat; strain and set aside. When cooled, run a flexible spatula around the sides of the mold(s) and invert. Remove the waxed paper. Spoon some of the raspberry glaze over each serving, and serve either warm or cold.

Serves 6 to 8
Recipe by Simone Beck

Passion Fruit-Filled Beignets

Light-as-air beignets are not normally filled. Here, though, adding an exotic passion fruit curd creates a new combination that's reminiscent of lazy days on a South Sea island.

1½ teaspoons active dry yeast	½ teaspoon vanilla extract
¼ cup warm water (105° to 115°)	1½ to 1¾ cups all-purpose
¼ cup warm milk (105° to 115°)	flour
2 tablespoons honey	1½ quarts vegetable oil, for
½ teaspoon salt	deep frying
1 egg	Passion Fruit Curd (recipe
1½ tablespoons unsalted butter,	follows)
melted and cooled	Confectioners' sugar

1 In a large bowl, sprinkle the yeast over the water; set aside to proof for 5 minutes.

2 Stir in the milk, honey, salt, egg, butter and vanilla. Stir in 1 cup of the flour and when fully incorporated, add enough of the remaining flour, ¼ cup at a time, until the dough becomes stiff and difficult to mix.

3 Turn the dough out onto a lightly floured surface and knead in enough of the remaining flour to make the dough firm but still slightly sticky. Continue to knead for 3 to 4 minutes. Lightly oil a large bowl and place the dough in it; turn to coat with oil and cover with a damp towel. Set aside in a warm place until doubled in size, about 1½ hours.

4 Punch down the dough and divide in half. Using your hands, roll each piece of dough into a long cylinder 1 inch in diameter. Cut the cylinder into 1-inch pieces and roll each into a ball. Place the balls of dough 2 inches apart on a lightly floured baking sheet. Cover with a damp cloth and let rise in a warm, draft-free place until almost doubled in size, about 45 minutes.

5 In a deep-fat fryer or deep wide saucepan, heat the oil to 350°. Fry the beignets in batches without crowding. Cook until golden brown on one side, about 2 minutes. Using a slotted spoon, turn the beignets and cook until golden brown, about 2 minutes longer. Transfer to a plate lined with paper towels to drain and cool slightly, 5 to 10 minutes.

6 Using a metal skewer or the tine of a fork, pierce a deep hole in the side of each beignet. Fit a pastry bag with a plain tip and spoon the passion fruit curd into it. Place the tip of the pastry tube in the hole of each beignet and fill with fruit curd. Dust the beignets with confectioners' sugar; serve warm or at room temperature.

Makes about 16 small beignets
Recipe by Marcia Kiesel

Passion Fruit Curd

4 to 5 passion fruits
2 egg yolks
⅓ cup sugar

2 tablespoons unsalted butter, cut into 4 pieces

1 Cut the passion fruits in half and scrape the seeds and pulp into a fine strainer set over a medium bowl. Using a wooden spoon, press the passion fruit seeds against the strainer to extract all the juice. Measure out ¼ cup of juice and reserve any excess for another use.

2 In a small heavy nonreactive saucepan, combine the passion fruit juice, the egg yolks and the sugar. Cook over low heat, stirring constantly, until the mixture begins to thicken, about 5 minutes. Add the butter and continue to cook, stirring, without boiling, for 1 minute.

3 Remove the mixture from the heat and pass it through a strainer set over a medium bowl. Let cool to room temperature. Refrigerate, covered, until ready to use. (The fruit curd can be made up to 1 week ahead.)

Makes ⅔ to ¾ cup
Recipe by Marcia Kiesel

Cinnamon Knots, Raspberry Snails and Aunt Irma's Sour Cream Twists

These fancifully shaped cookies will make even the knottiest days run more smoothly; their recipes follow, and two are based on this cream cheese dough.

1 Cut the cream cheese into 8 pieces and let stand at room temperature for 10 minutes.

2 Cut the butter into tablespoons and let stand at room temperature for 10 minutes.

3 Put the flour into a food processor. Scatter the cream cheese and butter over the flour and process, turning the machine quickly on and off 6 to 8 times. Then let the machine run until the dough resembles large curds, stopping to scrape down the sides of the bowl once, about 15 seconds; do not let the dough form a ball on the blade.

4 Turn the dough out onto a work surface and gather into a ball. Divide the dough in half and shape each piece into a 4-x-5-x-1-inch rectangle. Wrap the dough tightly in plastic wrap and refrigerate for at least 2 hours before using. (The dough can be refrigerated for up to 3 days or frozen for 1 month.)

Note:

To make the dough by hand or with a mixer, first cream together the butter and cream cheese. Then blend in the flour to form a smooth dough.

Cream Cheese Dough:
½ pound cream cheese
½ pound unsalted butter
2 cups all-purpose flour

Makes about 1½ pounds
Recipe by Dorie Greenspan

Cinnamon Knots

These are the cookies for which the "bet-you-can't-eat-just-one" wager was meant. Equally at home with coffee, tea or mugs of steaming cider, the knots may be made with ginger-sugar for a spicy change. If you don't want to bother with ornate folding and twisting, just cut the dough into long, thin strips and knot in the center or twist into pretzel shapes.

½ **recipe of Cream Cheese Dough**   1 cup sugar
   (preceding recipe)   ¼ cup ground cinnamon

1 Remove one portion of the dough from the refrigerator and let stand at room temperature for about 10 minutes, until malleable.
2 In a small bowl, combine the sugar and the cinnamon. Sprinkle about ¼ cup of the mixture on a work surface. Put the dough on the sugared surface and sprinkle with about 2 tablespoons of cinnamon sugar. Roll out the dough into a 13-inch square, sprinkling with more cinnamon sugar and turning dough several times as you roll until all of the sugar is incorporated. The dough will become dark brown.
3 Trim the dough into a 12-inch square. Cut in half crosswise and, working with one half of the dough at a time, fold each piece lengthwise in half into a 12-x-3-inch rectangle. Cut crosswise at 1-inch intervals into 12 strips.
4 Knot simply, twist into a pretzel shape or using a small paring knife, cut a slit through the center of the folded side of each strip, leaving a ½-inch margin at the free ends.
5 Fold back one layer of dough and pull it through the slit and back down to form a knot. Put the cookies on a buttered baking sheet, preferably nonstick, and refrigerate for at least 30 minutes, until firm, before baking. Repeat with the remaining dough.
6 Preheat the oven to 375°. Bake the cookies in the middle of the oven for 10 to 12 minutes, until slightly puffed and browned. Transfer to a rack and let cool before serving. (After baking, the cookies can be frozen for up to 3 months.)

Makes about 2 dozen
Recipe by Dorie Greenspan

Raspberry Snails

Chocolate, which is a traditional companion to raspberry, seems pleasantly surprising in these intensely flavored small packages.

½ recipe Cream Cheese Dough (page 197)	¼ cup currants
⅔ cup seedless raspberry jam	⅔ cup mini-chocolate chips or chopped semisweet chocolate
4 tablespoons sugar	
½ teaspoon ground cinnamon	1 egg

1 Remove one portion of the dough from the refrigerator and let rest at room temperature until malleable, about 10 minutes. Meanwhile, in a small saucepan, melt the raspberry jam over low heat, stirring frequently. Remove from the heat and let cool while you shape the dough.

2 On a lightly floured surface, roll out the dough into a 10-inch square. Using a pastry brush, spread a thin coating of jam over the dough.

3 Combine 2 tablespoons of the sugar with the cinnamon and sprinkle half of the mixture evenly over the dough. Scatter half the currants and chocolate over the dough. Cover the dough with a sheet of waxed paper and, using your hands, gently press the ingredients into the dough.

4 Mark the top and bottom edges of the dough at 2-inch intervals. Using these marks as guides, cut diagonally across to make a harlequin pattern. Then cut the dough in half crosswise to make 18 equal triangles. There will be 2 odd pieces of the dough at either end. These can be pieced together to make nibbles for the baker.

5 Starting at the wide base of each triangle, roll up the dough. Place the triangles on a buttered baking sheet, preferably nonstick, with the points tucked underneath. Refrigerate the cookies for at least 30 minutes before baking, or freeze. (Shaped cookies can be frozen and baked without thawing.) Repeat with the remaining dough, jam, cinnamon-sugar, currants and chocolate chips.

6 Preheat the oven to 350°. Beat the egg with 1 teaspoon of cold water to make a glaze. Brush the glaze over each cookie. Sprinkle with the remaining 2 tablespoons sugar.

7 Bake for 25 minutes, or until golden. (Frozen cookies will take 5 to 7 minutes longer.) Transfer to a rack and let cool before serving. The baked cookies can be stored in an airtight container for 2 to 3 days or frozen for up to 1 month.

Makes 3 dozen
Recipe by Dorie Greenspan

Aunt Irma's Sour-Cream Twists

Jim Fobel's Aunt Irma served these flaky yeast-based cookies every time friends came over for coffee or tea. The sour cream makes the flaky layers tasty, while the sugar coating keeps the outside crispy. The sweetness comes from the sugar coating, as there is no sugar in the dough.

1 envelope (¼ ounce) active dry yeast	¼ pound unsalted butter
3 tablespoons lukewarm water (105° to 115°)	½ cup white vegetable shortening
1 cup plus 1 teaspoon sugar	2 egg yolks, lightly beaten
3¾ cups all-purpose flour	1 cup sour cream, at room temperature
1 teaspoon salt	1 teaspoon vanilla extract

1 Place the yeast, water and 1 teaspoon of the sugar in a small bowl and stir to dissolve the yeast. Let the yeast proof for about 10 minutes, or until foamy. If this does not happen, start over with fresh ingredients.

2 In a large bowl, combine the flour and salt. Cut in the butter and shortening until the mixture resembles coarse meal. Stir the proofed yeast and pour it over the flour. Add the egg yolks, sour cream and vanilla; stir to blend well; the dough will be soft. Cover the bowl and let it rest in a cool place (60° to 70°) for 2 hours.

3 Preheat the oven to 375°. Lightly grease two baking sheets. Divide the dough in half and reserve one half, covered, until needed. Reserve ½ cup sugar; place the remaining ½ cup on a small plate. Sprinkle the work surface with about 1 tablespoon of the sugar in the plate; place the dough on top of the sugar and pat it out to a rectangle about 4 by 5 inches; sprinkle the dough with about 1 tablespoon sugar and roll it out thinner, turning it over several times and sprinkling the top with about 2 teaspoons more sugar each time, until the dough measures 13 by 17 inches and is about ⅛ inch thick, or slightly thicker. Sprinkle the top with about 1 tablespoon sugar and trim the rectangle to measure 12 by 16 inches.

4 Using a pastry wheel with a crimped edge or a small sharp knife and a ruler, cut the dough into strips 4 inches long and ¾ inch wide. One at a time, pick up the strips, dip the bottom surface into the sugar remaining on the plate, turn one end over so that the dough twists in the middle and place on the baking sheet, half an inch apart.

5 Bake for about 15 minutes, or until crisp and golden brown. Transfer to racks to cool. Repeat with the remaining dough and remaining ½ cup sugar.

Makes about 10 dozen
Recipe by Jim Fobel

Chutney Steamed Pudding with Rum-Butter Sauce

In this partnership, an old-fashioned steamed pudding goes modern, lightened and simplified to suit the tastes and time of today's busy cooks.

1 cup all-purpose flour	2 eggs, at room temperature
½ teaspoon baking soda	⅓ cup fruit chutney (see Note)
¼ pound unsalted butter, cut into small pieces and at room temperature	⅓ cup chopped walnuts
	Confectioners' sugar, for garnish
½ cup (firmly packed) dark brown sugar	Rum-Butter Sauce (recipe follows)

1 Generously butter and flour a 1-quart steamed pudding or kugel-hopf mold; set aside. Choose a deep pot, large enough to afford good circulation around the mold, with a tight-fitting lid. Place a trivet or rack in the bottom of the pot; set aside. Put a kettle of water on to boil.

2 Sift the flour and baking soda onto a plate or a sheet of waxed paper; set aside.

3 In a medium bowl, cream the butter and sugar together with a wooden spoon until light and fluffy.

4 Place the eggs, chutney and walnuts in a food processor and process for 2 to 3 seconds just to mix; do not overmix or the nuts will be too fine. Gradually stir this mixture into the butter mixture. Gradually add the flour mixture, about a third at a time, mixing after each addition.

5 Pour the batter into the prepared mold and tap the mold on the table a few times to settle the mixture. The mold will be only two-thirds full. Cover the mold with a fitted lid or a sheet of buttered waxed paper and a sheet of aluminum foil. Twist and crimp the foil tightly around the rim to seal. Place the pudding on the rack and add boiling water to reach halfway up the sides of the mold.

6 Cover the pot with a sheet of aluminum foil and the lid; steam over moderate heat for 1½ hours, replenishing the boiling water as needed about every 30 minutes. Insert a skewer into the center; it should come out almost clean. If wet batter clings to it, re-cover and steam the pudding a bit longer. Remove the pudding mold from the pot and let cool on a rack for 15 minutes. Invert onto a serving plate and tap lightly to loosen the pudding; let rest with the mold over it to keep warm until serving time. Sprinkle the pudding with confectioners' sugar and accompany with Rum-Butter Sauce.

Note:
This pudding tastes best when made with a thick homemade peach, pear or gooseberry chutney. If none is available, use a commercially prepared one.

Serves 6
Recipe by Lee Bailey

Rum-Butter Sauce

¼ pound unsalted butter, at room temperature	1 tablespoon grated orange zest
¾ cup sifted confectioners' sugar	½ teaspoon freshly grated nutmeg
2 tablespoons dark rum	

1 In a medium bowl, cream the butter and sugar together until light and fluffy. Gradually beat in the rum. Stir in the zest and nutmeg.

2 Transfer the mixture to a small serving crock and let stand in a cool place, covered with waxed paper, or refrigerate for longer storage. Let stand at room temperature until it reaches a soft and spreadable consistency.

Makes 1 cup
Recipe by Lee Bailey

Savories

Savories

In a burst of atypical eloquence, Webster's defines a savory this way: "Brit (1661): a dish of stimulating flavor served usually at the end of dinner but sometimes as an appetizer." And that's precisely it. Savories, which can range from something as simple as melted cheese on toast to *chou profiteroles* with cheese have this in common: They finish off the palate and set the stage for the port or brandy to come. If you as host or hostess so choose, a savory dish can end a meal with élan, adding the correct finishing touches, but without even a hint of sugar.

Traditionally, the Italians and the French follow the entrée with a salad course, then a cheese course, then a fruit course. Sweets, if they are served at all, are the final course, which may be followed by coffees and dessert wines, liqueurs or brandies. The British, famed for their sweet tooths, lump those first three courses together (including, if you're lucky, a chunk of Stilton) before the sweets begin. And then, after dessert they serve the savories.

To avoid sweets, we Americans, on the other hand, may just skip dessert. But there's no need to do without; a savory can provide an appealing and imaginative conclusion to the meal.

This chapter, then, is for those who aren't fond of sugar or who are doing their level best to avoid it. It's for those who have just had a rich dinner of sea scallops or sweetbreads and can't abide the thought of anything sweet. And it's for those who still have the better part of a great bottle of wine open and want to savor it slowly before moving on.

Though technically salad is a separate course, it works beautifully as a savory because its flavors are astringent, clearing the palate of what came before. Certain salads offer sweet with the savory either because they have a sweet element in them or will be followed by a special bottle of dessert wine. And there are all sorts of salads – simple ones, such as the Green Salad with Three Oils or the Salad of Bitter Greens with Grapefruit Vinaigrette, and colorful ones, such as the naturally sweet Beet and Chicory Salad or the Sicilian Citrus Salad, and ones with fruit or cheese, the Port and Stilton Salad with Port Dressing or the Romaine, Orange and Watercress Salad with Mustard Cream Dressing.

We've also collected some luscious baked savories that can conclude a meal – tangy, smooth Tyropita (Feta Cheese Triangles) are delicious, as is the chilled creamy Montrachet Cheesecake or rich Deep-Dish Vidalia Onion Pie, a heart-stopping rendition based on the famed sweet onions from Georgia. Serving a lightly golden Almond Gougère Ring or Feta Cheese Tart will allow even the most peripatetic host to sit down and relax.

Fruit served alone or with cheese (try the Lavender-Pepper Pears) is as classic a dessert as you'll find, always presenting the opportunity for imagination and experimentation, a way of "stretching" the palate into new territory.

Much has been written about the profusion of "new" fruits and vegetables in our markets. Indeed, produce that was once highly regional, completely foreign or extremely rare might be available year-round these days in three colors or sizes. Asian pears are round perfect-looking fruits that are sweet and delicious. Carambolas (a.k.a. star fruit) make a tart addition to salads or a unique garnish when sliced crosswise to show their star shape. Pummellos, the largest of all citrus fruits, look much like enormous grapefruits with very thick, almost spongy peel; not surprisingly, their fruit resembles grapefruit as well. The tasty juice and flesh of the ugli fruit should not be missed; it makes a pleasant addition to salads or can be peeled and eaten as you would an orange. We urge you to give these newcomers a go; their textures, flavors, shapes and colors are exciting and new, and you'll be surprised at how versatile they can be.■

Fresh Pear with Roquefort Cream

A classic combination: complex, rich Roquefort cheese offset by
sweet pear. In the best of all possible worlds, you'd want to serve it
with a glass of Sauternes.

**2 tablespoons crumbled
  Roquefort cheese,
  at room temperature
2 tablespoons heavy cream
1 tablespoon dry white wine
Pinch of cayenne pepper
1 ripe pear
½ lemon**

1 With a wooden spoon, mash the cheese and cream together until
   blended. Add the wine and cayenne and blend until smooth.
2 Cut the pear in half lengthwise and remove the core. Rub the cut
   sides of the pear with the lemon to prevent discoloration. Spoon
   half of the cheese mixture into the center hollow of each pear. Serve
   slightly chilled.

Serves 2
Recipe by Emalee Chapman

Sicilian Citrus Salad

The resting time really lets the flavors in this salad reach their peak.

5 medium navel oranges
½ cup olive oil, preferably extra-virgin
2 tablespoons fresh lemon juice

½ tablespoon peppercorns, coarsely cracked
2 tablespoons finely shredded lemon zest

1 Using a knife, peel the oranges; there should be no white membrane left. Slice the oranges crosswise into ¼-inch rounds and arrange, overlapping the slices, on 6 plates.

2 Drizzle the oil and lemon juice over the orange slices. Sprinkle with the cracked peppercorns and lemon zest. Cover the plates with plastic wrap and set aside to macerate at room temperature for 2 hours before serving.

Serves 6
Recipe by Deidre Davis and Linda Marino

Romaine, Orange and Watercress Salad with Mustard Cream Dressing

A *salade composée* with an old-fashioned cooked dressing that's just ever-so-slightly sweet.

Mustard-Cream Dressing:
¾ teaspoon salt
1½ teaspoons sharp mustard
1¼ teaspoons sugar
1 tablespoon melted unsalted butter, cooled
1 egg, beaten
⅓ cup heavy cream
2½ tablespoons cider vinegar
⅛ to ¼ teaspoon freshly ground pepper, or ½ teaspoon crushed green peppercorns

Salad:
3 or 4 navel oranges
2 small heads of romaine lettuce, washed and dried
1 bunch of watercress, washed and dried
4 scallion tops, thinly sliced
2 tablespoons fresh orange juice

Make the dressing:

1 Combine the ingredients, in the order listed, in the top of a double boiler. Mix well with a whisk. Set over simmering water and stir constantly until the sauce thickens, about 5 minutes. Scrape into a dish and chill for up to a day.

Make the salad:

2 Remove the peel and pith from the oranges. Cut them in half lengthwise, then into crosswise slices. Place in a bowl, cover with plastic, and refrigerate until serving time.

3 Tear the romaine into bite-size pieces and toss in a serving bowl with the watercress. Cover with plastic and refrigerate until serving time.

4 To serve the salad, arrange the orange slices on the greens and sprinkle the scallions over them. Stir the orange juice into the chilled dressing and adjust the seasoning, if necessary. Pour the dressing over the salad and toss at table.

Serves 8 or 9
Recipe by Elizabeth Schneider

Deep-Dish Vidalia Onion Pie

Vidalia onions are so marvelously sweet they'll satisfy even the most ardent sweet tooth. This pie is a triumph of great flavors. When Vidalias are out of season, look for Walla Wallas or Mauis.

Crust:
1 envelope (¼ ounce) active dry
    yeast
¼ cup lukewarm (105° to 110°)
    water
¼ teaspoon sugar
⅓ cup milk
2 tablespoons unsalted butter,
    cut up
1 teaspoon salt
½ teaspoon caraway seeds
About 2¼ cups all-purpose flour

Filling:
2 tablespoons unsalted butter
4 medium-large Vidalia onions,
    cut into ½-inch dice (about
    3 cups)
1½ tablespoons all-purpose flour
¾ cup milk
¼ teaspoon salt
8 ounces cottage cheese
3 eggs

Make the crust:

1 In a small bowl, dissolve the yeast in the water with the sugar. Let proof until foamy; if the mixture does not bubble up, begin again with fresh ingredients.

2 In a small saucepan, heat the milk, butter, salt and caraway, stirring, until the butter almost melts. Pour the liquid into a large bowl.

3 Stir in ¾ cup of the flour, then the yeast mixture. Stir in 1 cup more flour, then knead in however much more flour is easily absorbed to make a medium-soft dough. Turn the dough out onto a floured surface and knead until it is medium-firm, smooth and no longer sticky, adding flour as needed. Place in a buttered bowl and turn to coat the dough. Cover the bowl with plastic and let the dough rise until at least doubled in bulk, about 1 hour.

Meanwhile, make the filling:

4 In a large heavy skillet, melt the butter over moderately low heat. Add the onions and cook, stirring frequently, until the onions are golden and soft, about 30 minutes (reduce the heat if the onions begin to brown).

5 Add the flour and cook, stirring, for 2 minutes. Add the milk and salt, increase the heat to moderate and cook, stirring, until the mixture is thick, almost pasty, 2 to 3 minutes.

6 Blend together the cottage cheese and eggs. Stir in the onions. Season to taste with salt.

7 Preheat the oven to 375°. On a lightly floured surface, roll or pat the dough to form a rectangle slightly larger than the baking dish or pan you'll be using, which should be about 12 x 8 x 2 inches. Butter the dish and press in the dough to extend about three-quarters of the way up the sides of the dish. Press the dough well into the dish to cover evenly. Pour in the onion filling.

8 Bake in the center of the oven for 45 minutes, or until the crust is nicely browned and the filling is golden brown. Let cool in the pan for 15 minutes, then gently lift out the pie with large spatulas and let cool slightly on a rack before cutting into serving pieces. (The pie can be made ahead of time.) Serve at room temperature or reheat in a 350° oven for 15 minutes.

Serves 6
Recipe by Elizabeth Schneider

Feta Cheese Tart

A savory blend of rye, sesame and feta cheese flavors that's extraordinarily easy to prepare.

3 tablespoons unsalted butter
3 tablespoons sesame seeds
½ cup plus 1 tablespoon finely crushed rye cracker crumbs, made from all-rye crackers, such as Finn Crisp
6 ounces (1 cup lightly packed) feta cheese, patted dry and crumbled

6 ounces cream cheese, at room temperature and cut into small pieces
2 eggs, at room temperature
1 tablespoon minced fresh basil or 1½ teaspoons dried
2 teaspoons minced fresh rosemary or ¾ teaspoon dried
½ teaspoon freshly ground pepper
½ cup sour cream

Prepare the crust:

1 Preheat the oven to 325°. In a small heavy saucepan, melt the butter over low heat. Add the sesame seeds and sauté, stirring, until lightly browned, about 2 minutes. Remove from the heat and stir in the rye crumbs to moisten them.

2 Pat the crumbs into a 9-inch pie pan. Place another 9-inch pie pan on top of the crumbs and press down to pack into a firm crust.

Prepare the filling:

3 In a large bowl, beat the feta cheese and cream cheese with an electric mixer until smooth and light. One at a time, beat in the eggs. Beat in the basil, rosemary, pepper and sour cream until blended. Pour into the pie crust and smooth the top.

4 Set the pie pan inside a roasting pan and add enough hot water to reach halfway up the sides of the pie pan. Bake for 1 hour, until a knife inserted in the center comes out clean. Serve warm or at room temperature.

Serves 8 to 12
Recipe by Dani Manilla

Spinach Salad with Warm Balsamic Dressing

The balanced, mellow flavor of balsamic vinegar makes possible a one-to-one, vinegar to oil ratio. The warm dressing softens the spinach slightly without wilting it, and the sliced toasted almonds are deliciously crunchy. All in all – a most fitting end to a summer meal.

½ pound fresh spinach, torn into bite-size pieces
1 large red bell pepper, cut into thin strips
¼ cup balsamic vinegar
¼ cup fruity olive oil

2 garlic cloves, minced
¼ teaspoon freshly ground black pepper
½ cup sliced toasted almonds

1 In a medium bowl, combine the spinach and bell pepper.

2 In a small heavy saucepan, whisk the vinegar and oil until well blended. Whisk in the garlic and black pepper.

3 Warm the dressing over low heat, stirring, until heated through, about 1 minute. Pour the warm dressing over the spinach and red pepper and toss until coated. Just before serving, add the almonds and toss to mix.

Serves 6
Recipe by Anne Montgomery

Zucchini Ribbons with Arugula and Creamy Goat Cheese Sauce

Lavender-Pepper Pears

Gastronomic greatness. A most pleasing mélange of textures, flavors and dramatic presentation.

1¼ cups heavy cream
½ cup finely chopped onion
3 sprigs of fresh thyme plus
  ½ teaspoon minced fresh thyme
  (or a total of 1½ teaspoons
  dried thyme)
3 parsley stems
3 black peppercorns
2 medium garlic cloves, unpeeled
  and lightly crushed

3 ounces mild goat cheese
4 teaspoons balsamic vinegar
Salt and coarsely cracked pepper
16 lengthwise slices of zucchini,
  cut ⅛ inch thick (from about
  3 medium)
3 tablespoons extra-virgin
  olive oil
1 bunch of arugula, large stems
  removed

1 In a heavy medium saucepan, combine the cream, onion, thyme sprigs (or 1 teaspoon dried), parsley stems, peppercorns and garlic. Bring just to a simmer, cover and cook over low heat until the garlic is very soft, about 20 minutes. Strain into a small saucepan; discard the garlic and herbs.

2 Place the saucepan over low heat and whisk in the goat cheese, 1 teaspoon of the vinegar and the minced thyme (or ½ teaspoon dried). Stir until the sauce is smooth. Season with salt and pepper to taste.

3 Meanwhile, heat a large heavy skillet over high heat. Brush both sides of the zucchini slices with the olive oil and place in the skillet. Cook until lightly browned, about 1 minute on each side. Remove and keep warm.

4 To assemble, toss the remaining 3 teaspoons vinegar with the arugula. Gather together 3 arugula leaves and place crosswise on one of the zucchini slices; fold the zucchini slice over the arugula. Repeat with the remaining zucchini and arugula. Arrange four zucchini bundles decoratively on each serving plate. Spoon about one-fourth of the sauce over each serving and top with additional cracked pepper.

Serves 4
Recipe by Anne Disrude

For an intriguing dessert to round out a light meal, try this perfumed fruit with a wedge of Italian Fontina or other mild semisoft cheese.

1 tablespoon fresh lemon juice
2 large ripe Bartlett pears, peeled
⅛ teaspoon lavender*, crumbled

½ teaspoon coarsely
  cracked black pepper
*Available at spice markets
  and specialty food shops

Sprinkle the lemon juice over the pears. Combine the lavender and pepper and sprinkle over the pears. Serve on a plate with a knife and fork.

Serves 2
Recipe by Anne Disrude

Salad of Bitter Greens with Grapefruit Vinaigrette

Simple, simple, simple. Tasty, tasty, tasty.

1 medium head of chicory or escarole, or 2 large bunches of arugula	1½ teaspoons fresh lemon juice
2 Belgian endives, halved lengthwise and cored	¼ teaspoon salt
Juice of 1 small grapefruit (about ½ cup)	⅛ teaspoon freshly ground pepper
	6 tablespoons olive oil

1 Rinse the chicory under cold water. (Do not soak – it will become more bitter.) Dry thoroughly, tear into bite-size pieces and place in a large bowl. Cut the endives lengthwise into ⅓-inch strips and add to the greens.

2 In a small bowl, combine the grapefruit and lemon juices with the salt and pepper. Gradually whisk in the oil. Pour the dressing over the greens and toss well.

Serves 6
Courtesy of Deidre Davis and
Linda Marino

Almond Gougère Ring

A splendid cheese dessert pastry to serve with fresh fruit of the season.

¼ pound unsalted butter, cut into bits	1½ cups (6 ounces) freshly grated Gruyère cheese
¼ teaspoon salt	Pinch of freshly grated nutmeg
¼ teaspoon freshly ground pepper	1 egg yolk
1 cup all-purpose flour	1 tablespoon milk
4 whole eggs	½ cup slivered almonds

1 Preheat the oven to 375°. Butter a baking sheet. In a heavy medium saucepan, combine the butter, salt and pepper with 1 cup of water. Bring to a boil over high heat. Remove from the heat and add the flour all at once. Using a wooden spoon, beat until the mixture is smooth and pulls away from the sides of the pan to form a ball. Continue to beat over low heat for 1 minute.

2 Remove from the heat and let cool for 1 minute. Beat in the whole eggs, 1 at a time, making sure each egg is completely incorporated before adding the next. Stir in 1¼ cups of the cheese and the nutmeg. Mound large heaping spoonfuls of the mixture on the prepared baking sheet to form a wreath; the inside edges should measure about 7 inches across.

3 In a small bowl, lightly beat the egg yolk with the milk. Using a pastry brush, paint the top of the wreath with this glaze. Sprinkle the remaining ¼ cup Gruyère and the almonds over the wreath.

4 Bake the gougère for 15 minutes, until puffed and set. Reduce the heat to 350° and cook for 45 minutes longer, until golden brown and firm to the touch. Let cool for 10 minutes and serve warm.

Serves 8 to 10
Recipe by W. Peter Prestcott

Port and Stilton Salad

This classic combination is terribly British.

1½ tablespoons unsalted butter	2 small heads of Bibb lettuce,
2 teaspoons safflower oil	separated into leaves
1 garlic clove, unpeeled	Port Dressing (recipe follows)
but bruised	2 Belgian endives, cut into
¾ cup walnuts	thin julienne
1 large head of red leaf lettuce,	½ pound Stilton cheese,
separated into leaves with	coarsely chopped
tough ends removed	

1 In a medium skillet, melt the butter in the oil over moderate heat. When the foam subsides, add the garlic and cook for 2 minutes. Discard the garlic.

2 Add the walnuts and cook, shaking the pan frequently, until toasted to a dark golden color. Drain the nuts on paper towels.

3 In one bowl, toss the lettuce leaves with ⅔ cup of the Port Dressing. In another bowl, gently toss the endive julienne with the remaining dressing.

4 On each of 8 chilled salad plates, place 1 large leaf of red lettuce. Arrange 3 Bibb lettuce leaves in a cloverleaf shape on top. Neatly bunch the endive julienne in a fringe below the Bibb.

5 Place a heaping spoonful of the Stilton in the middle of each salad and top each with 1½ tablespoons toasted walnuts.

Serves 8
Recipe by W. Peter Prestcott

Port Dressing

1 tablespoon Dijon-style mustard	1 tablespoon fresh lemon juice
½ cup fragrant olive oil	3 tablespoons tawny port
1 tablespoon walnut oil	¼ teaspoon salt
1 tablespoon safflower oil	⅛ teaspoon finely ground pepper
1 tablespoon tarragon	
wine vinegar	

Place the mustard in the jar of a blender or food processor. With the machine on high speed, slowly add the olive, walnut and safflower oils; then add the vinegar, lemon juice, port, salt and pepper. Mix well and adjust the seasonings, if necessary.

Makes about 1 cup
Recipe by W. Peter Prestcott

Leek Salad and Savory Cheese Soufflé

This unusual salad comes from a very old "salet" recipe, which in the Middle Ages would have been garnished with nasturtium, borage or marigold blossoms. Use only the tender and delicate part of the leek; if the green is too strong (try a nibble), use only the white. Serve this alone or as shown with individual Savory Cheese Soufflés (recipe follows).

Leek Salad:
1 cup thinly sliced leek, tender part only (white and mild green)
1 cup chopped celery (2 medium ribs)
1 cup (5 ounces) frozen peas, thawed
1 tablespoon finely chopped fresh mint or fennel leaves
Small bunch of chicory, torn into bite-size pieces (about ½ pound)
4 or 5 thin rounds of red onion, separated into rings
1 small navel orange, peeled and cut into thin rounds
¼ cup plus 2 tablespoons vegetable oil
2 tablespoons cider vinegar
1 teaspoon Dijon-style mustard
1 teaspoon minced fresh dill, or ½ teaspoon dried dillweed
¼ teaspoon sugar
¼ teaspoon paprika
¼ teaspoon salt
⅛ teaspoon freshly ground pepper

1 Place the sliced leek in a colander; pour 2 cups of boiling water over it. Rinse under cold water and drain well.

2 In a medium bowl, combine the leek, celery, peas and mint. Divide the chicory among 6 salad plates. Toss the vegetables together and arrange on the chicory. Arrange the onion rings and orange slices on top.

3 In a small bowl, whisk together the oil, vinegar, mustard, dill, sugar, paprika, salt and pepper until blended (or place in a small jar, cover and shake well). Drizzle the dressing over the salad.

Serves 6
Recipe by Geraldine Duncann

Savory Cheese Soufflé

Give rise to your spirit with this savory soufflé. Light as air, puffed and golden straight from the oven, it makes a deliciously dramatic conclusion.

8 tablespoons (¼ pound) unsalted butter	Pinch of cayenne pepper
6 tablespoons freshly grated Parmesan cheese	½ teaspoon freshly grated nutmeg
⅓ cup all-purpose flour	1 teaspoon Dijon-style mustard
1¾ cups milk	6 whole eggs, separated
1 teaspoon salt	1¼ cups grated Gruyère cheese (about 5 ounces)
⅛ teaspoon freshly ground black pepper	1 egg white

1 Preheat the oven to 400°. Use 2 tablespoons of the butter to thoroughly grease a 2-quart soufflé dish or 6 individual ramekins. Sprinkle evenly with 2 tablespoons of the grated Parmesan cheese and set aside.

2 In a heavy medium saucepan, melt the remaining 6 tablespoons butter over moderate heat. Add the flour and cook, stirring, for 3 minutes without allowing the mixture to color to make a roux.

3 Meanwhile, in another medium saucepan, scald the milk over moderately high heat. Gradually whisk the hot milk into the roux. Bring to a boil, whisking constantly. Cook, stirring, until the béchamel thickens, about 2 minutes. Stir in the salt, black pepper, cayenne, nutmeg and mustard.

4 Remove from heat. One at a time, beat the egg yolks into the béchamel base.

5 Stir in the grated Gruyère and 2 tablespoons of the remaining Parmesan cheese. (The soufflé can be prepared ahead to this point. Simply cover the surface with waxed paper or plastic wrap to prevent a skin from forming. If held for more than 1 hour, refrigerate. Let return to room temperature before continuing.)

6 Beat the 7 egg whites until stiff but not dry or grainy. Stir about one-fourth of the beaten whites into the soufflé base. Working quickly and lightly, blend the lightened base into the remaining egg whites. Turn the mixture into the prepared soufflé dish or ramekins. Smooth the top with a spatula and run your thumb around the soufflé to form a groove around the top about 1 inch in from the rim; this will form the classic "top hat" when the soufflé rises.

7 Bake the soufflé(s) in the lower third of the oven for 35 minutes. Sprinkle the remaining 2 tablespoons Parmesan cheese over the top and bake for about 5 minutes longer, until the cheese is melted. Serve immediately.

Serves 6
Recipe by John Robert Massie

Chèvre Mousse

Autumn Apple, Beet and Walnut Salad

This fragrant herbed cheese mousse is made on the same principle as *coeur à la crème.* Make it the night before so that the whey has a chance to drain. Serve with fresh fruit and light biscuits or crackers.

If you can find golden baby beets in your market, this is definitely the salad they were grown for. Leave a couple of them whole with their tops for garnish.

½ pound Bûcheron or other mild goat cheese, at room temperature	¼ teaspoon freshly ground white pepper
¼ cup sour cream	3 teaspoons Calvados or apple brandy
¼ cup walnuts, coarsely chopped	1 cup heavy cream
½ teaspoon dried rosemary, crumbled	Bay leaves and walnut halves, for garnish
1½ teaspoons salt	

1 In a medium bowl, using an electric mixer, beat the goat cheese with the sour cream until smooth. Stir in the walnuts, rosemary, salt, white pepper and 2 teaspoons of the Calvados.
2 In another bowl, beat the heavy cream until almost stiff. Blend in the remaining 1 teaspoon Calvados. Gently stir half the whipped cream into the cheese mixture to lighten it; then fold in the remaining cream.
3 Line a 4- to 5-cup wicker basket with three layers of dampened cheesecloth, cutting the cloth large enough to overlap the mousse. For garnish, arrange bay leaves and walnut halves upside down on the cheesecloth in a decorative pattern.
4 Carefully turn the cheese mixture into the mold and smooth the surface. Fold the cheesecloth over the mousse. Place the basket on a rack set over a bowl to drain in the refrigerator overnight.
5 Unmold, fold back the cheesecloth. Place a serving plate over the top of the basket and invert carefully. Peel off the cheesecloth. Serve chilled.

Serves 12
Recipe by W. Peter Prestcott

1 head of Boston lettuce, separated into leaves	¼ cup buttermilk
1½ cups coarsely shredded raw beets	¼ cup mayonnaise
2 medium tart, firm red apples, such as McIntosh or Empire, diced	½ teaspoon prepared horseradish
¾ cup broken walnut halves	1½ tablespoons fresh lemon juice
	Freshly ground pepper
	1 teaspoon grated lemon zest, for garnish

1 Line a serving platter with the lettuce leaves. Gently squeeze the shredded beets in paper towels to absorb as much juice as possible. In a large bowl, combine the apples, beets and walnuts and toss to mix.
2 In a small bowl, whisk the buttermilk, mayonnaise, horseradish and lemon juice until smooth. Season to taste with pepper.
3 Pour the dressing over the apple mixture and toss gently until coated. Mound the salad in the center of the platter and sprinkle with the grated lemon zest.

Serves 6 to 8
Recipe by Jennifer Marshall

Portsmouth Salad

Serve this salad with or without its dressing for a crunchy sweet "pseudo" dessert.

2 medium cucumbers, well washed
1 small ripe pineapple, cut into ³⁄₈-inch dice
2 tart red-skinned apples, such as McIntosh, cut into ³⁄₈-inch dice
¼ cup olive oil
½ teaspoon brown sugar
¼ teaspoon salt
¼ teaspoon freshly ground pepper
1 head of Bibb or Boston lettuce

1   Using a fork with sharp tines, score the skin of the cucumbers. Cut in half lengthwise; scoop out the seeds with a spoon. Cut the cucumber into ³⁄₈-inch dice; place in a large bowl.
2   Using your hands, gently squeeze handfuls of the pineapple over a small bowl to collect 2 tablespoons of fresh juice; reserve the juice. Add the pineapple and the apples to the cucumber.
3   In a small bowl, combine the oil, brown sugar, salt and pepper with the reserved pineapple juice. Beat until blended; pour over the salad and toss lightly to mix.
4   Arrange several lettuce leaves on 6 small plates or in 6 saucer champagne glasses. Divide the salad evenly over the lettuce and serve at room temperature.

Serves 6
Recipe by Jim Haller
Blue Strawbery Restaurant
Portsmouth, New Hampshire

Green Winter Salad with Three Oils

In this recipe, Jonathan Waxman uses the flavors of nut oils to their greatest advantage. Serve after a rich beurre-blanc sauced entrée.

1 small bunch of arugula
1 head of radicchio
1 Belgian endive
1 small head of red leaf lettuce
4 ounces mâche (lamb's lettuce)
1 tablespoon sherry vinegar
1½ teaspoons minced shallots
¼ teaspoon salt
⅛ teaspoon freshly ground pepper
¼ cup extra-virgin olive oil
1½ teaspoons hazelnut oil
1 tablespoon walnut oil

1   Carefully wash the salad greens, drain and pat dry. Tear into bite-size pieces and place in a large bowl.
2   In a small bowl, use a whisk to blend the vinegar, shallots, salt and pepper. Gradually whisk in the oils, from the heaviest to the lightest: first, the olive oil, then hazelnut and finally the walnut. Drizzle the dressing over the greens, toss and serve.

Serves 4
Recipe by Jonathan Waxman

Beet and Chicory Salad

The sweet beets and bitter chicory are offset nicely by the crunch of fresh-toasted pecans.

3 pounds fresh beets (weighed without tops)
1 teaspoon grated lemon zest
¼ cup fresh lemon juice
3 tablespoons olive oil
1 teaspoon salt
½ teaspoon freshly ground pepper

1 head of chicory, torn into bite-size pieces
¼ cup chopped fresh parsley
Red Wine Vinaigrette (recipe follows)
½ cup toasted coarsely chopped walnuts, for garnish (see Note)

1 Preheat the oven to 450°. Wrap the beets tightly in aluminum foil. Place on a baking sheet and bake for about 45 minutes, or until tender when pierced with a small knife. Let cool slightly.

2 Slip the skins off the beets under cold running water. Cut in half crosswise; cut each half into ¼-inch slices. In a medium bowl, toss the beets with the lemon zest, lemon juice, olive oil, salt and pepper. Let marinate at room temperature for at least 20 minutes, or up to several hours.

3 In a large bowl, toss the chicory and parsley with enough of the Red Wine Vinaigrette to coat lightly; place in a serving bowl or on a platter. Remove the beets from the marinade and arrange them over the greens. Scatter the walnuts over the top, if desired. Drizzle any remaining beet marinade over the salad. Pass any remaining Red Wine Vinaigrette separately.

Note:

To toast the walnuts, preheat the oven to 350°. Scatter the nuts in a baking pan and bake, stirring the nuts frequently, until lightly toasted, about 10 minutes.

Serves 6 to 8
Recipe by John Robert Massie

Red Wine Vinaigrette

2 tablespoons red wine vinegar
1½ tablespoons fresh lemon juice
1½ teaspoons Dijon-style mustard
½ garlic clove or small shallot, minced
¼ teaspoon salt
¼ teaspoon freshly ground pepper
¼ cup olive oil
¼ cup vegetable oil

In a small bowl, whisk together the vinegar, lemon juice, mustard, garlic, salt and pepper until blended. Gradually whisk in the oils in a slow, thin stream.

Makes ⅔ cup
Recipe by John Robert Massie

Montrachet Cheesecake

Serve this mild, elegant goat cheese pie as a cheese-based savory dessert. Sliced papaya or other sweet fruit makes an excellent accompaniment. Or, you might want to make tiny individual tarts and decorate with fresh berries.

1½ cups all-purpose flour
⅛ teaspoon salt
⅛ teaspoon sugar
6 tablespoons unsalted butter
2 tablespoons solid
   vegetable shortening
2 to 3 tablespoons ice water
1 log (11 ounces) Montrachet
   blanc goat cheese, at room
   temperature

2 large packages (8 ounces
   each) cream cheese, at room
   temperature
3 eggs
½ teaspoon chopped fresh
   rosemary or ⅛ teaspoon dried
   crumbled
¾ cup (¼ pound) pine nuts,
   lightly toasted

1 In a large bowl, combine the flour, salt and sugar. Cut in the butter and shortening until the mixture is the consistency of coarse meal. Add 2 tablespoons of the ice water and toss to moisten the flour. Gather the pastry into a ball. If any flour doesn't adhere, sprinkle with up to 1 tablespoon more water. Flatten into a 6-inch disk, wrap well and refrigerate for at least 1 hour, or overnight.

2 Roll out the pastry to a thin round 14 inches in diameter. Place it in an 11- to 12-inch tart pan with a removable bottom, fitting the pastry against the sides and trimming any overhanging edges. Refrigerate the pastry-lined pan for at least 30 minutes. Preheat the oven to 350°.

3 Cover the pastry with parchment paper or foil and fill with pie weights or dried beans. Bake in the center of the oven for 30 minutes, or until golden around the sides. Remove the weights and liner and bake for about 5 minutes longer, until the center is dry. Leave the oven on.

4 Beat together the Montrachet and cream cheeses until light and fluffy. One at a time, beat in the eggs and blend in the rosemary.

5 Fill the warm pie shell with the cheese mixture. Sprinkle the pine nuts over the top. Return the pie to the oven and bake for 25 minutes, until set. Let cool to room temperature. Cut into thin wedges to serve.

Serves 16 to 20
Recipe from Piret's
San Diego, California

Tyropita

These flaky, buttery phyllo triangles have a tart feta cheese filling that's an ideal ending for a light, cold main course. They can be completely prepared ahead and frozen. Keep the phyllo dough covered with a damp kitchen towel to prevent drying out while you are working with it.

¼ pound plus 3 tablespoons unsalted butter	1 egg yolk
¼ cup all-purpose flour	3 tablespoons minced chives
1 cup milk, at room temperature	¼ teaspoon freshly ground pepper
1 pound feta cheese, crumbled	12 sheets of phyllo dough

1 In a heavy medium saucepan, melt 3 tablespoons of the butter over moderately low heat. Whisk in the flour and cook, stirring, for 2 minutes without coloring to make a roux. Slowly whisk in the milk until smooth. Bring to a boil, reduce the heat slightly and cook, whisking frequently, until the sauce is thick, about 2 minutes.

2 Add the feta cheese and cook, stirring, until smooth. Whisk in the egg yolk, chives and pepper and cook over low heat, stirring, for 3 minutes. Remove from the heat and scrape into a bowl. Let cool to room temperature, then cover and chill until firm, about 45 minutes. (The filling may be prepared a day ahead to this point.)

3 Preheat the oven to 375°. In a small heavy saucepan, melt the remaining ¼ pound of butter over low heat. Brush a baking sheet with about 2 teaspoons of the butter and set aside.

4 Lay 1 sheet of phyllo dough on a flat surface. Lightly brush with about 1 teaspoon butter. Cut the sheet lengthwise in half; fold each strip in half lengthwise again. Brush the tops of each lightly with butter.

5 Mound 1 rounded teaspoon of cheese on the bottom left-hand corner of both phyllo strips. (Too much filling will cause the pastries to leak when baking.) Loosely fold up each strip, using the classic flagfolding technique, to make a triangular pastry. Transfer to the baking sheet and lightly brush with butter. Make the remaining pastries in the same way. (The recipe may be made ahead to this point. Wrap and freeze the pastries. If frozen, allow an additional 5 to 7 minutes baking time.)

6 Bake for 12 to 15 minutes, until crisp and golden. Serve warm.

Makes 24 triangles
Recipe by Rux Martin

Cheese

All attempts at being encyclopedic on so huge a subject as cheese have failed. We won't even begin to try. What we do want to give you is the confidence to go into a store and make some cheese choices that will not disappoint you, plus guidance in choosing groups of three or four cheeses that will provide an interesting mix of flavors and textures. We urge you to use our recommendations merely as guides; feel free to strike out on your own, tasting what's available to you.

To prepare this chapter, we tasted a dozen or so cheeses specifically with dessert in mind. Some – the subtle flavor of blue-veined Fourme d'Ambert, creamy, rich, wonderful Saint Nectaire and silky and delicate goat's-milk Caprella – were perfect as is, accompanied by nothing at all save a good loaf of bread. Others, Basque sheep's-milk Pyrénées or a nutty and wonderful three-year-old Gouda, for example, go perfectly with Queen Anne cherries, while the Gouda is just as good on its own or with wedges of melon. We found the fabulous texture of aged Cantal to be ideal with melon, Caprella to combine nicely with pears, and

the mild but very flavorful Fontina d'Aosta to go with anything – especially peaches. (Make sure to buy real Italian Fontina d'Aosta, not some of the far blander cheeses that are called Fontina; this cheese has considerable character.)

Then there's Morbier, a cheese with a great story. Early in its history, Morbier was made in two layers, separated by a thin layer of ash. The bottom one consisted of curds made from the mellower morning milk. A layer of ash or soot – usually birch ash – separated it from the top layer of curds, made from the more acidic evening's milk. Morbier is good, mellow cheese that will taste great with green grapes or ripe, sweet nectarines or whatever other fruit is on hand. It'll taste even better if you tell your guests its story.

By and large, goat cheeses are popular partners for fruit, along with any and all of the rich double- and triple-crèmes. Those who truly love blue cheeses – Stilton, Roquefort and Gorgonzola among them – sometimes tend to think the only reason to eat a meal is to get to the cheese that follows – and they do have a point. Gorgonzola blends perfectly with a full-bodied red wine such as Barolo. Roquefort, made from ewe's milk, pairs traditionally with Sauternes to make a brilliant combination, especially if the wine is Château d'Yquem. Stilton isn't complete without a glass or two of vintage port.

Generally speaking, in choosing a cheese for dessert you should try to avoid strong cheeses, such as Limburger, Livarot and many of the aged grating cheeses, especially Pecorino. On the other hand, an aged Asiago from Italy is a hard cheese that is a marvelous addition to any after-dinner assortment of cheeses. Stay clear of cheeses that have even the slightest ammonia-like odor, as well as cheeses that may be mild but have rinds that are not. Keep in mind, though, that what pleases your palate is just fine – regardless of outside opinions. Take advantage of locally-made cheeses and taste before you buy.

Deciding which cheeses to serve for dessert is not a mysterious problem. You should set up a group of cheeses that progress from a smooth, mild example to something more assertive, then perhaps, to a goat cheese or triple-crème and finally to a well-aged blue cheese or hard cheese. You'll probably want to include examples from different countries or regions and keep an eye on what you choose to guarantee a variety of textures, colors, shapes and sizes of cheese.

If any of the cheeses you buy is strong, place it on a separate tray, away from the milder cheeses. Take the cheese out of the refrigerator at least one hour before you plan to serve it (leaving it out up to three hours is okay). It is vital that the cheese be at room temperature for its full flavor to develop and come through on the palate. Serve the cheese on rather plain, not "busy" trays – marble or wood or rattan is fine – and try not to let the presentation detract from the cheeses themselves. Set the cheeses on large shiny non-toxic leaves (or silk imitations) and keep them apart from each other; have a separate knife for each cheese. Serve your cheese tray with good crusty bread and, usually, unsalted crackers (the cheese will be salty enough).

Don't forget, however, the classic fruit and cheese combinations – berries spiked with aged Balsamic vinegar or served lightly sugared alongside small rounds of Caprella, Fagottino or a triple-crème such as Gratte Paille, or maybe topped with dollops of Mascarpone. Fresh pineapple begs to be paired with a soft, mild cheese such as a Bel Paese, Robiola or Valençay. Papaya mixes well with a variety of types, from a blue-veined goat cheese to an Aged Monterey Jack or a nutty Tomme de Savoie. Golden, red or purple plums love cheese. They can take on creamy cheeses such as a classic Gorgonzola as easily as a Taleggio or Alpistella. Melons – especially cantaloupe with its pronounced flavor – are fit partners for wedges of Aged Gouda (look for three-year-old Gouda – it's brilliant), Mimolette or any Cheddar-style cheese. And, on the subject of Cheddar, go for the golden richness of a real English Farmhouse Cheddar or a high-quality cheddar from Oregon or Vermont. Once you have had the real thing, you'll wonder what that orange and yellow stuff at the grocery is all about.

If you are not overly familiar with a wide variety of cheeses, be brave and try new types when you have guests. Cheese is appropriate after virtually any meal. Common sense will tell you to take it easy with triple-crèmes if you just served tortellini with cream sauce, or to steer clear of buttery style cheeses after Chicken Kiev. Seldom will you find a cheese that's actually inedible, and, if you're lucky, you might just happen upon one that's inspired. Buy your cheese at a reputable cheese shop or specialty store from people who know how to treat it and do a thriving business. Only if it is handled and stored properly will cheese be at its height when you want to serve it. Like wine, cheese is a living thing, constantly evolving with time and temperature; take good care of it. ∎

Served alone or with fruit, a selection of cheeses can end a meal simply but with style. Clockwise, from top left: Fourme d'Ambert (on pedestal), Shropshire Blue, Gorgonzola, Asiago Americano, Saint Nectaire, Pyramide du Valençay, Fontina d'Aosta; and in the center, Caprella.

Liquid Assets

Liquid Assets

■ The beverages you serve when you're entertaining say a good deal about the festivities. Only the most hedonistic (and wealthiest) among us can afford to drink the finest

wines and brandies all of the time, and, in fact, the world supply can't handle too many of them. Like any other "natural resource," the supply of top-notch wines, brandies and liqueurs is limited – usually by nature. Winegrowers on some of the tiny plots of land on the Burgundian Côte d'Or use only the grapes they can grow on their own plots of land. Since the space is so drastically limited (vineyards vary in size from about two to 125 acres), so too is the production of wine made from the grapes grown on it. And then, these *vignerons* must live with the fear that something will go wrong in the winemaking process. Not until the wine is safely bottled and aged can they begin to relax, but even then, they'll only be happy if what's inside is an outstanding example.

Great vintages are the equivalent of endangered species, rare and beautiful and worthy of preservation. That's why some of Burgundy's best – the Montrachets, Chambertins, Clos de Vougeot, Romanées, Echézeaux and Cortons – are so valued by connoisseurs.

When Champagne recently began to enjoy an upsurge in sales, lifelong Champagne drinkers feared their supply would be disrupted as increasing numbers of wine drinkers began to seek top labels. Certainly, Champagne production is limited, especially among the best and oldest houses, and, since true Champagne can be made only from grapes grown within the delimited Champagne region of France, production is finite. However, new labels of sparkling wines are coming on the market every day, made by the *méthode champenois*, from practically every grape-growing country in the world, including some splendid examples from California vintners.

All this is to say, simply, that a great wine or brandy should be treated as the special thing that it is, savored slowly and enjoyed to the fullest. What's fundamentally important is to offer a beverage that is in line with the other foods at the table. You wouldn't want to serve a fine Bordeaux with pizza, nor a jug white with a whole poached salmon. Likewise, when you're serving a beverage to accompany or follow a savory or sweet dessert, there are several issues to consider. First and always, choose a beverage you like. If you are serving a cheese from the Loire valley of France, you might select a crisp, dry white Loire wine, such as Sancerre, to go with it. (In fact, whenever you're choosing wine to go with cheese, select the cheese first and then the wine. All cheeses enhance wine; they are a perfect complement. You can't go too far wrong if you select a bottle that's made in the same region as the cheese; chances are they'll have a natural affinity for one another.)

If your guests try to avoid sugar, you know that a sweet liqueur won't thrill them, but a glass of one of the many *eaux-de-vie* (fruit brandies), a brandy or a sip of well-aged port might well be appreciated. If a sugary flavor does appeal, a world of sweet wines and liqueurs awaits. Liqueurs aren't called "after-dinner" drinks for nothing; however, you should feel free to serve them with dessert if you wish (especially if the dessert happens to include that particular liqueur).

You really have to taste liqueurs to find out which ones you like, though they can be classified generally by flavor. Fruit-flavored liqueurs include orange ones, such as the French Grand Marnier, Mandarine Napoléon, Curaçao and types of Triple Sec such as Cointreau; cherry ones, as well as examples flavored with apricot, melon, banana, coconut, raspberry, crème de cassis, blackberry, peach and sloe gin. Many liqueurs are based on the flavor of herbs: anisette, Drambuie, Chartreuse, Benedictine, Galliano, Strega, Ouzo, Pernod, Sambuca, Crème de Menthe and Kümmel. Still others are made from beans or kernels, such as the coffee flavored Kahlúa and Tia Maria, the cocoa-accented Crème de Cacao, or almondy Amaretto. Cream liqueurs – such as Bailey's Irish Cream – have taken a strong hold on American after-dinner drinkers.

Eaux-de-vie make for interesting after-dinner drinking since their intense aromas are almost equivalent to eating the fruit from which they are distilled. Look for Kirsch, Framboise, Quetsch, Mirabelle, Poire William and Slivovitz at your liquor store.

As any Sauternes devotee will tell you, who needs dessert when you can get your hands on a bottle of Château d'Yquem? They're so, so right. A first sip of this unbelievably wonderful honeyed wine is almost a shock to the system. Who would have guessed that all those flavors and scents could be tied up in a single, drinkable substance? Now this is not meant to denigrate other fine Bordeaux or Burgundies, but in terms of dessert, sweet wines deserve focus.

A fine way to acquaint yourself with sweet wines is to visit a wine bar or restaurant that serves wines by the taste or by the glass. Try a top-notch French Sauternes (beware of a generic California bottling called Sauterne – without the *s* – that in no way compares with the real, French, thing), a German *Trockenbeerenauslese*, a Hungarian *Tokaji Aszú* or *Eszencia*. Closer to home, there's American Essensia from Washington state or California, or late-harvest Gewürztraminer or Zinfandel.

Dessert wines, however, can wreak havoc on elaborate dessert plans since unless you plan to serve just a small amount of plain fresh fruit, you may have too much of a good thing. If you are serving dessert wine, go easy on the sweetness and quantity of food you serve. Keep it simple; leave the creamy and chocolatey concoctions for times when you plan to serve liqueurs and coffee afterward.

If you are planning to serve a Celebration or a Work of Art dessert, you can follow it with a liqueur or brandy that should finish off the evening very nicely (beware, however, a tendency to finish off the evening a little too nicely). Liqueurs – from Chartreuse to Crème de Menthe to Grand Marnier – offer small sweet sips of intense flavor. If you want to stay away from sweetness, try a *Marc de Bourgogne* or one of the many *eaux-de-vie*, perhaps some Poire William or a touch of framboise. These "waters of life" will act as restoratives to a spirit already sated by a great dinner.

A very serious final touch to a fine meal comes in the slow and easy appreciation and enjoyment of a great port or brandy. Again, whatever pleases you will do just fine, whether it's an unaged, sharp, relatively inexpensive Italian grappa or the finest, rarest Cognac or Armagnac. Each type of brandy has its disciples, who will argue the merits of their favorite quite convincingly.

If you like brandy, look into the finest examples from almost any country in the world. However, France is known for its great Cognacs with good reason; they are magnificent. All Cognacs are brandy, but not all brandies are Cognac – only those grown within a geographically delimited region of France can call themselves by that name. The secret to great brandy is in its cooperage and its aging – the type of wooden casks used to hold it during cellaring and the length of time and conditions under which it is stored. Fine Cognacs are aged in Limousin oak barrels that are made from the oak trees of the Limoges region of France. They derive character and flavor from the tannins in the wood and from contact with whatever oxygen seeps through the wood to the wine. The barrels are stored in dark cellars. The color of Cognac is derived from the wood; it starts out as a pure, colorless liquid. Cognacs available in the United States must be aged for at least two years, though many spend up to four years in cask. The rarest and finest

Cognacs improve during their 40 to 50 years in cask – a long time to wait for a return on an investment. If you have not yet been offered a 100-year-old Cognac, some day you probably will be. Remember that regardless of its age, the brandy will be only as good as it was the day it was bottled. Therefore, if it was aged for 45 years, it's probably great; if it was in wood for only two years, it's not a bit better than it was the day it was bottled 98 years ago.

Portugal's most famous sweet wine – Porto – is appreciated more in Great Britain than probably any other place in the world. It's time to catch on to this fascinating and delicious wine. A vintage year for port is declared only sporadically, when the shippers find the wine to be exceptional. Excellent port vintages include 1945, 1947, 1948, 1950, 1955, 1958, 1960, 1963, 1966, 1967, 1970, 1975 and most recently in 1977 and 1982. As you can see, a vintage year is comparatively rare, making the wines very popular to aficionados. Port is bottled after two years and then needs time to age and gather together its character. The smartest shoppers will buy port when it is released and put it away, undisturbed, for 20 years or more.

The most extraordinary, ultra-fine examples of wines, liqueurs and brandies deserve unfettered time in the spotlight, for each of them represents the culmination of centuries of time and care and triumphs and errors in learning how to produce the best. We don't think it's possible to purchase a prime example of any one of these wines or spirits and not feel better for it. We urge you to explore this interesting world of rare potable liquids to discover which ones do something special for you. ■

Index
of Recipes

Index of Recipes

Photography Credits

12 Hazelnut Succès
Glasses: Braid Black by Mikasa. Tray: Axis from DAPY.

16 Chocolate Cake
Plates from Zona; Background from Jerrystyle; Flatware: Torun by Dansk; Napkin from Henri Bendel.

21 White Chocolate Mousse
Glasses, left to right: Cowdy from Hot House; Tunbridge Glassworks, Steven Smyers, Cam Langley, Cowdy from Rogers-Tropea. Shelf from Jerrystyle.

28 Three-Layer Celebration Cake
Punch Set: Mirage from Toscany Imports.

33 Chocolate Chip Fudge Cake
Tray by Brightman Design. Cups and spoon by Robert Davis. Plate by Ann Morhauser. Vases by Ronit. All from Rogers-Tropea.

37 Madeleines
Tea set by Roger Michell from Hot House.

46 Milk Chocolate Cake
Cake plate and small plate: Blue Dots from Gmundner Keramik.

53 Strawberry Peach Pie
Pie plate and spatula from Garrett Brown.

56 La Galette Pérougienne
Fabric: Reputation from Hot House. Scandinavian chair from Evergreen Antiques.

63 Rhubarb and Strawberry Pie
Plates: Sweet Briar by Johnson Brothers of the Wedgwood Group. Large and small baskets from Evergreen Antiques.

69 Pear Brandy Tart
Plate from New Glass; Glasses from Barneys New York; Flatware by Georg Jensen from Royal Copenhagen; Canvas background by Cynthia Kinsley.

84 Berry Custard Tart
Small plate by Ann Morhauser from Rogers-Tropea. Aqua glass by Philip Muller Glasses for Gear Stores. Sunglasses from Joël Name Optique de Paris.

91 Sorbets and Ices
Table and doors from Le Bris Antiques Ltd. Spoons by David Tisdale from Rogers-Tropea.

99 Oeufs à la Neige
Serving bowl by Fiesta, dishes by Riviera and spoon, all from Mood Indigo. Fabric and wicker wreaths from Gear Stores.

104 Almond Cookies
Scandinavian table from Evergreen Antiques. Haws watering can and garden tools from Zona. Basket from Wolfman Gold & Good Co.

111 Ambrosia Mariposa
Ceremonial tea set and tray by Marek Cecula from Contemporary Porcelain. Fork: Trylon by Ward Bennett from Sointu.

123 Zauber Torte
Covered dish by Jerrystyle. Backdrop by Pauline St. Denis.

126 Chocolate Leaf Cake
Silver dish from Platypus. Candlesticks from Sointu.

132 Fruit Loaf
Alvar Aalto dish from Ahlström-Iittala.

137 Ice Cream and Sherbet Bombe
Espresso pot from Platypus.

142 Coeur à la Crème
Plate by Michael Lambert, fork and spoon by David Tisdale, from Rogers-Tropea. Table by Elizabeth Jackson from Clodagh, Ross & Williams.

151 Sparkling Spiced Strawberries and Chocolate Truffles
Table: Neophile from Clodagh, Ross & Williams.

155 Cantaloupe with Port Wine
Plate by Peter Greenwood from Wallengren/USA. Decanters: Ebony from Theresienthal, distributed by Hutschenreuther. Chair from Clodagh, Ross & Williams.

Ahlström-Iittala Inc.
41 Madison Ave., New York, N.Y. 10010

Baccarat Inc.
55 E. 57th St., New York, N.Y. 10022

Barneys New York
Seventh Ave. and 17th St.
New York, N.Y. 10011

Henri Bendel
10 W. 57th St., New York, N.Y. 10019

Cardel Ltd.
621 Madison Ave.
New York, N.Y. 10022

Civilization
78 Second Ave., New York, N.Y. 10003

Clodagh, Ross & Williams
122 St. Marks Place
New York, N.Y. 10009

Contemporary Porcelain
105 Sullivan St., New York, N.Y. 10012

Dansk International Design
Radio Circle Road
Mount Kisco, N.Y. 10549

DAPY
431 W. Broadway, New York, N.Y. 10012

Elite Limoges
225 Fifth Ave., Suite 622
New York, N.Y. 10010

Evergreen Antiques
120 Spring St., New York, N.Y. 10012

Fairway Fruits & Vegetables
2127 Broadway, New York, N.Y. 10023

Garnett Brown
119 W. 23rd St., New York, N.Y. 10011

Gear Stores
110 Seventh Ave., New York, N.Y. 10011

Gmundner Keramik
6 Lake Dr., Darien, Conn. 06820

Harvey Electronics
2 W. 45th St., New York, N.Y. 10036

Hutschenreuther Corp.
41 Madison Ave., New York, N.Y. 10010

Hot House
345 W. Broadway, New York, N.Y. 10013

Jerrystyle
34 E. Fourth St., New York, N.Y. 10013

Cynthia Kinsley
70-13 Caldwell Ave.
Maspeth, N.Y. 11378

Le Bris Antiques Ltd.
510A Broome St., New York, N.Y. 10013

Charles Lamalle
36 W. 25th St., New York, N.Y. 10010

The Mikasa Retail Store
30 W. 23rd St., New York, N.Y. 10011

Mood Indigo
181 Prince St., New York, N.Y. 10012

Joël Name Optique de Paris
65 W. Houston St., New York, N.Y. 10012

New York Marble Works, Inc.
1399 Park Ave., New York, N.Y. 10029

New Glass
138 Wooster St., New York, N.Y. 10012

Janice Parker
Landscape Flower and Party Design
117 W. 17th St., New York, N.Y. 10011

Il Papiro
1 Herald Square, New York, N.Y. 10001

Platypus
126 Spring St., New York, N.Y. 10012

Retroneu
225 Fifth Ave., New York, N.Y. 10010

Rogers-Tropea, Inc.
1351 Third Ave., New York, N.Y. 10021

Royal Copenhagen/Georg Jensen
683 Madison Ave.
New York, N.Y. 10021

Sointu
20 E. 69th St., New York, N.Y. 10021

Pauline St. Denis
461 First St., Hoboken, N.J. 07030

Toscany Imports Ltd.
386 Park Ave. S., New York, N.Y. 10016

Villeroy & Boch/Heinrich
41 Madison Ave., New York, N.Y. 10010

Wallengren/USA
72 Thompson St., New York, N.Y. 10012

Wedgwood
41 Madison Ave., New York, N.Y. 10010

Wolfman Gold & Good Co.
484 Broome St., New York, N.Y. 10013

Zona
97 Greene St., New York, N.Y. 10012

Contributors

Recipes by Diana Sturgis, John Robert Massie, Anne Disrude and Marcia Kiesel were developed in the course of their work in Food & Wine's test kitchen. Other former or current Food & Wine staff members who contributed recipes include: W. Peter Prestcott, Jim Brown, Kate Slate, Maria Piccolo Stern, Rosalee Harris, Anne Montgomery and Bette Duke.

Food professionals who have contributed to this book include the following:

Jean Anderson is a cookbook author, food and travel writer and photographer. Her most recent book is The Food of Portugal (Morrow), published in the fall of 1986.

Lee Bailey is best known for his books, Country Weekends, City Food, Country Flowers and most recently, Great Parties (all with Clarkson Potter). New Yorkers are familiar with his stylish home furnishings shop in Henri Bendel.

Simone Beck (a.k.a. Simca) teaches cooking classes and is the author of many cookbooks, among them Simca's Cuisine (Knopf) and New Menus from Simca's Cuisine (Harcourt Brace Jovanovich).

Rose Levy Beranbaum is a cookbook author, consultant and owner of her own cooking school, Cordon Rose.

Emalee Chapman is a San Francisco based food writer and the author of three books on fast and fresh cooking.

Diedre Davis and Linda Marino are both food writers who are based in Boston.

Jim Dodge and Gayle Henderson Wilson: Jim Dodge is pastry chef at San Francisco's prestigious Stanford Court Hotel. Gayle Henderson Wilson is a Bay Area food consultant.

Geraldine Duncann is a cookbook author and food and travel writer.

Jim Fobel is an artist, food journalist and cookbook author of Beautiful Food (Van Nostrand Reinhold) and Heirloom Baking, slated for publication in 1987.

Arthur Gold and Robert Fizdale are famed as duo-pianists. Their Gold and Fizdale Cookbook (Random House) was extremely well received when it was published in 1984.

Dorie Greenspan is a freelance food writer currently hard at work on her own dessert cookbook.

Christopher Idone is the author of Glorious Food (Stewart, Tabori & Chang) and Glorious American Food (Random House). He also acts as a food and restaurant consultant.

Quinith Janssen is a food writer based in Shepherdstown, West Virginia.

Sarah Kelly is a talented baker who specializes in the food of Germany, Austria and Switzerland.

Lydie Marshall is a cooking teacher in New York City. Her most recent book is Cooking with Lydie Marshall (Knopf).

Rux Martin is a food writer who lives in Vermont.

Michael McLaughlin is chef/owner of Manhattan Chili Co. in Greenwich Village, as well as author of The Manhattan Chili Co. Southwest American Cookbook (Crown) and coauthor of The Silver Palate Cookbook.

Perla Meyers is a cookbook author, cooking teacher and consultant to companies in food and food-related industries.

Maurice Moore-Betty is a cookbook author and cooking school teacher who lives in New York City.

Leslie Newman, a New York-based food writer and novelist, is working on a cookbook entitled Feasts.

Judith Olney is a cookbook author, food writer and media spokesperson who lives and works in Durham, North Carolina. Her books include The Joy of Chocolate, Judith Olney's Entertainments, and Judith Olney on Bread.

Molly O'Neill, a former professional chef, is now the restaurant critic for New York Newsday.

Jacques Pépin, former chef to Charles DeGaulle, is the author of several books on cooking and technique as well as the star of his own PBS cooking series, "Everyday Cooking with Jacques Pépin."

Joanna Pruess writes regularly for various food magazines and she directs The Cooking Studio at King's Supermarket in Short Hills, New Jersey.

Elizabeth Schneider is a food journalist. Her most recent book, A Commonsense Guide to Uncommon Fruits and Vegetables (Harper & Row) received considerable acclaim when it was published early in 1986.

Joan Scobey writes about food and entertaining from her home outside of New York City.

Ruth Spear is a food writer and cookbook author who resides in New York City.

Barbara Tropp is chef/owner of China Moon, a Chinese bistro in San Francisco and author of The Modern Art of Chinese Cooking (Morrow). She was named one of the "Great Chefs of San Francisco" in the PBS series of the same name.

Paula Wolfert is a food writer, cooking teacher and the author of The Cooking of South-West France (Dial Press).

We also wish to thank the restaurants and individuals whose names follow:

Sally Darr of La Tulipe, New York City; Narsai David of San Francisco, California; Sirio Maccione and Alain Sailhac of Le Cirque, New York City; Peter Sussman of The Phoenix Restaurant, Warren, Vermont; Wild Wind Farm, Naples, New York; Pat Buckley of New York City; Chefs Paul and Jean-Pierre Haeberlin of l'Auberge de l'Ill, Illhaeusern, Alsace; Chef Nicholas Gill of Hambleton Hall, Hambleton, England; Liz Smith, New York City; Katharine Hepburn, New York City; Chez Eddy, Houston, Texas; James Nassikas of The Stanford Court Hotel, San Francisco, California; Gian Marino Restaurant, New York City; Chuck Williams of Williams-Sonoma, San Francisco, California; Margaret Fox of Cafe Beaujolais, Mendocino, California; Catherine and Ghislane de Vogüé, Paris, France; The Chanticleer Restaurant, Nantucket, Massachusetts; Mark Carrozza of Cafe Renni, Lambertville, New Jersey; John Bruno of The Pen and Pencil Restaurant, New York City; Georges Blanc of La Mère Blanc, Vonnas, France; George Lang of Café des Artistes, New York City; Jane and Ben Thompson, Cambridge, Massachusetts; Chef Patrick O'Connell of The Inn at Little Washington, Washington, Virginia; The Fork Shop Restaurant, Brookfield, Vermont; Stephenson's Restaurant, Kansas City, Missouri; Leona Foote, Charlotte, Vermont; Jimmy's Place, Chicago, Illinois; Maggie Waldron, Ketchum Communications, San Francisco, California; Dario Mariotti of The Mayfair Regent Hotel, New York City; Helen Fioratti, New York City; Margaret Romagnoli, Boston, Massachusetts; Vincenzo Buonassisi, Milan, Italy; Barry Wine of The Quilted Giraffe, New York City; Jonathan Waxman of Jam's, New York City; Dani Manilla, Huntington Beach, California; Piret Munger of Piret's, San Diego, California; Jim Haller of The Blue Strawbery, Portsmouth, New Hampshire; Jennifer Marshall, Philadelphia, Pennsylvania; Henry Koehler, New York City; Bun's Restaurant, Delaware, Ohio.